The Markets Never Sleep

Founded in 1807, John Wiley & Sons is the oldest independent publishing company in the United States. With offices in North America, Europe, Australia, and Asia, Wiley is globally committed to developing and marketing print and electronic products and services for our customers' professional and personal knowledge and understanding.

The Wiley Trading series features books by traders who have survived the markets' ever-changing temperament and have prospered—some by reinventing systems, others by getting back to basics. Whether a novice trader, professional, or somewhere in-between, these books will provide the advice and strategies needed to prosper today and well into the future.

For a list of available titles, visit our Web site at www.WileyFinance.com.

The Markets Never Sleep

Global Insights for More Consistent Trading

THOMAS L. BUSBY

with Patsy Busby Dow

BICENTENNIAL
1807
WILEY
2007
BICENTENNIAL

John Wiley & Sons, Inc.

Published by John Wiley & Sons, Inc., Hoboken, New Jersey
Published simultaneously in Canada

For general information on our other products and services or for technical support, please contact our Customer Care Department within the United States at
(800) 762-2974, outside the United States at (317) 572-3993 or fax (317) 572-4002.

Wiley also publishes its books in a variety of electronic formats. Some content that
appears in print may not be available in electronic books. For more information
about Wiley products, visit our web site at www.wiley.com

Library of Congress Cataloging-in-Publication Data

Busby, Thomas L., 1951–
    The markets never sleep : global insights for more consistent trading /
Thomas L. Busby with Patsy Busby Dow.
        p. cm. — (Wiley trading series)
    Includes index.
    ISBN-13 978-0-470-04946-4 (cloth)
    ISBN-10 0-470-04946-4 (cloth)
    1. Capital market 2. Stock exchanges. 3. Investments I. Dow, Patsy
Busby. II. Title.
    HG4523.B873 2007
    332.64—dc22

                                                                2006026722

Printed in the United States of America
10 9 8 7 6 5 4 3 2 1

Contents

Preface

Trading is competitive. It is a zero-sum game—for every winner, there is a loser. And, if that is not challenging enough, some of the brightest people in the world are professional traders. When trading the financial markets, the retired attorney, former marketing executive, or housewife is akin to David squaring off against Goliath. At first glance, it appears that the little guy has no chance to succeed. However, remember that when the biblical battle ended, it was David who was still standing.

David's success came from training, experience, and divine intervention; the average trader's power comes from education, training, and experience. To succeed in the financial marketplace, traders need to fully understand it and know how to survive and thrive in it. The more knowledge you have, the more powerful you become. That is the purpose of this book: to help traders gain insight into the 24-hour nature of the financial markets so that they can benefit from that information and use it to help them make money and be more consistent.

Both the novice and the advanced trader can benefit from the information provided. Beginners may not have considered the significance of the 24-hour nature of the markets, and advanced traders may not be using that knowledge to its maximum potential. Due to the competitive nature of trading, if you gain only one helpful insight from this book, you will likely cover the purchase price many times over. Every strategy, technique, and idea that helps your trading is valuable. If a running shoe improves the runner's stride by the slightest bit, every serious runner wants the product. Likewise, if an idea or strategy improves your trading, you need to know it and use it.

The world is a big place. However, many U.S. traders act as though it is not. They tend to focus only on the day markets in Chicago and New York. When the opening bell rings at the NYSE and the bulls and bears fill the floors of the CBOT and the CME in Chicago, thousands and thousands of traders from California to the Carolinas begin their workday. In reality, their day began many hours before, but they did not know it.

Beginning the trading day with the opening bell of the NYSE is like showing up for your eight-to-five job around two in the afternoon—you are late. The financial markets have been trading for hours. In Paris, London,

Tokyo, China, and around the globe there are major financial centers and exchanges where traders have been executing orders for hours. While most of the traders on our shores were sleeping, the stock, bond, options, futures, and commodities markets around the globe were operational. In fact, by the time our financial centers join the game, most Asian and many European exchanges have already closed or are nearing their end. That means that traders across the oceans have already evaluated the financial scene and expressed their views about it. Traders in the United States who realize that fact and use it to their advantage have an edge. That edge may be just what some traders need to become and stay profitable.

OVERVIEW

The book begins by noting the inherent risks involved in long-term trading. In our age of rapid communications, a disaster thousands of miles away has the ability to torpedo our financial markets and send them into a tailspin. Consider the events of September 11, 2001, or Black Monday of 1987. Therefore, knowing about the 24-hour nature of the markets offers protection and allows the savvy trader to hedge positions or seek some other form of protection, should there be a need to do so. In the first chapter, I discuss my trading day and how I use time and the 24-hour nature of the markets to help me become profitable and gain greater consistency.

Chapter 2 focuses on how the global markets work. It surveys some of the most important aspects of the financial landscape, such as interest rates, national debt, trade imbalances, energy availability and costs, precious metals, bonds, and geopolitical events. As a trader, it is not necessary to hold a Ph.D. in finance, but it is essential to have a general understanding of economic forces and the likely effect on the markets if those forces get out of balance. For example, if oil prices are too steep or interest rates too high, other aspects of the economy will respond. Traders must know that reality and incorporate that knowledge into their trading.

Technology connects our world like never before. A significant event that occurs thousands of miles away will have almost instantaneous effects on our financial markets. A tribal conflict in the jungles of Nigeria, an economic sanction leveled against a huge multinational corporation by the EU, an interest rate hike by the Central Bank of China—all of these events and countless others affect prices of equities and other products traded on our exchanges. Chapter 3 explains the significance of understanding global connections and why traders need to know them.

The United States boasts the world's leading economy. Therefore, it is often easy for many of us to discount the effect and significance of other financial centers. Chapter 4 looks at Asia from two standpoints. First, each trading day begins in the Land of the Rising Sun. It is here that the sun first passes across the morning sky. Traders in Tokyo, Singapore, Hong Kong, and across the Asian continent have the first opportunity to express their views and move prices up or down. That fact offers traders on our shores a preview of what might be coming our way. Also, some of the world's major economies are in the East. China is a growing economic power-house, and Japan has long been an important financial and economic center. Traders must be aware of the significance of Asia to their portfolios.

After Asian traders start the day, Europe is the next bustling trading center to get going. The FTSE in London, the CAC-40 in Paris, the German Dax, and other major indices reflect and report the action. In our computer age, traders have the ability to sit at their desks at home and virtually travel to the markets across the Pacific and Atlantic. In fact, each morning, I generally do just that. I frequently trade the German Dax, an equity index futures market. With just a click of my computer mouse I buy and sell contracts and profit from my global knowledge. Other traders may enjoy trading a Parisian product, or perhaps one traded on the London exchange. With knowledge, training, and experience, the Internet age allows it. The economy and trading products of Europe are the focus of Chapter 5.

After Asia has closed and Europe is winding down, exchanges in the United States get going. Chapter 6 gives an overview of our nation's major exchanges and indices. It also explains the significance of time in my trading and how I use the element of time to help me make money. Especially in the morning hours, I take advantage of information from Asia and Europe to improve my trading odds.

In Chapter 7, I explain some of my short-term trading strategies. In particular, I outline the criteria I use for trading equities, and I describe the process that I use for buying and selling stocks. Also, I discuss my techniques for trading equity index futures like the S&P 500 futures, Dow futures, or Dax futures contracts. Time and the 24-hour trading clock help me determine the best times for me to trade, and also assist me in being profitable and gaining greater consistency.

I enjoy day trading; most of my plays are short-term ones. However, many traders cannot or do not want to trade intraday. Therefore, Chapter 8 discusses some swing trading strategies across time zones that may be helpful for these traders. In particular, insights are given for the gold and precious metals markets, the equity markets, equity index futures, and options. These strategies, if executed correctly, may open new opportunities and increase profits.

Chapter 9 shifts to long-term strategies. Many traders enjoy holding positions longer than I typically do. And, many of these traders are also profitable. However, you must remember that it is unwise to buy or sell any financial product and forget it. Always monitor trades and be prepared to take defensive action if necessary. This chapter suggests some long-term plays to consider. In particular exchange traded funds, options, and mutual funds are discussed.

The "Golden Keys to Unlocking the Secrets of the Financial Markets" are the focus of Chapter 10. Time, key numbers, and market indicators open the doors to financial success. Having already stressed the significance of time, this chapter deals with the major statistical indicators and explains how to read them. In addition to market indicators such as the NYSE TICK and the TRIN, other market clues are explained. The significance of fuel prices, precious metals, and index futures are noted. The chapter also discusses key numbers and their significance. It is impossible to be consistently profitable without understanding and using key numbers.

Risk is a major aspect of trading. Managing risk with each trade is critical. If you do not respect and manage the downside of trading, you will not be trading for the long-term. You will likely be broke. Therefore, Chapter 11 discusses some strategies that I use to manage risks. Some are simple and basic, like using stop orders for protection and diversifying a portfolio, and others are more advanced, like hedging losing positions with index futures or with a LEAP. The big idea here is that you must always know your risk and limit it as much as possible. If you control risk first, then you will be in a position to take profits. I am a firm believer in the view that if risks are managed and controlled, the rewards will come.

When I speak at seminars and money shows, I often hear traders express a desire to become more consistent. Many are profitable on Monday and in the red on Tuesday. They have a great deal of difficulty staying on an even keel. And, regrettably, new traders often suffer huge losses but reap relatively low profits. That ratio of losers to winners means that the trading account is all too soon empty. Therefore, the goal of Chapter 12 is to offer some guidance for gaining consistency. Using a 24-hour trading clock and taking advantage of global information is part of the solution. Other helpful ideas include having a plan and following it, using good money management techniques, keeping emotions in check, discarding bias, and setting realistic goals. If you employ these techniques, consistency should greatly improve.

Trading is my job, and I approach it like a job. Each day, before I place my first trade, I am prepared. Chapter 13 reviews the steps that I take in order to be ready for my battle with the bulls and the bears. I check for scheduled news, gather key numbers, test my equipment, and prepare myself mentally and emotionally for battle. If I am ready, I know my chances for success are tremendously increased.

Every experienced trader knows that psychological factors play an enormous role in trading. When money is on the line, greed and fear often step into the picture and reason and sound judgment step out of it. Traders must find the middle ground and balance greed and fear. In Chapter 14, I offer some strategies for dealing with the greed/fear dilemma. I also share some techniques that I use to stay mentally positive and psychologically up to the task. Each day offers new challenges, and winners must be ready.

Trading is a difficult job. Financial markets trade around the clock. How is one to deal with markets that never sleep? When I began my trading career, it was not so time intensive. Computers and the Internet were not yet bringing the world into my trading room. In those days, I worked frantically from the time the exchanges opened until they closed, but then I went home. Today my schedule is different. It is easy to become preoccupied with the markets and overtrade. Traders must guard against that tendency. Even though I monitor global markets around the clock, and sometimes trade some of the products on foreign exchanges, my life is actually more relaxed that it was in those early days. That is because I use technology to help me keep an eye on the world, but I select trading times that fit my schedule, my trading strategies, and my lifestyle. I still have time to sleep, play golf, and enjoy my life. Chapter 15 explains how I do it.

Chapter 16 identifies the traits of a winner. Trading success requires persistence, a desire to win, discipline, flexibility, composure, and some other important characteristics. Those who do not possess these characteristics and are unwilling to develop them will not succeed.

Finally, Chapter 17 wraps up the book and briefly surveys the high points. The financial markets never sleep, and modern technology allows traders to take advantage of that fact. By using a 24-hour trading approach, educated and skilled traders are able to expand their world, have more trading opportunities, and achieve more consistency. It is my sincere hope that by reading this book, your trading will become more profitable, more consistent, and more enjoyable.

About the Authors

Thomas L. Busby, the founder and CEO of the Day Trading Institute (DTI) has been a professional securities trader for more than twenty-five years. He began his trading career with Merrill Lynch, and before DTI opened its doors in 1996, he was a vice-president with Salomon Smith Barney.

Tom earned a bachelor's degree in Business Administration from the University of Georgia and a Juris Doctorate degree from Oklahoma City University School of Law. He was a distinguished graduate of the United States Air Force Budget Officer School, and served seven years as an officer in the United States Air Force prior to becoming a professional securities broker and trader. Tom is well respected in his field and is a member of both the Chicago Mercantile Exchange (CME) and the Chicago Board of Trade (CBOT).

Tom suffered a great financial setback during the crash of 1987. When the market tanked, he was over-leveraged in the options market. Many traders would have left the arena after such a loss, but not Tom. He persisted and immersed himself in his work by studying and analyzing the markets. Out of his defeat came a new determination to improve his approach and become a better trader. Over the years he has developed a unique method whereby the avoidance of risk has become his primary focus and profit taking has assumed a second-row seat. This approach has served him and his students well. Tom's trading method incorporates more than two decades of experience; he is a veteran of many bullish as well as bearish cycles, and he freely shares his knowledge and experience with his students.

Tom is a frequent contributor to a variety of trading publications. Over the years Tom has written many articles covering a wide array of trading topics. He is also the co-author of *Winning the Day Trading Game*, which was published by John Wiley & Sons in late 2005.

Tom has been married to Paula for more than two decades. Their sons, Winston and Morgan, are also traders. They work with their father at DTI.

Patsy Busby Dow holds a Juris Doctorate degree from Tulane School of Law. She is a former assistant district attorney and a former assistant

United States attorney. Several years ago, when making a career change, she began learning the art of trading. Her cousin, Tom Busby, was, of course, her mentor. Patsy is co-author of *Winning the Day Trading Game* and is currently the staff writer at DTI.

In addition to her degree in law and her trading education, Patsy holds a master's degree in education and a master's degree in history from the University of South Alabama. She has been married for 36 years to Mike Dow, a former four-term mayor for the City of Mobile. They have three children.

Acknowledgments

The students and staff of Day Trading Institute (DTI) are major contributors to this book. I have been a trader for more than two decades, so certainly my trading methods, approaches and ideas are presented. Patsy, one of my first cousins and a dedicated writer, has done a good job of capturing my thoughts and trading strategies. As always, I deeply appreciate her efforts. Patsy penned this book. Geof Smith, chief instructor at DTI, has carefully reviewed all of the information presented, especially all technical data, and he has assisted with other significant ideas. Jeanette Simms, our COO, has contributed both ideas and editorial guidance. I appreciate her efforts and contributions. Chuck Crow and Anna McConnell have lent their hands to graphics designs, and I want to thank them. However, it is to the students of DTI that I owe special thanks. As they come through the classes and learn, question, and consider various trading strategies and ideas, they teach me many invaluable lessons. To all of them I give a special "Thank you."

CHAPTER 1

Let's Rock and Roll

Why I Like the Global Beat

Tokyo's lively tempo hits its first beat at 6:00 PM Central Time. Two hours later, traders in Hong Kong start dancing to the tune when the Hang Seng opens. It's only a few hours later when Germany's toe-tapping rhythm chimes in and trading begins on the Dax. By the time the buying hits the open outcry pits of the New York Stock Exchange (NYSE), I'm dancing—rocking around the clock to the markets' beat.

In 1955, Bill Haley and his Comets ignited the popular music scene with their rendition of "Rock Around the Clock." The recording was a tremendous success, and it soared to the top of the charts. The lively lyrics of the song transported listeners around the clock as the words jumped from hour to hour—rocking 'til broad daylight. When twelve o'clock struck, the rocking just started all over again. The tune was one of America's most popular hits for almost two months. Trading the global markets and jumping to their beat has been a hit with me for about two decades.

Not only was "Rock Around the Clock" a sensation in the United States, but its success echoed around the globe. The tune soon appeared at the top of music charts across the Pacific and the Atlantic. Twenty years after its release, moviegoers were still "rocking around the clock" with the tune in *American Graffiti,* and television audiences were enjoying the beat with each weekly episode of *Happy Days.* "Rock Around the Clock" has remained a global favorite, and some music aficionados claim that every minute of the day, somewhere in the world, it is possible to dance to that old Bill Haley classic.

I've always liked dancing, and I like "rocking around the clock," too. I just don't do it very often with my dancing shoes; I do it with my computer and my knowledge of the global financial markets. Virtually every hour of the day and night, a financial center somewhere on the globe is popping. The most active area for trading is the one where the sun is shining the brightest. Therefore, I rock with the markets and take advantage of their 24-hour beat.

LEARNING THE 24-HOUR ROCK MAKES LIFE EASIER

"Markets Crash: Dow Jones Loses More Than a Trillion Dollars of Asset Value." What if this was the headline tomorrow or next week? What would happen to your portfolio if some geopolitical or economic event sent prices on Wall Street into a tailspin?

Most traders forget that the markets never sleep. The financial markets operate 24 hours a day. During virtually every hour of the day and night, someone, somewhere is trading. Oblivious to that reality, most traders buy and hold large positions of equities and other financial products without thinking about protecting themselves against the potentially destructive forces that prowl in the darkness. Years ago, I asked a veteran trader, H. L. (Mac) McFarland, to help me decide if my overnight exposure was too great. At that time, Mac had been trading for almost 50 years, and he was both my friend and mentor. Mac taught me how to handle a trade and how to handle people. Mac responded, "Tom, if a trade interferes with your sleep, you are too exposed. Any risk that makes you toss and turn at night is just too great." In other words, if a market position is large enough to make you fret about it overnight, it needs to be pared down or the trade avoided. The way for global traders to get a good night's rest is to plan and prepare so as to be protected should a nightmare tiptoe into their portfolios while they are snoozing. And, part of that preparation involves learning to step to the global beat.

Are your overnight market risks too great?

If a trade interferes with your sleep, you are too exposed. Any risk that makes you toss and turn at night is too great.

I vividly remember a night in December 1996, when my knowledge of the 24-hour nature of the financial markets helped me greatly. I was sitting in my office trading the night markets on the Globex and watching television with a friend and fellow trader. My friend Bill is a really big guy who stands well above six feet tall and registers more than a few pounds on the scales. Bluntly, he dwarfs me. On this night we both had a nice size position in the S&P 500 futures; we were long and feeling very confident about our bullish positions.

Then we heard the news: Alan Greenspan, the chairman of the Federal Reserve, was delivering a speech in Washington, D.C., and referred to the markets as *irrationally exuberant*. To be exact, Greenspan asked his audience how one knows when irrational exuberance has unduly escalated asset values. Thanks to the power of the electronic media, my friend and I were among millions of viewers who quickly heard about the words Greenspan had chosen. As soon as the significance of the message hit my brain, I lunged across my big burly friend as though he weighed no more than a small rag doll. His arm rested on the back of a chair and blocked my path to the computer screen, but I flung it away with ease. My adrenaline was rushing—I knew that a statement that powerful from Alan Greenspan was taking the markets down. Remember, I was long a good-sized position. I grabbed the mouse and took our long contracts to the market. Then I reversed, going short. Soon my winnings from my shorts more than covered the losses we initially suffered before I was able to exit, shift gears, and jump on the new winning team.

At the time Greenspan spoke, the open outcry pits in New York and Chicago were closed, but live markets were trading in Asia. The stock market in Tokyo immediately responded and took a dive. In fact, following the Greenspan speech, the stock exchange in Tokyo saw its greatest loss of the year. Prices on exchanges in Hong Kong also fell; a 3 percent loss was recorded before the market closed. The scare that ignited selling in Asia traveled to Europe, where the exchanges in Frankfurt, Germany, and London, England, also experienced a sell-off.

I was able to take defensive action because I was trading the S&P 500 futures on an electronic trading system that operates virtually 24 hours a day. When the NYSE opened for business on Friday, December 6, 1996, traders rushed to sell their holdings and prices fell almost 150 points on the Dow in only half an hour. Glad I wasn't on the wrong side of that avalanche. Before the day ended, the Dow had recouped much of the loss, but it was a rough journey indeed for the bulls. While they were sleeping, an unsuspecting asset assassin (Mr. G. himself) had crept into the global markets. Figure 1.1 shows how this affected the S&P 500 futures. Figure 1.2 shows the market's recovery in the days following Greenspan's now-famous remarks. Admittedly, it was the short-term traders who really suf-

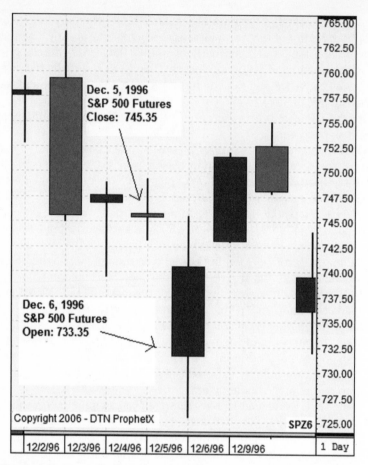

FIGURE 1.1   The price gap in the S&P futures following the Fed chairman's remarks. Luckily, the markets were able to recover quickly. (*Source*: Copyright 2006-DTN ProphetX)

fered from the drop. Those who were holding long positions that were margined found themselves in a squeeze. Many of them likely got a call from their brokers to meet margin calls. For them, it was time to pay the piper because they had been hit by a major sell-off while they were sleeping.

Even though the markets recouped rather quickly, for those who had to meet those margin calls, that fact was irrelevant. They deposited additional cash in their accounts or their positions were liquidated immediately. Brokerage houses do not give traders a chance for the markets to

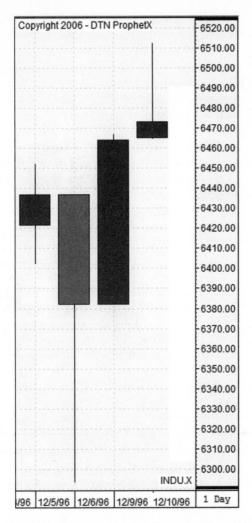

FIGURE 1.2 The market's recovery. A few days after the well-remembered speech, prices were moving up again. (*Source*: Copyright 2006-DTN ProphetX)

readjust. That is not the way the game is played. The remarks by the Fed chairman cost them dearly.

Also consider September 11, 2001. When traders slipped under the covers on the night of September 10, all seemed to be well and the markets were trading as usual. Suddenly, on the morning of September 11, investors turned on their televisions to see two huge airliners plowing into the Twin Towers. It was a horrifying event for all Americans. The safety of our nation and our sense of security was shattered forever.

I was teaching a class that day. I operate an educational trading facility, Day Trading Institute (DTI), in Mobile, Alabama. The students had come early and we had taken a long position in the S&P futures. Due to my trading method, we had exited part of our initial purchase and had done so profitably. We were still holding a small part of the original buy and were expecting prices to continue to rise. With a protective stop in place to preserve our assets, we were hoping to add a little more to our account balance. Suddenly, the market shifted and prices inexplicably dropped. Generally, when markets move in such an erratic manner during this time of day, the reason is news. Therefore, I asked Geof Smith, DTI's chief instructor, to go into my office and check the television for news. Had there been some negative economic report or other event that had taken the markets south? Within a minute or so we knew the story. After a quick check, Geof alerted us to the disaster, and we clicked on the set and turned the volume up to hear the shocking details. Because we had taken defensive steps to safeguard our money and limit our risk, we were removed from the market with only a small profit on our remaining position. However, many buy-and-hold traders and investors did not do so well.

Figure 1.3 tells the story. After the attack, the Chicago Mercantile Exchange (CME) stopped trading activities for a few minutes. Then the exchange opened for a very short time to allow traders to clear their positions or take whatever defensive measure could be taken. Following that few minutes of trading, the exchange and all other major U.S. exchanges closed for a week. The third bar from the left depicts the price action on September 11. The gap between the third and fourth bars represents the week when the exchange was closed. The bars that follow that gap show how prices fell during the days immediately following the attack.

Again, it was the short-term players and those who were highly margined who felt the greatest pain. Equities are often margined 50 percent and futures are margined much, much more than that. For a good faith payment as small as 2 to 3 percent of the total asset value, a trader has the ability to control some commodity futures. That means that when prices fall that far that fast, it causes dislocations in the market and many traders receive margin calls. For them, the downtrend may be short lived, but it is final. They must either put more money in their accounts or liquidate their positions. That reality means that those traders need to have the ability to immediately react to a crisis—even if that crisis should happen in the middle of the night, and often even if it is only short-term. It gives me great satisfaction to know that despite the devastation of September 11th, our method preserved our capital and helped us manage our money.

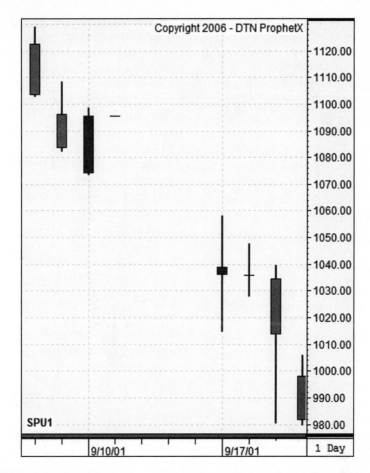

FIGURE 1.3   The high on September 11 is around 1100.00. By September 21, the market hit a low around 940.00—a drop of about 160 points. That represents a loss of approximately $8,000 for each S&P 500 futures mini-contract. I had a protective stop in place and I was removed from the market without a financial loss. (*Source*: Copyright 2006-DTN ProphetX)

Following September 11th, prices fell dramatically for five days or so. Then they began to recoup some of the losses. In November, prices on the S&P actually rose above their pre-attack highs and stayed buoyant for several months. Then, in March 2002, with geopolitical problems on the horizon, the bears gained the upper hand and prices started falling. They continued their fall for months. Figure 1.4 follows the action for a year and graphically explains how the S&P 500 futures traded from the beginning of September 2001 through September 2002. Prior to the terrorist attack, the financial markets had been going south. There was a brief rally from

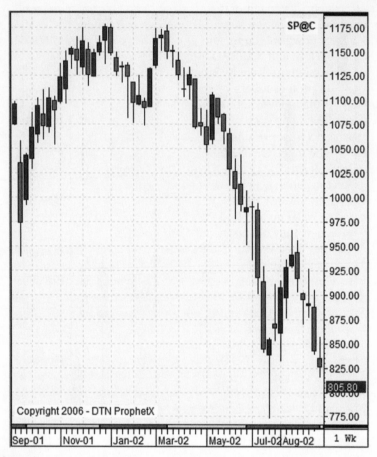

FIGURE 1.4 With prices trading in the 1,100 range in early September 2001, they initially dropped significantly. Perhaps it was a patriotic rally, but prices recouped in November 2001 and stayed high for several months. Then in March 2002, prices again began falling and dropped dramatically for months. (*Source*: Copyright 2006-DTN ProphetX)

November 2001 until March 2002. Then a big downhill trend began and lasted for many months.

The attack on the Twin Towers happened in the morning hours shortly before the major trading centers in the United States opened their trading sessions. After the destruction, the exchanges closed for a week. Only traders with knowledge of global markets were able to hedge any long positions by using exchanges operating off our shores. Those doing business exclusively in U.S. financial products that were traded on U.S. exchanges were effectively locked out of the markets. I was able to continue my business because I shifted my activities to a German product—the Dax. The Dax is a very powerful, large, and globally respected index. Just as with our S&P 500, Dow, and NASDAQ, there is both a cash index and a futures index. I trade the futures equity index. If necessary, I was able to hedge my positions and protect assets or make money on the short side because I understood that somewhere around the globe trading was active, and I sought and found one such market.

By using a 24-hour trading clock, you can see the immediate effects of an event on the markets. The tape expresses the world's view. For example, if Microsoft (MSFT) receives a sanction from the European Union, and news of that negative event is aired while Asian markets are still trading, prices in Tokyo for MSFT stock will fall. Traders in the United States may be stunned to wake up and find that their shares have lost value. Because they were asleep, they did not hedge their positions or take any protective action. Had they been watching, they would have known what was happening because the markets give instant feedback. The bad news would have been immediately expressed in Asian trading. No one can watch the markets 24 hours a day. Therefore, experienced traders use protective stops to remove them from the market if there is an unexpected market shift. They do not assume a heavy load of stock, bond, or futures positions and forget them. That is a sure way to lose money.

Assume that you are holding a large short position and good news breaks at 8:00 PM when U.S. exchanges are closed. Prices take off and losses mount in your bearish portfolio. You can twiddle your thumbs and wait for New York and Chicago to open for business the next morning to respond to the news and lose a princely sum. Or, you can trade the night markets. If possible, you can exit your shorts and possibly shift your position. If you are unable to liquidate your holdings after hours, you can hedge by buying futures contracts in the S&P 500, Dow, Nasdaq, or some foreign market. You can even hedge with a commodity like gold or oil. By using a global approach, you have a wide range of opportunities to limit your losses and maybe even make some good profits.

The biggest challenge for a trader is to maximize profits while limiting risk and protecting assets. Having knowledge of the global markets gives traders a better chance to achieve that goal. I know well the importance of limiting risk. Believe me, I learned that lesson in 1987. If you read my first book, *Winning the Day Trading Game,* you know that I was a victim of the '87 crash; at least, I made myself a victim because I was too exposed. I was foolishly overleveraged in the options market. When the right combination of economic forces united, a storm blew down Wall Street and I was in its path. I was wiped out. When calm returned, my finances were in shambles and my self-confidence destroyed. It took years for me to get back on my feet, but I finally made it. Now I am aware of those lurking dangers in the market and I work hard to protect myself against them. I still play the game, but I am a much more cautious player.

I am a trader and proud of it. When my older son, Winston, started college, I drove him to Auburn, Alabama, and attended the usual parent orientation sessions with him. I remember Winston telling me that I should not introduce myself as a trader. He thought other parents would not understand the term and they would be less than respectful of my occupation. I told him that in Chicago, traders were kings; nonetheless, in Auburn, Alabama, I would respect his wishes. Today, Winston, too, is a trader.

My favorite markets are equity index futures like the S&P 500, Dow, NASDAQ, and Dax. I have traded the S&P 500 futures since the very first day they traded. I especially like the mini contracts like the S&P e-mini. However, I trade or have traded just about everything. If I see an opportunity in the commodities arena, I trade it. In early 2006, gold and oil grabbed my attention. If a stock looks promising, I enter the equities market. I trade stocks both ways: long and short. It all depends on the play that is offered. I have traded more than a few options in my day, and the currency market is not a stranger to me. Although I do not consider it to be my strongest suit, I have made some money there.

Many traders believe that futures are too dangerous and risky. Admittedly, the futures markets have some unique and potentially deadly pitfalls. However, I see more danger in the traditional "buy it, hold it, and forget it" strategy of most traders. With futures, I generally enter and exit the market quickly. I may hold positions during most of a trading session, but as a rule I do not hold futures overnight. If I trade the night or Globex market, I exit my day's positions and then reenter once the night session has opened. Then, I monitor the play and always use protective stops to help me look after my interests. In sharp contrast, the buy-and-hold traders put on positions and forget them. When the night assassin comes prowling around the markets, they just get slaughtered.

Because the financial markets are dynamic, they constantly change. A day in the life of a global trader is never the same. That is probably why I love trading so much. Every sunrise brings new challenges and new experiences. Some days are great for shorting everything in sight and making a lot of money. Other days are filled with the exuberance of good financial news and a buyer takes home the big paycheck. Then there are those days when prices bobble up and down—a seesaw syndrome that leaves even the most astute short-term trader scratching his head and looking for some divine sign to enlighten the path and lead to profits. When the markets are active and when they are dormant, when profits are big or little, when money is made or lost, I am still a trader. I constantly look for winning opportunities where profits can be made.

I am a professional trader, and I trade almost every day. When I see a bull, I grab it by the horns, and when I spot a bear, I get in the cave with it. The challenge is, of course, to identify the move and dive into the market on the right side of it. That may sound easy, but believe me, it is not. Using a 24-hour trading clock helps me get and stay on the winning team. My RoadMap™ software is designed to follow the 24-hour markets and track their paths while I am sleeping. It saves time and gives me an edge with my analysis.

HOW I MAKE MONEY USING GLOBAL KNOWLEDGE

Rewind to April 2000. Americans were caught in a dot-com frenzy; investors purchased every Internet stock in sight. Many market commentators warned that the "New Economy" was nothing more than a veil for overpriced equities that were breaking all of the rules. Dot-coms with no business plan, no earnings, and no track record were going public, and everyone seemed to be buying. Hopes and expectations were the real commodities being traded, as droves of investors rushed to put their money down for every Internet-associated IPO. Never mind that many of the high-tech investments were nothing more than castles in the sky, sprinkled with fairy dust and built on clouds of dreams. They lacked foundation, but no one cared.

On March 10, 2000, the Nasdaq reached an all-time high as prices traded around the 5,132 mark (see Figure 1.5). Many decided the naysayers were wrong. Perhaps traditional thinkers did not understand the significance of the Web and its future money-making potential. Wall Street was conducting business differently, and most traders believed there was no problem. Investors who bought technology and the dot-coms were like King Midas; their holdings turned to gold. Apparently, there was no reason to worry—at least not on March 10, 2000. Markets were strong, and the bulls were stampeding to higher prices. However, Freddy Krueger crept into the markets in April, and the Nasdaq took a dive.

Toby Keith, one of my favorite country-music entertainers, has an album titled *Dream Walking*. In one of the songs, Toby talks about knowing when the dream ends. In April 2000, the dream was coming to a close for the high-tech traders, but few realized it. My first clue came from across the Pacific. Around 4:00 AM Central Time. I do not remember the exact day, but it was in mid-April—the 14th or 15th, as I recall. I learned that the Nikkei and the Hang Seng had suffered major losses during their trading

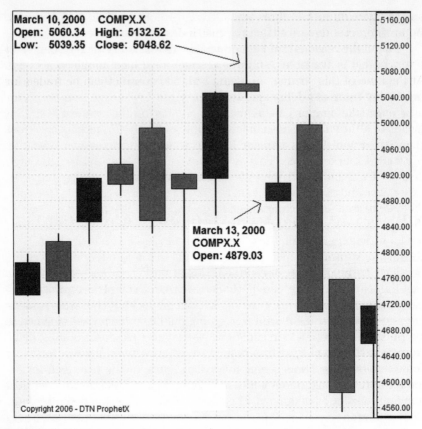

FIGURE 1.5   The high-techs were soaring in the early part of March 2000. But, the picture soon changed. (*Source*: Copyright 2006-DTN ProphetX)

sessions. The Nikkei is an index located in Tokyo; Hong Kong is home to the Hang Seng. Both the Tokyo and the Hong Kong indexes ended their sessions with extraordinary declines. The sell-offs in Asia piqued my interest; perhaps a global move was in the making. Asian markets were being hit by some severe winds; would those winds die down before traveling to western shores, or would they intensify? Would Europe have the strength to buck the Asian trend or follow it? I dressed and headed for the office.

I worked out of a couple of small rooms a few miles from my home. My trading school was in its infancy, and I used the rented space as my personal trading headquarters. At the office, I had several monitors and I easily viewed the action on the futures markets. For a number of reasons, I like trading and following the index futures like the S&P 500 futures, the Nasdaq, and the Dow futures. Futures are, after all, predictors of the cash markets. Futures forecast the prices that the cash index expects, at least in theory.

One of the reasons that I am drawn to this market is the high degree of leverage that is available. A futures account must be a margined account. At the time of this writing, an e-mini S&P 500 contract can be traded for only a few thousand dollars per contract (some brokerage houses require an even smaller margin). Currently, the e-mini is trading around 1,400. That means that the value of one contract is about $70,000. Translation: For just a few thousand dollars a trader has the ability to control approximately $70,000 of market value. That is a great deal for me because the high degree of margin allows me to leverage my skills. With margin, one with experience and expertise is able to get the most bang for his buck. However, the uneducated and inexperienced lose their hides. Because I have traded the S&P futures since they first began in 1982; I believe that I have more than a little experience in this field. Therefore, on this day my focus was on the index futures.

Once in the office, I concentrated on Europe. To my delight, the weakness exhibited in Asia repeated itself in Europe; London, Paris, Frankfurt—everywhere the skies were gray and getting grayer. Not only was the sell-off moving across the Pacific westward, but the downward spiral was accelerating. Europe's percentage of loss was greater than Asia's. The storm winds were moving faster and gaining strength by the minute. I was delighted, because I was seeing a potentially trending market. Because I trade futures, I make money in a market that goes up or down, and in a trending market I make a lot of money. Therefore, I began paying very close attention.

At 8:30 AM Central Time, when the U.S. day markets opened, prices immediately headed south. There were no buyers—everyone was a seller. There was no premium in the futures markets. I watched and waited; I sat in front of my computer screen reading the tape and watching the indicators get weaker and weaker. Generally, I consider the first five minutes of the day's trading session to be very important. During this time I determine if the bulls or the bears are in charge. In that first few minutes, the line is drawn in the sand, and each side dares the other to cross it. Today, I wanted to know if the bulls could exert enough strength to pull the markets back up to their opening prices. But, there were not enough buyers for prices to rebound. After five minutes of trading, none of the index futures—the S&P 500, Dow, or Nasdaq—were able to rise. Not even one of them bothered to put up an effort to challenge the day's preliminary prices. The index futures knew only one direction, and that was down.

Get short. Sell something. That was my immediate reaction. I knew the bears were in control, and the profit takers from this move were the shorts. I started selling and selling hard. I identified the weakest market. Which one was selling off the fastest? That was where I wanted to put my money down. I identified my play and sold, and then I watched the profits start rolling in. As the minutes passed, I knew I was watching an unusual event because weakness was evident across the board and things appeared to be getting worse by the minute. I looked at the S&P 500 futures; a support level was hit and I expected some attempt by the bulls to regain control. I knew that if the market was responding normally, buyers should be stepping in at this level. But, that was not happening on this day.

Generally, in a healthy market, when support is touched, there is an attempt to rally or retrace. The rally may not be successful, but there is a valiant effort. For example, the number 37 tends to be a key number in the S&P futures. It does not matter if trading is at 1,037, 1,137, or 1,237. That 37-price point is going to serve as a key number. When that price is hit in a falling market, one expects it to prop prices up. In other words, at that point one generally expects buyers to step in and pull prices skyward.

Not that day, though—when the S&P or the Nasdaq hit key numbers, prices just sat and churned away for a short time. Then, the support level broke and the markets tumbled to the next support level (see Figure 1.6). That important 37 on the S&P yielded quickly and prices collapsed to the next key number of 35 and quickly fell to 32. At the new point, the process repeated itself, until the market again dropped to the next level of support.

Hour after hour, I kept shorting the futures, loading the boat with more and more contracts and making more and more money. At one point, I had about $50,000,000 in asset value riding on the bears. But, the play kept paying me. The buy-and-hold traders were suffering more by the minute while I was making thousands. As the session continued, the debacle kept unfolding and my money continued pouring in.

At midday, I prepared for a possible turnaround. I know that generally, during the middle of the day, there is a reversal or retracement. At least there is an attempt made to flip the coin. In anticipation, I lightened my load, watched, and waited. No reversal. No attempted rally. The bears were conquerors, and the bulls were in hiding. A meltdown was in progress.

Because I recognized the signs early and I knew the significance of the Asian and European sell-offs, and because I was always ready to make money, it was a great day for me. Air was leaking from the dot-com bubble. I, like many traders, had been waiting for it, and my knowledge and skill allowed me to take advantage of it. By the time the market closed in the afternoon, I had made a lot of money. The numbers told me what the next day's financial news would report. A storm had hit Wall Street.

During those fateful days in April 2000, the Nasdaq lost more than $2 trillion of market value. In one week it dropped over 25 percent from its highest prices. In March, prices were nearing the 5,050 price on the Nasdaq, and by the end of the first week in October, they sat at 1,114. April 14 was

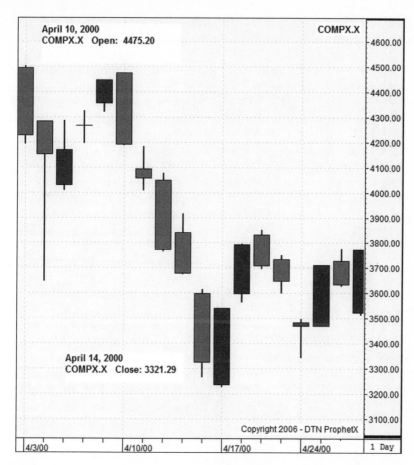

FIGURE 1.6 Daily price action on the Nasdaq. Look at prices on April 10, 2000. Note how they fall on April 14 and 15. My 24-hour trading clock gave me a good tip as to the expected market direction. (*Source*: Copyright 2006-DTN ProphetX)

one of the days in that timeframe that saw a hefty price drop. I know that many traders around the country and across the world were in a state of panic on April 15, 2000, and throughout that entire time period (see Figure 1.7), because I remember all too vividly the panic I felt following October 19, 1987. I am glad to report that this time I was on the winning team. Unlike scads of investors, I had not been taken by surprise, because I saw and properly interpreted the storm warnings. A storm on Wall Street is not always a bad thing. If the winds are blowing your way, you can enjoy the breeze.

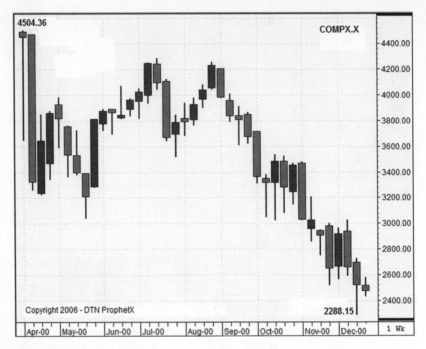

FIGURE 1.7 The Nasdaq fell from April 2000 until the end of the year. Prices continued to go down day after day. Remember, my first big hint that the day of reckoning was at hand came from across the Pacific and Atlantic. When I saw prices falling dramatically in Asia and Europe, I knew the U.S. markets were in for a rough ride. (*Source*: Copyright 2006-DTN ProphetX)

THE WINNER GETS THE CASH

The winner gets a toy: A shiny red Corvette convertible was my trophy for the day's work. In celebration of my winnings, I was able to get a new ride with a big price tag and no guilt attached. I selected red in honor of the shorts. The bulls had paid me big. In the aftermath of the initial Nasdaq fall, there was a lot of talk about the big winners and the big losers in the dot-com fiasco. It seems that some of the greatest minds in their respective fields were like lambs strolling to the slaughter. Bill Gates, Charles Schwab, and Michael Dell were multibillion dollar losers during the week of April 15, 2000. Warren Buffet, by contrast, was a big winner. His net worth was reputed to have increased by more than $500 million. I certainly made nowhere near the money Buffet made and the news media was not pounding down my door to get an interview, but I was definitely in the winner's circle. I enjoyed earning enough for my Corvette and having money left over to put in the bank. It was a great trading day!

The bull market did not end in a day. Unlike the strong winds of a hurricane that blow through in a few hours, the doldrums of the market continued for months. I shorted the Nasdaq futures and other index futures many times between April and October and reaped the rewards. Bad weather on Wall Street can destroy those who are unprepared, but those who see the storm clouds coming can earn their keep.

Rocking Around the Clock Brings Home the Bacon

Few days are like those profit-making sessions in April 2000. Most days one has to work hard to bring home a little bacon. Take this example of a random day in the markets.

"Dad, everything's up. Talk to you later."

It is a few minutes past 4:00 AM Central Time, and Morgan, my younger son, is reporting on the action in Asia and Europe. When Morgan, was in high school and college, he checked the index futures around the world each trading day. If financial markets across both the Pacific and the Atlantic were trading in the same direction, he called me.

On this day, his call is my cue to get to my computer and check out the situation for myself. I'm not the only one getting a call. In fact, a lot of folks received phone calls because at that time Morgan had been operating his little "fee-for-notification" service for some time. He had built up quite a clientele. His message tells me that Tokyo and Hong Kong closed their sessions up; and London, Paris, Germany, and Switzerland are also all trading up. However, it does not matter what the direction of the move is; the significant thing is that all of these futures markets in major financial centers around the world are following the same track. This day, their direction happens to be up. I slip out of bed and head downstairs. I have several monitors in my home office and can easily survey the landscape. With a few clicks of my mouse I get a panoramic view.

The Dax, a powerful German index, has been moving up since its open at 2:00 AM Central Time (since May 2006, the Dax opens at 1:00 AM Central). It is nearing a key resistance level of 6,350. Therefore, I pick 6,351 as a likely place to buy some contracts. I want to see resistance broken before I join the fray, and 6,351 is just across the line. Then I turn my attention to the S&P, Dow, and Nasdaq futures. Like the Dax, the charts are all moving up. Quickly, I identify the next level of resistance on the S&P. Again, I want resistance to be broken before I make a purchase. The market moves up to my entry points, and now I dive in. I take some Dax contracts and some S&Ps. Within a minute or so, I am taking down profits and lightening my load. Trading the Dax increases my accuracy with the S&P; it takes only a trained eye to see the connection between the two indexes and gain the benefit of using both for guidance.

I plan to hold some futures contracts in both indexes and try to catch the momentum of a bullish move and, I hope, a trending day. If the bulls are really strong, this could be one of those days when prices keep going up and up as the minutes and hours pass. The possibility excites me. I put in my protective stops and head back to bed. I need more rest before going to work.

At 6:00 AM, I check the markets again. Things are still looking good and the markets are strong. Both my S&P and my Dax contracts are making me money. The 6:00 AM Central Time price on the Dax futures is one that I consider to be important. Some years back, one of my students, Ron McDow, spent a great deal of time studying the Dax. Ron pointed out to me the importance of the 6:00 AM price. I began watching and analyzing it. I realized that the 6:00 price-point is very important. I rely on that price as a major pivot. I often determine my entry price based on it and I use it for 24 hours. (My rationale for honoring this particular price point is that I consider it to be a benchmark for afternoon trading in Germany. Traders are returning from lunch and reevaluating the day's move.) Within seconds, the Dax is trading above the pivot and I jump in again, adding to my positions. A couple of minutes pass and again I am able to lighten my load and exit some of my contracts with a small monetary gain from each contract. I am still long the S&P and the Dax and I tighten my protective stops, dress and head to the office.

Some big economic news is being released at 9:00 AM Central. I know the markets might react violently to the numbers. Therefore, I plan to monitor my trade carefully. However, by 7:30 AM, the markets' upward momentum appears to be sputtering. Things start moving down, and my stops are hit on both the Dax and the S&P. I am taken out of the markets.

At 9:00 AM, the data are released and the numbers are not as good as predicted. Suddenly, there is a sell-off in progress. No worry for me, because my protective stop has already taken me out of the action. The sunny blue skies of early-morning trading are now mixed with scattered clouds, so I go to the sidelines to analyze and consider my course of action. What appeared to be a major gust from across the Pacific and the Atlantic has died down. Faced with some economic reality from our shores, this storm has fizzled with no great move. The upward surge stalled and the market moved down. I made some money early in the day, but midday marked the end of profits for the session.

The above scenario is no particular day; it is many days. A trend appears to be developing across the oceans, but other factors or events stop the move and the market stalls. What appeared to be shaping up to be a bullish explosion is nothing but a dud. Every day is not like that fateful April day in 2000, when I correctly identified a major global market trend and was able to ride the wave of the storm to reap some pretty big profits.

On days like these, I generally make a little money but it's not enough to brag about. These times remind me more of a Ford Taurus than a shiny red Corvette. I play the game and struggle with the bipolar tendencies of the financial markets. With a little luck, I take home a few bucks. I'd like to make more, but I know that a lot of days filled with consistent small profits may result in a Corvette buy. Being consistent on these average days is the name of the game. Using a global clock helps me stay consistent. Figure 1.8 shows how this worked on July 12, 2006.

> *Using a 24-hour trading clock minimizes risk, provides a market edge, and helps me achieve greater consistency.*

FIGURE 1.8 Prices on the S&P futures on July 12, 2006. Each bar represents 30 minutes of trading. The bar on the far left reflects the price action when New York and Chicago opened. Prices trend consistently downward until noon. Notice how sluggish the market gets at midday. My trading opportunities were basically over. The morning was my time to make a little money. Many days are like this day. You have to find trading opportunities and take them when you can.

TRADING IS NOT EASY

Trading is hard! Like any job, some days are more interesting than others; the market does not always put on a spectacular show. I am a trader. It is my profession, and I take great pride and pleasure in it. Every day I speak with people who want to make their living by trading. With hard work and perseverance, some of them will make it, but many of them will not. Over the years I have succeed at my quest. However, every day is not filled with bells and whistles. Some days are like those great shorting days in April of 2000, when the profits just kept rolling into the bank. But on other days— in fact, most days—one has to look for opportunities and make the most of them when they are spotted. Then there are other times when the markets do absolutely nothing; at least nothing that I can trade. So, I just sit, analyze, and wait. Like a sniper waiting to get his target in his sites, I focus and keep my powder dry.

One of the hardest things to do is to sit and wait. But as the years have passed, I have become better at it. Trading is all about identifying market moves and maximizing the money-making opportunities in them. And it is also about staying out of the market when there is no opportunity and always limiting one's risk and protecting oneself against a variety of potential nightmares on Wall Street. In the trading game, it is critical to manage your money so that when opportunity comes knocking, you can take advantage of it. If the best move of the year appears, you cannot play unless you have money in your account. Therefore, money management is critical, and I have devoted Chapter 11, *Managing Risk in Global Markets* to that topic. Financial markets continuously change. Sometimes there is a great deal of volume, other times very little. Events or economic data may spur prices upward or lagging indicators may pull things down. Markets are dynamic. For example, from the spring of 2005 until May 2006, the S&P futures had an average true range (ATR) of approximately 10 points. That is, on most days, prices moved only 10 points up or down from their highest point to their lowest. However, by early June the picture had changed and the ATR was 17 points, representing a 700 percent increase in volatility. Therefore, successful traders must adapt to the changes.

The market is different every day, but my routine is not. I trade during the same times and I follow the same strategy day in and day out. I believe that certain timeframes during the day are best for me, and that is when I will be sitting at my computer screen. At other times, I will be teaching my classes and running my school. I will not sit in front of my monitor all day and be lured into a mesmerizing unprofitable market.

MY TRADING ROUTINE ROCKS AROUND THE CLOCK

Market action follows the sun. Somewhere right now—day or night—the financial markets are active. Savvy traders use that action to make money. My trading routine incorporates the 24-hour trading clock and takes advantage of it to maximize my profits and expand my universe.

In order to become a consistent trader, one must follow a routine and a strategy, and I do both. Unless I receive one of those morning wake-up calls from Morgan, my trading day generally begins about 6:00 AM Central Time. I believe Benjamin Franklin had it right when he said, "Early to bed, early to rise, makes a man healthy, wealthy, and wise." Therefore, one of the first things I always do is step to the office down the hall and catch a quick look at the markets. Maggie, our English bulldog, seems to await my rising, and she follows me on her short little legs to my trading station. She is my only early-morning companion.

By 6:00 AM Central, a lot of information is available—remember that it is already lunchtime in Europe and the Asian markets have completed their trading day. I check to determine their direction. Asia ends trading around 3:30 AM Central (4:00 AM during Daylight Saving Time). Generally, my only concern is whether or not the East traded up or down, and if the move was significant. If Asia was very strong or very weak, I will look to Europe to see if the sentiment is contagious.

Germany, France, Switzerland, and London all begin trading around 2:00 AM Central Time. Sometimes, if I am anticipating a significant move, I may get up and make a very early morning trade. But, the older I get, the less interested I am in losing my sleep. Therefore, around 6:00 AM, when I am checking out Asia, I also review the European action. Are the major markets in Europe in agreement as to a direction? If so, I identify the direction and check to see if it is in sync with Asia. Then I look at the U.S. markets; I particularly want to check on the S&P futures, the Nasdaq futures, and the Dow futures. Are they agreeing with the rest of the world? Is a trend developing? Generally, at this time of day I consider trading two indexes— the S&P futures and the Dax futures. After placing my trades, I dress and head for the office. When I say that I placed my trades, understand that I have also placed protective stops. That is, if my order is elected and I am in the market, I also have a stop in place to take me out if I have made a mistake and the trade goes against me.

Once I get in the car, I phone the office and ask the early morning crew to fire up my machines. As soon as I step into my workspace, I glance at my trade. If things are going my way, I may leave the trade working until 7:00 AM or so. However, I will probably not make any other trades until after the

U.S. markets open. I use this time to gather key numbers. I look at yesterday's trading, as well as historical data. I consider yearly opening prices, monthly opening prices, and weekly opening prices, and I visualize today's action and place it in the bigger context of the market.

Gathering these numbers helps me identify points of support and resistance in the market. With that data, I plan some potential plays. At what point will I consider buying the Dax, the S&P, the Dow, the Nasdaq, or equities? At what point would I consider selling? If one of my hypothetical buying or selling points is hit, it may signal a breakout move and I am ready to take advantage of it. Once I am prepared, let the games begin.

When the Chicago Mercantile Exchange, or CME, opens for business, I return to my computer and watch. If I am able to identify an early move, I place a trade. Otherwise, I sit on the sidelines and check the indicators. Let me repeat, it is far better to stay out of the market unless you have a clear sense of where it is going.

I consider the 9:00 AM, 9:30 AM, and 10:00 AM Central Time price points to be important. Therefore, at these times I get far more serious about trading. If I see a trade, I take it. Otherwise, I wait. If I have not traded by 10:15 AM, I probably will not trade until after lunch. I busy myself with other things. I will not sit and stare at a computer screen or try to make a trade when there is none. Believe me, I used to do that. I traded like crazy all day and expended all of my emotional energy watching the market go nowhere. Now, I do not do it. I only trade when there are opportunities to make money. Due to the reduced volume in the market, I consider the time between 10:15 AM and 12:30 PM to be a difficult time to trade and I stay out. Generally, during this time I handle business issues.

At 12:30 PM, I return to my computer screen and get another look at the tape. At 12:30 PM the market tends to reset, and the afternoon action may be quite different from the morning moves. I like to observe from 12:30 to 1:00, and I often do not trade until 1:00 PM. Then, if I see a trade, I take it. However, unless the trade is going my way and I feel very good about it, I exit with my profits sometime before 1:30 PM Central. Between 1:30 and 2:00 PM Central, the market can be extremely volatile and dangerous—too volatile and unpredictable for my taste. Bonds are nearing their daily close, and experience has taught me that trading during these 30 minutes can be very risky. Therefore, I get away from the market and back to the rest of my life.

As seasoned traders know, the last minutes of a trading session may also be a good time for trading. Often, the volume picks up at the close because many traders realize that they are on the wrong side of the market and are forced to exit their positions. Therefore, there may be a lot of rapid price movement; if properly identified, the rewards can be worthwhile. If I see a move, I may trade again during this time.

The NYSE closes at 3:00 PM Central Time and the CME (the S&P and Nasdaq futures) closes at 3:15 PM Central. That is when most traders call it a day. They close their trading platforms and forget all about business until New York and Chicago come to life the next morning. That, however, is not my game plan. I know that the CME begins after hours, or Globex, trading at 3:30 PM, and the Chicago Board of Trade (CBOT) opens for trading at 6:00 PM Central. I want to know the opening price of the S&P during the Globex session, and I am interested in the first 30 minutes of Globex trading. That early-evening action may give me a hint as to what to expect during the evening session. Generally, I do not trade at this time, but I take note of how the market is acting and I store the information away to help me later.

I consider myself a global trader because I use international markets to help me trade. Sometimes I also trade foreign indexes. For example, I often trade the Dax futures. The Dax is located in Frankfurt, Germany, and it is a powerful index that may set the pace for trading throughout Europe. The Nikkei opens in Tokyo around 6:00 PM and the Hang Seng session begins in Hong Kong at 8:00 PM. Generally, I have no interest in these particular opening prices. My concern is with the close. I want to know if trading on these exchanges ended up or down. It is not necessary for me to watch them minute by minute. When I wake up at 5:00 or 6:00 AM Central, I check the prices. Then I determine whether I want to trade on the basis of them. If so, I do so—and if not, I walk away and wait for a better opportunity.

That, in a nutshell, is my trading schedule. It is relaxed and easy. I do not work at a frantic pace, and I do not trade continuously. I pick my trades carefully, and I trade during times when the odds are greatest that I can make money. I always know the risk of a trade, and I always take steps to protect my interests. Some days I am profitable, and other days I am not. The secret of trading is to win more often than not and to maximize profits and minimize loses. It is not easy. The markets are often unpredictable, and reading the indicators and joining the winning team is difficult. But, with persistence and hard work, the game can be mastered.

My Trading Day	
4:00 AM	If Asia and Europe are trending in the same direction, I identify a market entry price and place a trade. If there is no trend emerging, I go back to bed and get more rest. (Morgan's service is a real sleep saver on these days.)
6:00 AM	Note the 6:00 AM Dax futures price. Watch the Dax trade around this price. Is the Dax in sync with Asia and the United States? If so, I will probably trade the Dax.

(continued)

My Trading Day   *(continued)*

7:30 AM   Many times scheduled economic news is released at this time. If I am in the market from an earlier trade, I tighten my stop and watch carefully. I do not want a storm to blow through and destroy my resources.

8:30 AM   New York and Chicago open their sessions and the beat gets faster. I am very interested in the opening prices and the first five minutes or so of trading. I want to know whether the bulls or the bears are the strongest. That may give me a clue as to what to expect from the day's trading.

10:15 AM   Get away from the computer screen. This tends to be a difficult time to trade. Volume generally leaves the market and the probability of success is diminished.

12:30 PM   The index futures often reset and reverse or accelerate a morning move. If I am able to identify a play before 1:15 PM, I trade. Otherwise, I wait.

1:30 PM   I try to stay clear of the markets for 30 minutes. I refer to this time as the Grim Reaper because prices often jump erratically.

2:30 PM   The day sessions are ending. The open outcry pits of the NYSE close at 3:00 and in Chicago the S&P pits close at 3:15. If I see a late-day play, I trade. Otherwise, I wait for another opportunity.

3:30 PM   The Globex session opens and the S&P futures and the Nasdaq futures are open for electronic trading.

4:00 PM   The Dow futures close at the CBOT.

6:00 PM   The Nikkei opens in Tokyo.*

6:15 PM   Dow futures, bond futures, and gold and silver futures may be traded on the ECBOT.

8:00 PM   The Hang Seng opens in Hong Kong.*

2:00 AM   Many European indexes open. For years the Dax futures in Germany opened at 2:00 AM, but recently began opening at 1:00 AM.*

(continued)

My Trading Day *(continued)*

8:30 AM   The outcry pits open and the day trading session begins again.

*Because I am located in south Alabama, I use Central Time. All times on this schedule are Central.

Note: Asia does not use Daylight Saving Time. Therefore, hours of operation shift when we have Daylight Saving hours. Also, Germany has Daylight Saving time changes, but those dates differ slightly from those in the United States. Therefore, always check for exact hours of operation when trading these markets.

Trade Secret #1: Your trading day did not begin today; it started yesterday afternoon. When you learn that fact and use that information, your trading will become more consistent.

REVIEW

Wall Street may be open for business eight hours a day, but the global markets operate virtually 24 hours a day. Active trading follows the path of the sun as it moves from east to west. While Americans are eating their dinner on Monday evening, it is Tuesday in Tokyo and the financial markets are trading. When U.S. traders are snug in their beds and sleeping soundly, brokerage houses in France, Germany, and London are busy and the financial markets are alive with a flurry of activity. That simple bit of information helps me avoid risk, expand my trading horizons, and increase my profits.

Because I know that markets are trading 24 hours a day, I also know that bad things can happen to my portfolio while I am sleeping. Scary things frequently happen to global traders who are not prepared. A terrorist attack or a Fed chairman delivering a prepared speech during a dinner in Washington, D.C., may send financial markets crashing down. Therefore, global traders must know how to protect themselves in a 24-hour marketplace.

If you have a chance to make money from 8:00 to 5:00, think of how much more money you can make from 8:00 in the morning until 8:00 the following morning. Trading opportunities are greatly expanded. And, if there are money-making chances in the U.S., think how many more trading possibilities exist if you open up Asia and Europe. Having knowledge of global markets expands the playing field.

Finally, using a 24-hour trading clock may give you a heads up or a hint as to the course the U.S. financial markets may take during their trading session. It is true that sometimes Asia and Europe will trade in one direction and the United States will not follow. But, there are times when having knowledge of the action across the Atlantic and Pacific keeps you on track and steers you in the right direction. And, there are other times when knowledge of global market action keeps you from falling for a false play. Knowledge of the worldwide picture helps you reduce losses and stay more profitable.

Trading is a 24-hour game, and those who understand that fact will be in a better position to limit risk, increase their trading opportunities, stay on the right side of the action, and be more consistent and profitable.

 MARKET INSIGHT

- Financial markets operate 24 hours a day. Take advantage of that reality.

CHAPTER 2

Stepping to the Tune

Understanding How the Markets Work

The big boys in Chicago picked more than a few bucks from my pockets before I took my first swing. It was the early 1980s, and I was an arrogant young broker who thought I knew everything. I was vacationing in Maui and noticed that precious metals were bullish. I had been studying this particular area of the market for only a short time, but nevertheless, before I left my hotel room for the golf course, I bought some silver futures contracts. I did not understand much about silver—I knew just enough to pose a danger to myself. I do not know why it happened (my best guess now is that some important economic news was released), but once I was in the market, silver prices quickly tumbled. Before I had teed off, I lost $5,000 per contract. Believe it or not, my tee shot was even worse than my trading.

As I came to appreciate, commodities prices, including those for precious metals, are affected by many factors. I was not in step with the market's rhythm; I was having trouble dancing to its tune. Perhaps my loss was attributable to poor employment data or interest rate fears, who knows? At any rate, something spooked traders, and prices fell faster than Dale Earnhardt Jr. makes a lap at Talladega. And that is fast, real fast. From this lesson and many others along the way, I learned the importance of educating myself before putting my money on the line. A big part of that education is listening to the nuances in the tempo and properly reading the lyrics or language of the market. That language includes far more than ordering a meal in French or flagging down a cab in Spanish. I had to gain a basic and useful understanding of how the global markets work.

IT'S A SMALL WORLD, AFTER ALL

When it comes to financial matters, it is a small world, especially in this age of technology. If terrorists succeed in executing a major attack or inflation numbers confirm fears of escalating prices, or the gross domestic product (GDP) excites the market with signs of strength and growth, our advanced communication networks spread the word quickly. Then traders, with just a click of a computer mouse, have the ability to respond, and in seconds, they do so. Around the country and across the world they buy or sell on the basis of their interpretation of the events and their presumed effect of those events on the economy and the markets.

Generally, the initial response to economic data or news may be exaggerated, and after a few minutes or hours prices return to their pre-news levels. However, at other times news will result in a market shift. Prices that have been moving up or down for weeks or months may stop dead in their tracks and reverse; the entire landscape will suddenly change.

For example, on July 19, 2006, Ben Bernanke testified before Congress, noting that the economy had slowed somewhat, which would reduce pressure on inflation. He also said the Fed would be watching to see what effect previous rate hikes would have on future economic growth. The markets reacted strongly positive, as shown in Figure 2.1.

When I am trading, I have the television turned on, but I keep the sound off. If major news breaks, I touch the volume button to get the details. The tape tells the story; when news hits, prices react in a way that is abnormal for a regular trading session. I may have no idea what has happened, but I know that something big has sent the markets reeling. That is the point at which I turn up the volume on the television set and get the details.

Stocks, bonds, currencies, commodities, derivatives including futures and options—all of these are financial products traded globally. Like the famous shot heard round the world in 1776, economic, political, or social events that are significant enough will send a message heard around the world in the financial markets, and prices will respond quickly. Any trader with a little experience knows the power that news can exert on Wall Street. Never mind that the event took place in some remote village in Africa or some corporation headquartered in Hong Kong; if the news is considered to be of great consequence, it will affect prices in New York.

FIGURE 2.1 The first spike up on the left side of the chart shows the market's response to Ben Bernanke's July 19, 2006, message: Inflation may be under control and the incessant interest rates hikes may soon end. At least, that is how many traders interpreted the message. The Dow rose more than 200 points for the day, and the S&P 500 also saw a bullish move. Markets move quickly on news.

CAPITAL IS MOBILE

Money seeks opportunity. Investors from Alabama to Michigan and from the coast of South Carolina to the coast of California all want the same thing: They want the best money-making investment for the least amount of risk. And Americans are not alone; traders in Paris, London, Tokyo, and every other financial center also strive to maximize profits while minimizing risks. Therefore, those with capital and knowledge continuously seek the best investment opportunities. For example, if economic conditions favor corporate and industrial growth and expansion, equity prices will rise as investors, hoping to buy a piece of the action, put money into the stock market. Or, if inflation escalates and makes the cost of doing business too high, the economy begins slowing down and many investors abandon the equities markets and move investment dollars into precious metals or some other area in an attempt to hedge the inflationary blow to their portfolios.

Traders have a wide array of choices, including stocks, bonds, options, futures, real estate, commodities, currencies, precious metal, and others. If economic or political factors make one or more of these products too risky or financially unattractive, money will flow out of that product and into another one that offers better odds and better value. Likewise, if one area of the world presents superior chances for success, savvy investors will move their capital to that arena.

In its simplest form, the financial markets are like a group of kids playing tug-of-war. However, there is not one rope and two sides; there is a complex connection of many ropes and many sides. Players all want to be on the strongest team and have the ability to move from team to team as opportunities shift. For example, if bond prices are good and equities risky, more money will move into bonds. If interest rates are low and home prices are rising, money will move into that area. If a storm or bad weather condition destroys a significant amount of the corn crop so that demand far exceeds supply, buyers will step in to take a piece of that action because corn prices will likely rise. There are a variety of places where money can be placed, and the most attractive spot will draw the most investors.

Many factors affect investor decisions. Some of the most important of these are inflation, employment statistics, interest rates, commodities prices for raw materials and products like gold and precious metals, corn, wheat, and soybeans. Then there are trade balances and imbalances, deficits and surpluses, emerging economies, and developed economies and their needs. Add to the mix war and geopolitical conflicts—all of these and others play a role in the decisions that global investors make. Once investment or trading decisions are made, advances in technology allow transactions to be executed rapidly and easily. National borders, at least in developed countries, rarely pose a problem; many institutions and investors around the globe trade U.S. currency or stocks listed on the NYSE or some other U.S. exchange. Likewise, many Americans own equities in foreign corporations and trade the euro, yen, or other foreign currency.

The big idea is that capital is mobile and has the ability to flow from sector to sector and from nation to nation. Clearly, it is impossible to explain in one sentence, paragraph, or chapter all of the aspects of the global marketplace and how they work. It is too easy to say that the law of supply and demand explains everything, because political decisions and social and economic policies alter the supply and demand equation.

The good news is that one does not need a Ph.D. in macroeconomics to be a good trader. I am not an economist; I am a trader. I may flunk a macroeconomics exam on formulas or theories, but I know the importance of various elements in the economy and how Wall Street is likely to react if those elements get out of kilter. Good traders know the basic principles that make the financial markets keep on ticking, and they know what the implications of certain economic changes will likely be. With that said, let me explain some of the aspects of the global economy that I think are significant to most traders and why I think they matter.

THE POWER OF SUPPLY AND DEMAND

Supply and demand is the ultimate law of the global marketplace. Although it is an elementary concept, we cannot discuss how the global markets work without noting the importance of supply and demand. After all, it is this principle that governs prices. Markets respond dramatically to changes in supply and demand or events that are perceived to alter the supply/demand equation. Throughout time, scarce products or items have commanded the greatest price. Obviously, if there are many widgets, there is no need to spend a lot of money buying one; just find someone willing to sell cheap and pick one up. The tricky part is that subtle economic changes may have rather dramatic effects on supply and demand, or at least slight changes that may alter trader and investor perceptions of supply and demand. For example, if the Department of Labor releases a report confirming significant jobs creation during the last month, traders understand that the economy is growing. Economic growth means corporations will likely do well. Therefore, the equities markets may experience a rush of buyers. Corporate growth means more commodities needed by industries for raw materials. Greater demand translates into higher prices. Therefore, prices on the commodities markets, especially prices for those commodities deemed to be in short supply, will probably move up.

One prime example of the law of supply and demand is the petroleum market. Not too long ago, $50 a barrel for crude oil was thought by most traders to be a huge price. Then Hurricane Ivan came along, accompanied by a slew of geopolitical conflicts and problems. Crude oil prices sailed past the $50 per barrel resistance. Things got even worse when Hurricane Katrina hit in 2005. Supplies of both crude and refined products were threatened while demand increased. Then resistance was easily crossed to the upside and prices reached to the $75.00 per barrel area. Oil pressures eased during the late summer months of 2006, and again headed toward the $50.00 levels. By the end of September, oil was trading around $61.00 a barrel. However, if our nation is faced with a fuel shortage, prices will again escalate.

FACTORS IN THE SUPPLY/DEMAND EQUATION

As a trader, always remember that the law of supply and demand is the ultimate regulator of market prices. Understand the significance and market impact of economic data and political and social events, and know how they alter the supply/demand equation. With that basic principle in mind, let's move on to discuss some of the major aspects of the global economy that investors need to watch.

Interest Rates and Why They Matter

Alan Greenspan, long-time chairman of the Federal Reserve, had a watch, and he knew how to read it. He adhered to a strict time schedule with his news releases. Traders knew that if a Federal Open Market Committee (FOMC) report was to be released at 1:15 PM Central Time, at precisely 1:15 Central Time the information would be forthcoming. Following one of his first FOMC meetings on March 28, 2006, the new chairman, Ben Bernanke was not as precise. For several minutes after it was scheduled to release its report, the Fed was silent, and the markets waited and grew nervous. The brief delay resulted in a temporary sell-off in the equities markets. The momentary uncertainty sent some traders into a state of panic. That is how important interest rates are to the economy and to traders. A minute or two of delay in a news release and some traders hit the panic button.

Few actions have more repercussions on the global economy than interest rates. Rates have the power to move equity, commodity, currency, bond, and other prices. Interest rates determine the cost of borrowing; they dictate the price one must pay for additional cash. The flip side of the coin is that they also determine the rate of return that investors can receive for the money they lend. In other words, when rates rise, the lender wins and the borrower loses. Obviously, if the cost of borrowing is too high, consumers will borrow less, and so will business and industry. The auto manufacturing plant as well as the small, locally owned business may need funds for expansion and growth, but with high interest rates, their needs may not be met. The hiring of new employees or the purchasing of new equipment may be delayed until the price of borrowing the funds is reduced. If there is too much industrial and business shrinkage, unemployment numbers will likely rise and recession may follow.

The flip side of the equation is that cheap money encourages borrowing. When rates are very low, companies rush to get extra cash for anticipated needs and expansion. If growth is too strong, the labor market may be strained, pushing wages and salaries up and igniting inflation and thereby resulting in slowing growth.

The same scenario is true for consumers. As interest rates soar, fewer houses are purchased and fewer coats, appliances, automobiles, and other consumables move off the store shelves. With fewer dollars to spend, purchases are delayed. In early 2004, interest rates (federal funds rates) were at an all-time low of 1 percent. These low rates encouraged households to assume additional debt by buying on credit and refinancing real estate in order to get cash for new cars, or other consumables. For millions, the equity in their homes became their ATM. A recent commercial on television depicted a man who calmly explained that he has a beautiful home, new cars, membership in the country club, and debt up to his eyeballs. The commercial concluded with his plea, "Somebody help me." (Ironically, the suggested answer is another loan.)

Unfortunately, millions of Americans are in the same situation as the fellow in the commercial, and it is no joking matter. Excessive indebtedness of the average American places our economy at risk. If interest rates rise too quickly, many people will be trapped under a debt load that they cannot sustain. As more and more cash is used to pay interest on consumer debts, less cash is available for new purchases. As demand for new products decreases, supplies must also be reduced. Why produce more cars or televisions or appliances if consumers cannot afford to buy them?

Creditors may benefit from increased rates by earning more interest on loans, but if rates are too high, those same creditors may be faced with more and more defaulting debtors. Also, as rates rise, fewer home and other major loans will be made, and again, financial institutions will likely suffer as their bottom lines take a hit. Therefore, banking and financial products will have to become more creative and corporations better managed as interest rates rise.

When the Fed Speaks, People Listen

In the United States, the Federal Reserve has regulated interest rates and controlled our nation's monetary policy since its creation in 1913. The Federal Reserve System consists of 12 Federal Reserve Banks and a board of governors. Among its duties, the reserve banks serve as bankers for our national government and oversee and regulate the banking industry. One of the most powerful committees of the Fed is the Federal Open Market Committee. The FOMC meets regularly to assess and control our nation's monetary policy. To that end, the Fed has three major weapons in its arsenal: open market operations or control of the federal funds rate, the discount rate, and the reserve requirements. Of these three, control of the federal funds rate tends to be the most important and the most often used. The federal funds rate is the interest rate that is charged by depository institutions when money is loaned to other depository institutions overnight. That rate has a direct effect on interest rates charged for credit cards and other loans. After the Fed increased the federal funds rate to 5 percent on May 10, 2006, the prime rate charged by commercial banks rose to 8 percent. The federal funds rate has a direct relationship to rates charged to consumers.

In addition to setting the funds rate, the Fed regulates the discount rate or the interest rate charged to commercial banks and other depository institutions for loans made to them by their regional Federal Reserve Banks. Obviously, if money is cheap and available, customers will borrow more and spend more. The final weapon of the Fed is reserve requirements, or the amount of deposits that must be held in reserve by financial institutions. The Fed uses some complex formulas to determine the amount of cash that banks are required to keep in reserve. If this percentage is increased, banks must hold a greater amount of their depository funds in safekeeping. This action results in money being taken out of the economy because it is no longer available for lending.

In the spring of 2004, fearful that inflation was posing an economic threat and with rates down to an historic low around 1 percent, the Fed started raising rates, as shown in Figure 2.2. For 17 consecutive FOMC meetings, the federal funds rate ratcheted up another .25 percent. In the summer of 2006, with the funds rate at 5.25 percent and the corresponding prime rate at 8.5 percent, the Fed finally took a break. In the August and September meetings, rates remained unchanged. If the Fed fears that inflation is getting out of control, they will likely raise rates again. For a detailed look at the federal funds rate, go to http://www.federalreserve.gov/fomc/fundsrate.htm.

For those who remember the double-digit rates of the 1980s, a 5 or 6 percent rate may not sound too onerous. However, one must consider the rate in light of where it has been. A rate change from 1 percent to 5 percent is noteworthy. The economy is still growing rather dramatically in spite of the rate increases. Therefore, more hikes probably lie ahead in the near future. The financial markets will respond to rate changes. However, in reality, it is impossible to know what the response will be.

In addition, rates do not have to change for the market to gyrate. Mere rumor or anticipation of rate changes can also move prices significantly. During the morning of April 17, 2006, a member of the Federal Reserve board of governors publicly indicated that an end to rising rates might be near. The equity markets saluted the message by spiking upward. The S&P 500 Index futures climbed several points in seconds. A little later in the day, the minutes from the March FOMC meeting were made available to the public. Those minutes affirmed the earlier statements made to the

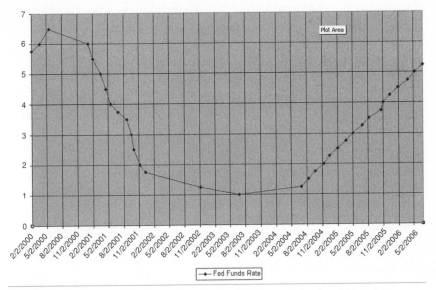

FIGURE 2.2   Notice the low federal funds rate in 2003. In June 2004, the interest rate increases began. Note the line heading up into 2006.

press by the board member. Again, stocks shot up in praise of the news. On that date, the Dow Jones rallied more than 200 points. Obviously, the equity markets consider interest rates to be very important, and at that time the market welcomed a halt to the increases. However, investors were disappointed again when the Fed did not stop the incessant hikes. The August meeting finally gave investors and traders the relief they wanted. When the Fed speaks—especially Ben Bernanke—the world listens. Following a statement by Bernanke in June 2006, indicating that the Fed would stay "vigilant" in its fight against inflation, prices in equity markets around the globe tumbled. In Tokyo, India, and across Asia and throughout Europe, the equity indexes reported the bearish news; the words of our Fed chairman sent prices down. Equity prices headed south because investors feared higher interest rates would bring our growing economy to its knees.

Another example of interest rate jitters was seen on May 17, 2006, when the Consumer Price Index (CPI), a report published monthly by the Department of Labor, confirmed inflation fears. The CPI is the most widely respected indicator of core inflation data. Knowing that the Fed is likely to respond to that information with more monetary tightening, traders took prices down with a vengeance. Across the board—the S&P 500, Dow Jones, and Nasdaq—the bears controlled the day, as Figure 2.3 shows.

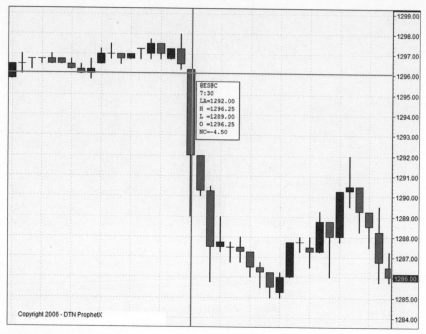

FIGURE 2.3 Notice how the S&P futures responded to the inflation fears. (*Source*: Copyright 2006-DTN ProphetX)

Macroeconomic changes like rate increases or decreases may have a delayed effect. Therefore, the real danger is too much tightening, which results in economic stagnation. Why are rates so important? Interest rates determine the cost of money, and that is critical around the globe. In Japan and throughout Asia, in Germany, Switzerland, France, and across Europe, in South America—everywhere—the cost of getting cash for business and consumers is important. Just as we have the Federal Reserve, other countries also have central banks that regulate rates. High interest rates in Tokyo or London will have a similar effect as high rates in New York.

I regularly trade after the FOMC reports. In fact, I execute the trade on the DTI chat. Readers interested in tuning into the action are welcomed. Just go to www.dtitrader.com to get our contact information. Believe me, the equities and bond markets care about interest rates. Once the FOMC news hits the airwaves, the markets start jumping (see Figure 2.4). It is exciting to watch the show. In my experience, as a general rule when rates increase there is an immediate sell-off in equities. Once the market digests the news, prices may quickly recoup. The reverse is also true; that is, when rates are lowered the immediate response tends to be higher equity prices, but again the euphoria may quickly end. Then there are times when the

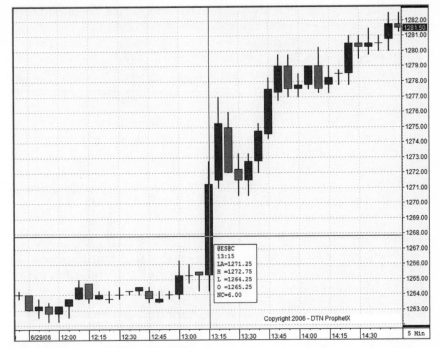

FIGURE 2.4 The chart depicts how the market started popping once the FOMC news aired. (*Source*: Copyright 2006-DTN ProphetX)

markets do the reverse of what is expected. That is the inherent danger of trading news. I have more than two decades of trading under my belt. I do not advice a novice to trade news, especially fed news.

Other Repercussions of Rate Increases

Inflation deteriorates the real value of bonds while rising interest rates translate into higher yields for newly issued bonds. In practice, that means that existing bonds paying lower rates are obviously less desirable. Why hold a bond paying 5 percent when newer bonds pay 6 percent, 8 percent, or more? Therefore, bonds with lower rates, when traded, must be sold at a discount. During times of rising rates, buyers tend to be hesitant to lock in capital in a long-term market; many hesitate and wait for higher and higher yields. The law of supply and demand means lower bond prices as rates rise. However, once bond traders and investors believe that rates are topping off, many will rush to the market in an effort to lock in those high rates. They know that once rates decline, those desirable rates will be golden and the bonds will be sold at a premium.

The currency market is also affected by rate changes. When rates rise, the U.S. dollar will have more appeal. Since capital seeks the best opportunities, if higher rates for investments are available in the United States, more foreign capital will likely find its way to our shores. The reverse may also be true; if rates decline here and higher rates are available in Europe or Asia, capital will likely travel across the Atlantic or Pacific and find its best opportunity.

Clearly one major factor that has serious effects on the financial markets is interest rates. The Fed's challenge is to balance rates so that full employment is attained but inflation is harnessed. If money is too tight, stagnation or recession will result. If it is too loose, inflation will deteriorate the real value of one's assets. The Federal Reserve's Web site contains a great deal of information. That site is www.federalreserve.gov.

> *Interest rates have serious effects on the financial markets. The Fed's challenge is to balance rates so that full employment is attained while inflation is harnessed.*
>
> *If money is too tight, economic stagnation or recession will result. If it is too loose, inflation will deteriorate the real value of one's assets.*

Trade Imbalances

It is no secret that the United States has become an importing nation. Since the 1970s, more goods have landed on our shores than have sailed away to world markets. China and other Asian economies have been the big winners in the trade shifts with China, boasting an enormous trade surplus while the United States repeatedly ratchets up a higher and higher deficit. Oil is a big import of the United States and Africa and eastern countries benefit greatly from that imbalance.

Our current deficit is somewhere between $700 billion and $800 billion. Economists debate the long-term effects of such a skewed trading situation but, in general, I am not sure that the markets care very much about it—at least not on a daily basis. The problem is that when countries sell to the United States, they acquire U.S. dollars in payment. That means that there are a lot of dollars in foreign hands. The Japanese own almost $700 billion in U.S. bonds and the Chinese own about $300 billion.[*] That is some serious money.

---

[*]Michael Kanell, "Trade Deficit Eases a Little," *The Atlanta Journal-Constitution*, January 13, 2006.

If those bond holders become unhappy and decide to cash in or demand more return on their investment, there will be hell to pay. As long as our national funders are happy, I guess all is well. However, eventually, there will likely be a day of reckoning. If we are lucky, the imbalance will be evened out gradually and with little pain. If we are not, there may be some major bumps along the way. Only time will tell that story.

However, the trade deficit is a lurking danger, and if faith is lost in the American economy and the U.S. dollar, traders will care, and care a lot. If foreigners holding U.S. paper decide to give us a real problem, prices on the financial markets will crash, and the result will be a global economic disaster.

National Debt

Our national debt and trade imbalance are two closely connected and related concepts. However, they are two distinct issues, so I want to briefly mention our national debt. Even the most strapped debtor is in great shape when compared to the U.S. Treasury. Our nation is carrying a heavy debt load. Citizens wishing to check up on the growing arrears can visit the site of the Bureau of Public Debt at www.publicdebt.treas.gov and obtain a daily accounting that claims to be to the penny. I recently checked, and the total national debt was $8,345,566,154,025.22. (If one is too concerned, he or she may visit the site and actually make a donation to reduce it. I'd bet there are not too many contributions rolling in.)

The national debt, like personal debt, is money owed; there is principal and interest that must be paid. As the debt rises, a greater and greater percentage of the GDP is required to service it. Like the trade deficit, the national debt does not really affect the markets on a day-to-day basis. However, the day may come when it does. As already noted, a great deal of our debt is in foreign hands. In fact, more than half of it is held by folks outside the United States. If those debt holders become worried about the stability of our economic situation and our ability to pay our obligations with interest, they could hesitate to assume the debt or demand higher interest rates for doing so. That, too, would send the markets and our economy racing down.

Oil and Energy Prices

A year or so ago, I did not pay attention to the weekly Oil Status Report. In fact, few traders did. Now, I never miss one of those news releases. The Energy Information Administration (EIA) reports each week on our nation's petroleum status. The report airs at 9:30 AM Central Time, usually on Wednesdays. The EIA is the statistical arm, of the Department of Energy and the agency monitors and releases data about our nation's petroleum inventories. The inventories consist of both domestic and imported products. Because petroleum prices, like prices for other goods and services, are determined by supply and demand, the markets respond to this report. The site for the EIA is www.eia.doe.gov.

In addition to oil inventories, a wide array of other factors can alter fuel prices. In early June 2006, eight foreign workers on an oil rig off the coast of Nigeria were kidnapped. Tribal fighting in Nigeria has resulted in the disruption of oil supplies to importing nations, especially the United States. A loss of Nigerian fuel means a tightening in our supply line and a rise in prices. The kidnapping signaled continued and possibly increasing instability in the area and oil prices raced up—light sweet crude increased by almost two dollars a barrel on the news. Foreigners abducted in Nigeria, oil prices soar in New York and Chicago.

Every nation in the world needs energy and fuel; some need more of it than others. The United States is by far the world's largest consumer of petroleum, with China coming in second. The United States consumes approximately 25 percent of the world's oil production. Major oil-producing nations include Saudi Arabia, the United States, Russia, Iran, Mexico, China, Norway, and Canada. Nigeria is Africa's leading exporter of oil, and a lot of this supply finds its way to the United States and Western Europe. Therefore, problems in Nigeria directly affect our nation's supplies. The United Arab Emirates and Venezuela also produce a small percentage of the world's petroleum. (For specific data regarding oil exports, one may wish to visit the CIA Fact Book online at https://cia.gov/cia/publications/factbook/index.)

A cheap source of abundant energy is vital for both developed and developing economies. The wheels of industry must have fuel to turn them, and consumers need energy to heat their homes and power their automobiles. Because Americans use so much oil, as a nation we are extremely vulnerable to escalating oil prices. Consequently, from Wall Street to Main Street citizens panic when fuel prices increase.

It seems like only yesterday when the price for a barrel of crude was a mere $50; then war in the Middle East and Hurricane Ivan altered the picture (see Figure 2.5). At the time of this writing, Iran, a significant supplier of crude, is threatening to retaliate against the West and increase prices if the United Nations imposes economic sanctions for its continuing uranium enrichment program. In Nigeria, tribal conflicts are causing disruptions as pipelines are blown up and supplies decreased. Obviously, as supplies are reduced, prices will rise. If investors and traders believe that fuel prices are draining too many consumer and industry dollars, equity prices will tumble.

> **In the months ahead, wise traders will keep a watchful eye on
> fuel prices.**

The flip side of the coin is that an overabundance in supply will reduce
prices. If too much oil is available, the law of supply and demand will kick
in and prices will fall. Therefore, in the current market, the price of oil is
something that I watch carefully. If prices are too high, equities will take a
dive and I will probably be joining the shorts. If prices fall and other
aspects of the economy are stable and strong, the cheap fuel prices will
spur the bulls to push equity prices upward.

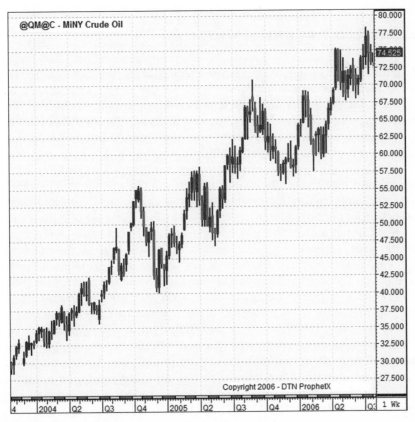

FIGURE 2.5 Note the upward move of crude prices. Those $50-a-barrel prices
are distant memories. (*Source*: Copyright 2006-DTN ProphetX)

DANCING TO THE BEAT OF A DIFFERENT DRUMMER

As you may have already guessed, if you can put a number on it, you can probably trade it. We just discussed that oil went from $50 to $75 a barrel. That's bad news—unless you were long crude oil futures. Market players can trade metals, commodities, and securities. They can short orange juice if they think there is going to be a bumper crop in Florida, or go long on bonds if they think the federal government is going to need to borrow more than expected. The important thing to remember is that prices are going to move in response to issues of supply and demand—real or perceived. Let's look at a few examples.

GOLD AND PRECIOUS METAL

Like Midas, many traders are obsessed with gold. In mid-May 2006, the precious metal was breaking 26-year highs. By the end of August, gold had fallen about 15 percent off its high and investors were not as bullish. Nevertheless, gold still has a lot of followers. Not since the early 1980s has the gold market seen prices like those now posting regularly on the tape. As Figure 2.6 depicts, gold surged in 2005.

Traditionally, gold is an inflationary hedge; traders seek its safety when they fear rising prices and the erosion of their portfolio values. Tellingly, gold began its most recent rise when the Federal Reserve launched its persistent interest rate hikes in June 2004. At that time, rates were sitting at an historic low of 1 percent and gold prices were in the 400.00 area. After 17 consecutive rate increases, current federal funds rates are 5.25 percent. At the time of this writing, gold prices are hovering in the high 500 to mid-600 area. The most important benchmark for evaluating gold is its yearly opening price. In 2006, gold opened around 500. As long as gold stays above its annual opening price, I will be bullish gold.

In the early 1980's, when Jimmy Carter sat in the White House and inflation was soaring, gold prices rose above $825.00 an ounce. If investors and traders get jittery about inflation and rising interest rates, prices will again move upward. When current prices are compared to those highs in the early 1980's,there seems to be plenty of room for the bulls to keep pushing prices higher. If gold becomes too attractive, capital will flow out of other areas and into the shiny metal. Remember, capital seeks the best opportunities, and if the precious metals market offers that opportunity, capital will be drawn to it like a metal paper clip to a magnet.

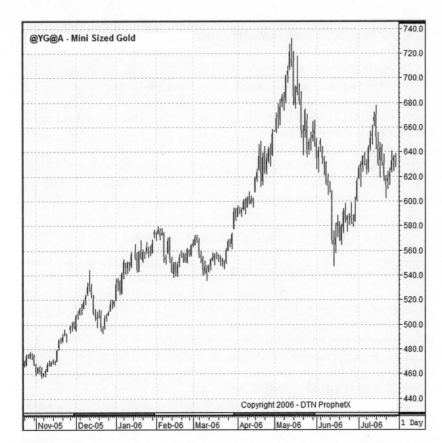

FIGURE 2.6 Note the upward climb of gold. The rise began in 2004. Then it leveled off for a few months. In 2005 through early-2006 the up-trend was dramatic. With inflation fears high, gold neared the $740.00 mark. Look at the price dip in the spring of 2006. The CPI, PPI, GDP, and Federal Reserve verbiage calmed investor fears and gold seemed less attractive. After hitting a low around $545.00, prices again started moving up and at the time of this writing are in the low $600.00 area. Even after undergoing a price correction, gold remained above its yearly opening price. (*Source*: Copyright 2006-DTN ProphetX)

Interest rates are not the only factor propelling gold and precious metals upward: escalating fuel prices and geopolitical concerns undoubtedly contribute to the bullish move. Historically, gold is a safe haven for investors fearing political or economic turmoil; when fears mount the nervous ones seek safety in gold and precious metals. There seems to be plenty of turmoil afoot, so the bulls will likely have no problem enlarging their herd in the near future.

Gold is an interesting market to watch because it mirrors investors' fears; the more fearful investors become, the higher gold prices tend to climb. Therefore, gold serves as an informal indicator of investor senti- ment. Astute traders and investors keep an eye on gold and precious met- als. If prices start rising too quickly, danger may be lurking on the horizon. Sometimes I trade gold futures and generally, even if I am not trading the metals market, I keep a close eye on gold prices. I know that if enough of the big boys are seeking safety in precious metals, I do not want to be too bullish with my equities or futures plays. Better safe than sorry. Gold prices alone will not lead me to buy or sell stocks or index futures, but I may use gold as a market indicator. A wise trader is aware of gold and its signifi- cance in the global marketplace.

Currencies and the Foreign Exchange Markets

The largest financial market in the world is foreign exchange or curren- cies. More than a trillion dollars of monetary value changes hands on a daily basis in this market. Monetary exchanges are made around the world for a variety of reasons including speculation. London, the United States, and Japan are the largest centers for the foreign exchange trade. The U.S. dollar is by far the world's most popular currency.

A nation's currency is the foundation for all of its financial markets. If its currency is stable and strong, investors will want to purchase and hold it; if it is weak and vulnerable to inflation, both foreign and domestic investors will want to stay clear. Although the U.S. dollar is the most widely traded currency in the world, the Japanese yen and European euro are also popular.

Throughout much of the twentieth century, our currency and the cur- rencies of other nations were tied to the gold standard. That is, the price of currencies on the world market were fixed or pegged to a set rate. The currency price on international markets was not allowed to float and nations could not print money at will and place it in circulation. President Richard Nixon abandoned the gold standard entirely in 1971, and today U.S. currency prices float on the world market and the Federal Reserve prints currency as needed.

Like gold, currency prices are also important to investors because they reflect the perceived soundness or weakness of a nation as viewed by the rest of the world. Our nation is currently carrying a huge debt load. Our balance of trade deficits are enormous and growing bigger every day. We are importing far more than we are exporting. This puts the United States at risk because it takes foreign dollars to support such debt. If foreign in- vestors sense weakness in the dollar or in the U.S. economy and pull away from American investments in stocks, bonds, and currencies, our nation will be in very serious financial trouble.

Most of us cannot alter the macroeconomic picture. However, as investors we need to have an idea of how our nation is perceived internationally. One way to get an idea is by watching the price of the dollar. If the dollar is weak on the world market in relation to the euro or the yen, it may be something to fear, or at least note. Likewise, if the dollar is relatively steady, the world is showing its respect for us and believes the economy that stands behind our greenbacks is strong.

Bonds and Bond Futures

Bonds are debt securities. They are loans to a governmental or corporate entity. Bond investors expect to receive the interest on their loan and a return of their principal when a bond matures or is paid. The federal government issues both short-term and long-term bonds and uses the borrowed money to finance the business of the government.

As already noted, the two greatest risks of investing in the bond market are inflation and rising interest rates. If rates rise, new bonds carrying the higher rate are the most attractive, and old bonds carrying a smaller rate are less popular. Obviously, investors want to maximize their investments. If a bond is purchased at a rate of 3 percent and rates rise to 4 percent, if the holder of the 3 percent bond wants to sell it, he or she must sell it at a reduced or discounted price. Who wants to have an investment that pays 3 percent when there is an equally safe investment that pays 4 percent?

Inflation also eats away a bond's investment value. If you were to buy a 30-year bond, and after the purchase inflation soars, the interest earned on the investment would be eaten away by the increased cost of living. In real terms, the value of the bond would decrease and fewer investors would want to hold it. Better investment opportunities may exist elsewhere.

Generally, there is an inverse relationship between bonds and equities. When bond prices rise significantly, equity prices tend to fall. In 1987, many traders considered high bond yields to be partly responsible for the October crash. Too much capital was flowing out of the equity markets and into the bond markets, and the result was disastrous.

Due to the relationship between bonds and equities, bonds may be used as an inverse indicator while trading stocks. If bond prices are rising, that may mean that equity prices are falling or will soon fall. Inversely, if bond prices are falling, that may mean that equity prices are rising. As noted earlier, the markets are a tug-of-war of interests. (Bonds are not *always* an inverse indicator, but often they are.)

Commodities

The world needs corn, soybeans, coffee, beef, pork, minerals, metals, and other commodities. Naturally, if there is a drought in our wheat-growing states and wheat crops are devastated, the demand for the wheat will rise in proportion to the scarcity. As these prices rise, money will be drained from other financial investment sectors into the commodities markets where top dollar can be demanded. Likewise, if there is a surplus in the market making the supply too great, prices will fall. The investment opportunities in this market sector will no longer be as great. The law of supply and demand regulates prices, and weather, world events, and governmental actions alter supply.

GEOPOLITICAL EVENTS

Markets like stability; they do not like uncertainty and doubt. Therefore, major political or social events around the world greatly impact financial markets. One never knows what the impact of a particular occurrence will be because no one knows how the event will be perceived. Take war in the Middle East. When there was talk of war and many people feared the United States would invade Iraq, the markets were squeamish. The situation was uncertain, and equity prices lagged. Once we entered the war and made the decision to take up arms, the question mark was removed. At the time of this writing the equities markets are strong and have been for many months. Equity markets were strong throughout 2005, and prices have continued to climb for much of 2006. However, with inflation fears mounting and interest rates rising, the picture may change. Again, time has to tell the story.

Consider also the presidential elections in 2000. As with most elections, there was a great deal of uncertainty. Remember that the markets do not like uncertainty, so prices lagged during the months before the election as polling numbers went up and down between the key contenders. Then there was the election. I traded that night. I confess that I was a Bush supporter, and I believed that the financial markets would favor a Bush victory. I also believed that Bush was going to win by a landslide, and the markets would rise to salute his victory. Therefore, I bought futures contracts, and I made a nice profit. The media announced Bush as the winner and the uncertainty was temporarily removed from the market. Prices went higher. (In fact, it was soon determined that the electoral votes in Florida were too close to call. For a full month the markets watched and waited. Finally, the presidential votes were certified and Bush was officially the newly elected President. It was a difficult time for most Americans and also for the financial markets.)

Wide arrays of factors contribute to how the global markets work. Traders need to understand them and their interconnections. That is the only way that they can step in tune to the market's beat.

> *Trade Secret #2:   Do not fight the Fed. It generally takes 6–12 months for the markets and the economy to feel the full effect of the actions of the Federal Reserve.*

REVIEW

A complex maze of interconnected factors causes prices of equities, bonds, commodities, futures, options, and other financial products to move up or down. Capital is mobile and seeks the best opportunities; everyone hopes to maximize profit and minimize risk. If the equities markets offer a greater return on investment, money will flow there; if bonds or commodities present a better deal, investment dollars will go in that direction. When inflation fears rise or geopolitical dangers threaten, the security of gold and precious metals lures investors. The bottom line is that there is a constant tug-of-war or competition between various investment opportunities based on the risk that one must assume and the reward that one anticipates.

The law of supply and demand rules the markets, but governmental policies may alter the supply/demand equation by imposing restrictions or implementing certain policies that interfere with the natural balance of goods and services and the need for them. Because investment dollars seek optimum money-making environments, astute investors and traders keep an eye open for noticeable shifts in strength among the various players. That is, if bonds are very strong, equities may weaken, if gold is rising, equities and bonds may appear less appealing, and so forth.

You do not need a doctorate in economics to trade. However, successful trading requires you to have a basic knowledge of how the markets work. Otherwise, you will find yourself waltzing to the jitterbug.

 MARKET INSIGHT

- Capital is mobile and seeks the best deal. That is, traders put their money in products that offer the greatest return for the least risk.

CHAPTER 3

Gettin' in the Groove

How to Think Globally

y first one was lime green and I kept it spinning for hours. In the late 1950s the hula-hoop craze swept the nation. Hula-hoops came in all colors and the only skill required to hula to greatness was a rhythmic gyration. Everybody owned at least one of the thin round plastic wheels, and some folks owned several. In the afternoons, all the kids in the neighborhood gathered in my backyard to spin their hoops. Sometimes a clock watcher was assigned to keep track of time and officially proclaim the *world champion*. Other times, we swiveled in pairs to establish the rightful titleholder. No trophy or prize came with the daily designation— just the satisfaction of knowing that the hoop stayed around your hips longer than it did around anyone else's. Each afternoon after walking home from school, we began another contest; at its conclusion, usually another world champion was declared.

It was many years ago and more than a few pounds back when I was watching those hoops spin. Now, it's not the neon lime ring that I keep an eye on but rather the global markets. Just as those mesmerizing toys kept spinning and spinning, so do the financial centers of the world as trading moves from one time zone to another and from continent to continent. However, playing the financial markets requires more than executing a good right wiggle to keep things spinning. A great deal of skill is essential, because a maze of complex factors sets prices and makes or breaks deals. To be successful as a worldwide trader, one must learn to think globally and gyrate with the markets' 24-hour swing.

GETTING WITH THE BEAT:
UNDERSTAND RELATIONSHIPS

China's Central Bank raises interest rates and the commodities market in the United States experiences a sell-off. It is 6:00 PM in Beijing and a few seconds past 6:00 AM in New York on April 28, 2006, when Chinese officials announce a small interest rate hike. Many commodity traders fear the increased rates will result in slower economic growth for China and thus lessen the demand for raw materials. That small rate change enacted thousands of miles and many time zones away sends tremors rumbling through the U.S. commodities markets. According to the *Wall Street Journal*, the Dow Jones-AIG Commodity Index, a broad-based commodities measure, fell by 2.3 percent based on that news[*]. Actions taken by the Central Bank of China jolted commodity prices in New York, and did so almost instantaneously (see Figure 3.1).

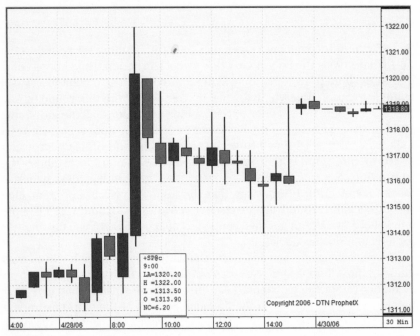

FIGURE 3.1   The S&P 500 futures respond to the rate increases reported by the government of China. (*Source*: Copyright 2006-DTN ProphetX)

---

[*]Andrew Browne and Michael M. Phillips, "China Raises Interest Rates to Rein in Galloping Growth," *The Wall Street Journal Online*, April 28, 2006.

May 17, 2006, the U.S. government released its monthly core inflation data. The Consumer Price Index (CPI) statistics acknowledged the threat of escalating prices. With inflation fears igniting, traders expressed their apprehension that the Federal Reserve would raise rates again at their June 2006 meeting. The dread of higher rates and inflation sent stock prices plunging. Bond prices also fell as traders expressed concern about the inflationary deterioration of the value of their fixed-income securities. The S&P futures took a dive. But, the dollar saw a small rally against the yen and the euro. Only one report—the CPI—but the result was many reverberations throughout the financial markets (see Figure 3.2).

On May 23, 2006, Bloomberg reported on bird flu and the possibility of its transmission to humans. Fearing the catastrophic consequences of the news, stock prices fall. A small group of sick people in Indonesia, and the scare that their disease might reach pandemic proportions brings out the bears on Wall Street. An illness in Asia seems to be taking a serious turn, and financial markets react quickly (see Figure 3.3).

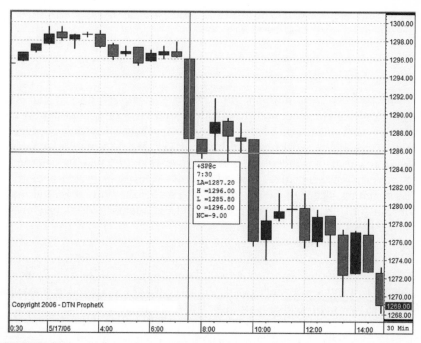

FIGURE 3.2 Note how the S&P futures fell in response to the CPI news. (*Source*: Copyright 2006-DTN ProphetX)

FIGURE 3.3   Reports of bird flu across the Pacific lead our financial markets to fall. (*Source*: Copyright 2006-DTN ProphetX)

The Federal Open Market Committee raises interest rates for the six-teenth consecutive time, and there is fear that emerging nations may be less attractive investment centers for available capital. Investing in developing areas of the world can be highly risky. Why assume added risk when one can gain a nice return on his investment by placing cash into U.S. government securities? A good return—less risk—seems appealing. A far-reaching effect of higher interest rates in the United States may translate into less capital for growth and expansion in less-developed areas of the globe.

Economic decisions by the major governments of the world have consequences that echo from continent to continent. Moreover, the boom is almost simultaneous with the action. Take the decision by the Bank of China: When rates were increased, Chicago and the commodity markets heard the news and headed south in the blink of an eye. Therefore, the first step to thinking globally is to understand the many interactions and intersections between and among economic events. The following chart expresses a few important relationships.

Relationships

As a general rule, the following tend to be true:*

Interest rates rise	Equities fall
	Bond prices fall
	Commodities fall
	Dollar strengthens
Interest rates decline	Equities rise
	Housing investments Rise
	Dollar Weakens
Inflation increases	Equities fall
	Bond prices fall
	Gold prices rise
Economic indicators (GDP, CPI, PPI, housing starts, employment data)	Strong data move markets up
	Weak data move them down
Uncertainty (political or economic)	Equities stall or fall
	Bonds stall or fall
	Commodities stall or fall
	Gold rises

Think of money flowing to the investment with the strongest growth trend.

*These relationships are general patterns on a short-term basis, and this list may not correctly reflect the patterns of all markets at all times.

STAY ALERT

Know what is happening. A major event of almost any kind can torpedo or energize your portfolio. On July 7, 2005, the world and the financial markets experienced a terrifying event. A group of suicide bombers attacked three underground trains and a double-decker bus in London. The attacks occurred during the morning rush hour as commuters were headed to work. In the United States, the tragedy occurred around 3:00 AM Central Time while the vast majority of traders were sleeping. Initially, the FTSE, the London exchange, took a downward move, but it remained open for business. Early morning traders in the United States may have noticed the FTSE taking a dive. Any experienced trader watching the tape did not need to hear the news to know what action to take—sell first and ask questions later. This was not a buyer's market. When the S&P, Dow, and Dax started going down in unison, it was time to sell. Even without hearing the news, the numbers alerted traders to the play because prices began falling quickly.

Anxious, alert, and savvy traders wanting to protect their portfolios and hedge their positions were able to do so in the index futures. Others, knowing that selling was likely to come into the market, shorted futures; it was highly unlikely that the bulls would win this battle, at least short-term. The point is that the 24-hour electronic market offered U.S. traders a chance to respond even though live markets in New York were closed.

On the afternoon before the bombings, when the S&P futures opened the Globex or night session at 3:30 PM, the trading price for an e-mini S&P futures contract was 1198.25. Before the markets stopped grieving the disaster, prices hit 1170.75—over a 30-point drop. (Thirty points on the e-mini S&P futures is $1,500.) This was a significant move for overnight trading. Again, only the 24-hour global traders saw much of it.

When New York and Chicago opened their trading pits the next morning, the action was over. Those who shorted the market early were getting out of their positions and the late sellers were paying them. Understanding the significance of political events around the world and having knowledge of global trading offered an opportunity to hedge positions or take profits.

Many readers may think that it is very callous to think about trading during times of catastrophe. Some may even believe that those who traded during a very sad and deadly event in England were taking advantage of tragedy. Actually, if you are a trader, you must be aware of such events and you must act upon them. Otherwise, you may well be caught on the wrong side of a big swing and lose your shirt. Traders cannot act as though the world does not exist. The financial markets are a microcosm of global sentiment. That is the way they work. If there is a disaster, sellers will run to sell and prices will move down; buyers will be few and far between. No one wants to be on the wrong side of a market avalanche; those who are will be buried.

Clearly, it is critical that traders know about significant geopolitical events and understand the likely effect that those events will have. Sometimes the events are good and it is time to buy; other times, there is bad news and only an ostrich with his head in the sand would be a buyer. Therefore, step two to thinking globally is to stay alert and be aware of events of significance around the globe and have a reasonable idea of their effect on the financial markets.

REMEMBER THAT THE MARKETS NEVER SLEEP

Financial markets never sleep. The trading pits in New York and Chicago may be active for eight hours a day, but that does not mean that trading stops when the pits close. First, there is the electronic market that trades after normal business hours. The Chicago Mercantile Exchange operates an electronic system known as the Globex. Trading on the S&P futures and the Nasdaq futures begins at 3:30 PM Central Time and electronic trading does not end until 3:15 PM the following day. The Chicago Board of Trade begins electronic trading on the ECBOT at 6:00 PM Central and trading on that exchange continues until 4:00 PM Central the following day. One can also trade bonds and commodities like gold and silver on the ECBOT. Just remember that this is a futures market so you need to know the unique features of futures as well as the risk and potential rewards.

Trading equities after hours is a trickier proposition. I believe that the easiest approach is to trade equity index futures like the S&P 500 futures or the Dow futures. If you wish to trade a Nasdaq stock, there is an after hours market that operates until 7:00 PM Central. However, remember that for every buyer there must be a seller and if there is a major disaster that takes prices down, buyers may be scarce. Also, only limit orders are accepted on this after-hours exchange. If you want to trade a stock listed on another exchange, like the NYSE, you have to wait for the exchange to open in the morning or trade through an international broker. Of course, only a stock that is internationally traded can be bought or sold through international brokers when the domestic exchange listing the stock is closed.

Because the markets never sleep, if some event—good or bad—alters prices, global traders can react to it and take necessary action to protect their assets, or they can trade the event, hoping for profits. You just have to know how and where to go about it.

UNDERSTAND TECHNOLOGY AND HOW TO USE IT

The vast majority of traders do not understand that futures, stocks, bonds, and other securities are traded virtually 24 hours a day. Just because the floor of the New York Stock Exchange (NYSE) or the Chicago Mercantile Exchange (CME) is vacant does not mean that trading has ended. Electronic opportunities exist somewhere in some product.

When I first began trading, I traded only during the day's session and I telephoned my orders to traders on the floor for execution. From the time the markets opened until the time they closed, I worked at a frantic pace and continuously bought and sold everything in sight. Over the years much has changed. In the mid-1990s the CME began selling a special machine for trading the night or Globex session and only professionals were able to obtain a machine. The device was, of course, called a Globex terminal. I got my first Globex in 1996. The equipment was pricy and hard to get but it was worth it for me; I gained the ability to place my own trades electronically during the night. I was so excited about the new technology that I often slept at the office and I hired Chuck Crow, still a DTI employee, and another college student to watch the market action while I rested on the sofa and closed my eyes. I did not want to miss anything. As with most electronic technology, the old bulky Globex soon became outdated. Today a special terminal is not needed—just a lap top and the other tools necessary for trading.

Many traders think provincially. That is, they fail to realize that trading is constantly occurring. When night is falling in the United States, Asia is waking up. Their financial markets are trading while we are sleeping. When Asian sessions end, Europe is trading. The German Dax, the London FTSE, the French CAC—all of these are important European indexes. Because the world is so economically connected, it is helpful to know what is happening across the oceans. Sometimes, the actions taken by traders in Tokyo or Paris may be irrelevant. However, there are other times when knowing about foreign markets will pay off. The information may point you in the right direction and let you know what to expect from domestic markets. Therefore, I use a trading strategy that takes advantage of a 24-hour trading clock. In other words, my trading system acknowledges the rest of the world and uses information from abroad to enlighten my path.

Technology opens the door. However, in order to take advantage of electronic markets, you have to have the right type of account, the right computer equipment, a broker and trading platform, and a good data feed system. You also need some experience operating all of it. If there is a huge market move after hours, only those who are ready will have the ability to take advantage of it. Therefore, I strongly suggest that if you think that you may want to trade when the open outcry pits are closed, get prepared for doing so. Once a crisis hits or a big opportunity presents itself, it is too late to get prepared. Remember that technology connects the world and opens the door for millions of traders to join the global trading game. With the right equipment and set-up, you can play with the big boys from your kitchen table.

Technology opens the door. Savvy traders enter.

FOLLOW THE SUN

The most active trading centers are those where the sun is shining brightly. Trading follows the path of the sun as it moves across the sky from east to west. Most traders act as though business stops when the pit bulls and bears leave the floors of the exchanges. Nothing could be farther from the truth. At 6:00 PM Central Time (7:00 PM Daylight Saving Time), the Tokyo exchange opens for business.

Later in the evening, around 8:00 PM Central Time (9:00 PM during Daylight Saving Time) stocks on the Hang Seng start changing hands. Just as Minolta and other large Asian corporations are traded on our exchanges, some U.S.-based corporations are traded in Asia. If Asian traders have an active trading session, prices will likely change overnight and American investors may have a surprise waiting for them when they check the value of their equity holdings. Also, if a world event, like the capture of Saddam or the bombing of a London subway occurs before exchanges open in the United States, Asian markets will be the first to respond. During 24-hour trading, Asia gives us our first indication of world sentiment.

When Asia nears the close of its trading day, action begins in Europe. Many major European exchanges open at 2:00 AM Central Time. Germany, Europe's largest economy, is home to the Dax. Trading also begins on the FTSE (London), the CAC (France), and the Swiss Exchange when most U.S. traders are sleeping. For years the Dax cash market closed at 10:00 AM Central and trading on the Dax futures closed at 1:00 PM Central. However, recently, electronic trading has been expanded and the Dax futures now close at 3:00 PM Central—just like the NYSE.

During pre-dawn hours in the United States the Dax tends to lead the way. The German economy is large and powerful and that is evident in the financial markets. As the sun continues its path across the sky, European trading remains the most active trading center of the world until the exchanges open in New York and Chicago. Then the United States takes the lead, and our markets are the center of attention. When our trading day draws to an end, major exchanges close for only a few minutes before the CME opens for business and the show begins again.

When I awake each morning, I want to know what the world markets had to say during overnight sessions. Was there a development that gives me an advantage when I start my day? A trader must answer one question correctly to be successful: Should I be long, short, or out of the market? Having insight into global markets and their trading patterns helps me answer that question.

Trading is a competitive field. Every time a trader places an order and enters the market, he or she is going head-to-head with some of the smartest and most skillful traders in the world. If you want to be success-ful, you need to be as prepared as possible and have as much knowledge and information as possible. Knowing how Asia and Europe are trading gives additional insight and adds another dimension to my trading.

Another reason for using a 24-hour trading clock that follows the sun is that there may come a time when one wants or needs to trade in the night market. For example, assume that Joe, a trader and investor is long a significant equities position. And, for his net worth, a big loss will be dev-astating. Now assume that terrorists strike major communication and trans-portation systems in the United States on a Sunday afternoon. Joe believes that the attack will cause a sell-off on Wall Street when trading begins on Monday and he fears that the selling will be strong. Joe fears that the dam-age to the nation and to the markets may be significant and long-term. Joe needs to immediately execute a defensive hedging strategy for his protec-tion. Therefore, he calculates the value of his long stock position and sells enough e-mini S&P 500, Nasdaq, Dow, or Dax Future contracts to off-set his losses. His equity account may go down the drain, but his profits from his futures account will offset the losses and give him some protection. Joe may not succeed in covering every single dollar, but, if done correctly, he has executed a workable strategy to protect the bulk of his assets.

The big idea here is that global trading follows the path of the sun. Where the sun is shining brightest, the markets are most active.

24-Hour Trading Clock Checklist

3:30 PM*	CME opens for electronic trading; S&P 500 & Nasdaq Index futures open.
6:00 PM	Nikkei opens**; ECBOT opens for electronic trading.
6:15 PM	Dow Index futures open.
8:00 PM	Hang Seng opens.**
1:00 AM	Dax opens.**
7:20 AM	CBOT outcry pits open.
8:30 AM	CME outcry pits open.
3:15 PM	CME & CBOT open outcry pits close.

(continued)

	24-Hour Trading Clock Checklist *(continued)*
3:30 PM	CME opens for night electronic trading on the Globex system and the 24-hour trading clock begins ticking anew.
4:00 PM	ECBOT closes.

*All Time is Central Time.

**Japan and Hong Kong do not participate in Daylight Saving Time. Therefore, during Daylight Saving Hours, the Nikkei opens at 7:00 PM Central and the Hang Seng opens at 9:00 PM Central. Also, Germany has Daylight Saving hours but the dates when the time changes to Daylight Saving Time are not identical to those in the United States.

GET OUT OF THE BOX

There may be a time when you need to think creatively. Perhaps a time will come when you need to hedge your positions. Maybe some economic factor or world event will raise your level of anxiety and you will want to get some financial cover.

With knowledge of the global marketplace, you have a better chance of devising a workable plan to protect your portfolio.

Some years back a cousin of mine, Jim, was the CEO of a publicly traded company that he had founded. The company manufactured and sold laser printers. Although Jim had originally designed the software, hardware components were imported from Japan. In order to get the most competitive price possible, Jim and the company entered into a large long-term contractual agreement for the equipment that they needed. Jim and the other company executives were very excited about the deal, but Jim worried about the exchange rate. The contract tied the company into some hefty purchases involving huge sums of money. If the dollar fell significantly in relation to the yen, he knew that the company would be in real trouble. The cost of the hardware would escalate in real dollars and profit margins would shrink at a time when the company was already engaged in fierce price competition with industry giants.

Jim was not a financial guru, but he understood the danger, he knew the global connections of the world markets and he knew that currency prices fluctuate 24 hours a day. Jim discussed his fears with a number of experts and considered hedging his position by buying yen futures. However, most of the professionals that he consulted warned him of the risks and discouraged his plan. One highly respected banker was certain that trading yen as an inflationary hedge against the escalating currency would lead to total disaster. However, in a casual conversation with a leading Japanese executive, Jim learned that he had a large long position in yen. Jim knew the man to be very savvy with financial matters. Because the gentleman was so well respected for his business acumen by both the Japanese and the Americans in the industry, rightly or wrongly, Jim put great stock in his opinion. Based on his personal research, along with his gut feelings and what he believed to be confirmation from someone who he deemed to have a real grip on the issue, Jim purchased futures contracts for yen. He purchased a large position for the company and a relatively small position for himself.

Time proved the purchase to be wise. The yen rose steadily against the dollar and Jim's profits grew month after month. When profits from the transaction reached $5,000,000, Jim liquidated the company position as well as his own. The $5,000,000 was used by the company to offset the rising price of the imported hardware and Jim pocketed over $350,000 on his smaller personal position. Luck or genius? Probably some of both; Jim understood the danger of doing nothing because he understood the connections between economic forces. At the end of the day, he successfully hedged the company's position. While he was sleeping, his investment in the world markets was working for him.

The action Jim took was risky. Those who advised him of the risk were right to do so. But, taking no action was equally risky. Jim needed a hedge to protect himself and the company he steered against inflationary forces. Luckily for him, he found the right hedge and made a great move. Without thinking globally, Jim would have been slaughtered.

I am not advising anyone to take a large position in yen or anything else. But, I am saying that by educating yourself and by having an understanding of global markets and a respect for the 24-hour nature of them, you will be far better off because you will be in a much more advantageous position to look after your own financial interests. At least with knowledge of global opportunities, you have the chance to hedge your bets if you wish to do so.

ENLARGE THE SPACE

World markets are vast. One having knowledge of them can use that information to trade foreign products. Thinking globally means considering the many trading avenues that are available around the globe, learning about them, and using them.

I began trading the Dax in mid-September 2001. After terrorists attacked New York, the American exchanges were closed for days. Trading is my business. Therefore, in order to continue working, I had to find another segue into the markets. If I did not, I was temporarily out of business. Therefore, I began studying European and Asian indexes in search of a trading venue that fit my needs. That night I traded the Nikkei, Hang Seng, and the FTSE. It was not until I traded the Dax that I made money, and the Dax is the market that I decided to master. Every morning I awoke a little before 2:00 AM Central Time and watched the action as the Dax opened. It was not long before I placed my first trade. Even after New York and Chicago got back up and running, I continued to study and trade the Dax. It has become one of my favorite trading vehicles. Prices move quickly, and traders have the opportunity to make (or lose) a lot of money in a short period of time. When I was pressed, I learned a great deal about it. I use it as a leading indicator for my trading strategy. Now I always keep an eye on it. It has become a source of profits for me.

I enjoy dancing with the Dax; other traders may prefer another index or international trading spot. One's individual preference is not the issue. What is important is that one knows that the world is a big place. Perhaps the currency market is your cup of tea, or the bond market. I like futures, and I like the index futures. I enjoy trading futures markets that are located in the United States and in Europe. Other traders may trade the Nikkei or take some other avenue to expand their reach. One needs to always remember that the United States and our exchanges and financial markets are just one slice of an enormous pie.

Remember that global trading is a lot like spinning the hula-hoop in the 1950s. Keep your eye on the circling ring of trading action and gyrate to its beat; follow the active centers of buying and selling as market momentum tracks the path of the sun.

> ***Trade Secret #3: Worry about risk. Reward will come.***

REVIEW

World financial markets form a big pie, and the United States constitutes just a slice of it. Those wanting to maximize their trading and enjoy a bigger helping of the pastry must learn to think globally. First, one must understand the relationships between economic factors and events. If interest rates rise in China, commodities prices in Chicago will likely fall. When the FOMC ratchets up interest rates there will be consequences: commodity prices, bond prices, equity prices, the housing sector prices, and other economic areas will be affected. Our economy is controlled by an array of complex and intersecting factors that move prices in the financial markets.

Global thinkers must be alert. If a major event occurs anywhere in the world, traders will voice their sentiment and reaction to it in the markets. A terrorist attack, bird flu, and a zillion other events have the power to move markets around the world.

Never forget that the markets do not sleep. Traders may snuggle under the covers and catch a few winks, but active trading follows the path of the sun from east to west and virtually during every minute of the day someone is trading somewhere. Trading in the major financial centers of the world affects prices of items traded on our markets. Therefore, to think globally, one needs to keep an eye on the action in Asia and Europe. It is not necessary to follow every price bobble on an hour-by-hour basis, but it is important to know the general trend of the markets and keep up with any major geopolitical or economic event.

Thanks to the power of technology, with the right equipment and setup, the world is open and available for trading. At DTI, we were able to develop proprietary software to organize market data and track prices 24 hours a day. Having global data expands our world. Those who know how to do so can hedge their positions, expand their opportunities, and gain additional indicators to lead them through the financial maze of the global marketplace.

 MARKET INSIGHT

- Thinking globally means considering the many trading avenues that are available around the globe, learning about them, and using them.

- Stay alert to any significant global event. If an event around the world is important enough, the markets will respond to it. Savvy traders should, too.

- Be savvy!

CHAPTER 4

Land of the Rising Sun

The First Tunes Are Asian

ysterious Asian tones drift across the Pacific and catch your ear. It is 6:00 PM Central Time and The Land of the Rising Sun is welcoming a new day. Each morning, the financial markets in the east are the first to open and view the world's financial landscape. Stock markets are closed in the United States, but if some important economic or political event occurs, Asian traders will respond to it. Because I understand the significance of global markets, I divide my trading clock into four time segments with Asia dominating the first of those segments (see Figure 4.1).

My first time segment actually begins a couple of hours before Japan markets open; it starts with the opening of Globex or trading in the United States (see Figure 4.2). The Globex or evening session on the CME begins at 3:30 PM Central Time. Traders wishing to buy or sell S&P futures, Nasdaq futures, and a number of other products, can log onto their computers and actively trade these indexes until 3:15 PM Central Time the following day. Even though you can trade some products based in the United States, I consider the first global time segment to be dominated by Asia. This is the case because Asian financial markets are actively trading during this time and the eyes of the world are focused there.

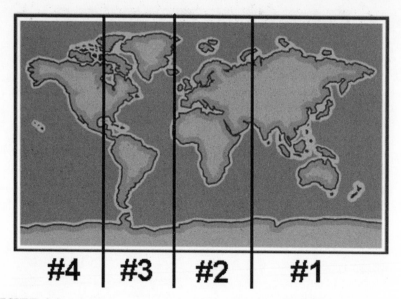

FIGURE 4.1 I divide my trading day into four time segments. The first segment begins shortly after the day trading sessions close in the United States. Asia dominates time segment one.

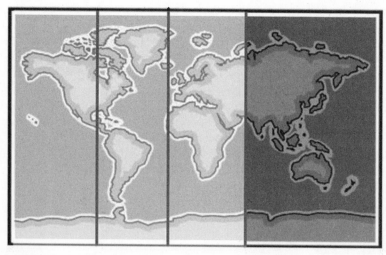

FIGURE 4.2 Time Segment #1: Asia dominates the action.

THE DAY BEGINS IN ASIA

The sun rises in the east and sets in the west; it is an elementary concept with vast implications. Over a hundred years ago, Jules Verne used
his knowledge of the movements of the sun to weave a clever tale about
Phileas Fogg and his adventures while traveling around the world. In Verne's
1873 classic travelogue *Around the World in Eighty Days*, Fogg reads
a news report about the possibility of circling the globe in only 80 days
and he shares the information with friends at his club. However, his fellow Londoners do not think such a journey possible. On a bet (a very large
bet for the times), Fogg and his servant Passepartout, set out traveling
eastward around the globe to prove the point. During the course of Fogg's
excursion, he passes from nation to nation and continent to continent,
always moving eastward. After having numerous adventures and encoun-
tering a host of memorable characters, Fogg finally returns to London.
However, based on his calculations and his watch, the journey has taken
81 days and he has lost the bet. It is Passerpartout, his faithful companion
and servant, who stumbles on the truth and realizes that the trip has,
indeed, been made in 80 days by London's standards; Fogg has won the
bet and earns a tidy sum. How? Due to his continuous journey eastward,
Fogg has gained a day and has actually arrived right on time! Jules Verne
explains,

> *"In journeying eastward he [Fogg] had gone towards the sun, and the
> days therefore diminished for him as many times four minutes as he
> crossed degrees in this direction. There are three hundred and sixty
> degrees on the circumference of the earth; and these three hundred
> and sixty degrees, multiplied by four minutes, gives precisely
> twenty-four hours—that is, the day unconsciously gained. In other
> words, while Phileas Fogg, going eastward, saw the sun pass the
> meridian eighty times, his friends in London only saw it pass the
> meridian seventy-nine times."*

Thanks to the international date line and the time zones that he crossed
during the course of his journey, Phileas Fogg achieved his goal. The
International Dateline sits on the 180-degree line of longitude in the middle
of the Pacific Ocean. It is the point that separates two consecutive days
from each other. It divides the Eastern and Western hemispheres; a traveler going west across the line gains a day and a traveler going east across
it loses a day. This means that Asia is the first to welcome each new
dawn. That fact had great significance for Phileas Fogg, and it has im-
mense significance for today's global traders. It means that informed

traders in the United States get a peek at Asia's trading day before ours even begins. Western traders have the chance to view a dress rehearsal of market sentiment without having to pay for the show.

Technology allows traders to move with the speed of their Internet connection. During the course of Fogg's journey from London to Asia and back, modern means of transportation were not available, and his trip was both long and tedious. Fogg had to use his ingenuity to find the fastest and easiest mode of transport. At various times he traveled by land and by sea. He sailed on a steamer, rode the rails, rumbled along in a carriage, cruised on a yacht, and was conveyed via an elephant. In sharp contrast, today we can travel around the world via jet or while sitting at the computer screen and making just a quick click of a mouse. In the blink of an eye, global traders can visit the financial markets in Japan or China, or elsewhere if they choose. And, just like Phileas Fogg, if they travel eastward, they may gain a tremendous time advantage.

> *In the blink of an eye, the global trader can visit the financial markets in Japan, China, or elsewhere. The right equipment and the click of a mouse are all that are required.*

A VAST AND DIVERSE CONTINENT

Asia is by far the largest continent, and it is home to a majority of the world's population. With its enormous landmass, Asia contains a slew of nations. Some are large or well developed, like Japan, China, and Singapore, while others are so small and relatively new that most Americans have not even heard of them. Due to its vastness and diversity, continental generalizations are impossible to make. Parts of Asia, especially countries in East Asia, are industrially sophisticated with powerful economies that are growing rapidly. Japan and China are two of the world's major economic centers. India is another country to watch. Parts of India are dominated by small farming villages while other areas are very modern with a great many industries and services. The population is highly educated and, following years of British control, many Indians speak fluent English. Therefore, software development and services are one of the nation's strengths. The GDP growth rate exceeded 7 percent in 2005, and the future appears to be bright. Pakistan also has experienced good economic growth in recent years, but the area is plagued with many problems, and its long-term future is far from predictable.

Many areas in Asia, including Iran, and Iraq, are unstable—politically and economically. Iran's uranium enrichment program has ignited global fears, and Iranian leaders threaten to reduce oil supplies to the West should the United Nations impose economic sanctions against them. From time to time, the effect of those threats has been reflected on Wall Street, as traders have feared higher oil prices and the consequent economic repercussions.

Iran continues to pose a major threat to world peace by funding the terrorist organization Hezbollah and persisting in its nuclear research and development. Only time will tell what will happen there and the effects of those actions on our financial markets.

North Korea, another Asian trouble spot, has also been dominating the news. The dictatorial policies and warlike actions of Kim Jong Il are doing more than raising a few eyebrows. The economy of North Korea is weak and the population suffers from poor agricultural practices and lacks the technological and industrial capabilities to compete globally. For a number of years, Jong has been experimenting with nuclear development—including nuclear weapons. Recently his efforts have become recognized by the world and he has declared his intent to create an atomic device and long-range missile with the capability of reaching targets in the United States. Needless to say, his posturing has generated concern across Asia and around the world. South Korea, Japan, China, and Russia have all weighed in on the side of the United States and have called for a halt in the armaments development. Many speculate that if North Korea continues in its quest, an arms race may begin in eastern Asia, and the results of such action would be widespread both politically and economically.

If all of those issues were not bad enough, now armed conflict has erupted in southwestern Asia between Israel and Hezbollah, a strong terrorist faction headquartered in Lebanon. For a while, the situation was very serious. Westerners were leaving Lebanon and Israeli citizens were seeking shelter daily in bunkers. There was talk of World War III. The United Nations succeeded in bringing about a cease fire, but who knows how long it will be before this or some other conflict begins again. Obviously, the Mideast is a very unsettled area of the world and its future is unknown. Not only is there great human suffering in the area, but there are also many economic problems resulting from the unrest. Specifically, the continued turmoil threatens oil exports, and with the United States being the world's most oil-dependent nation, the economic consequences may be significant.

JAPAN AND CHINA: ECONOMIES TO WATCH

Asia's economic issues and the financial markets reflect the enormity of that vast land space. Therefore, for my trading, I am aware of the big Asian problems but I focus on the financial markets in two of eastern Asia's most highly developed economic centers—Japan and Hong Kong. I personally believe that the Nikkei in Tokyo, Japan, and the Hang Seng in Hong Kong are good mirrors of Asian market sentiment, and these indexes, being more akin to those in the United States, reflect useful market sentiment of early traders in the east. Therefore, that is generally my focus.

JAPAN: A MAJOR ECONOMIC POWER

Defeated by war and having their nation literally reduced to ashes after World War II, the Japanese people quickly rebuilt their homeland and today Japan boasts a modern economy. The hard work and intelligence of the Japanese are respected around the globe. Since the late 1960s, Japan has held the title of the world's second largest economy. In spite of a shortage of raw materials, the small, mountainous island nation has become a powerhouse for technology and business. However, throughout the 1990s, the economy was sluggish and the GDP was disappointingly low. Nevertheless, recent economic data point to more prosperous days ahead.

Japan suffered greatly during the oil shortages of the 1970s and consequently took steps to become less oil dependent. Hybrid cars, alternative fuels, and governmental policies mandating conservation have helped Japan become more petroleum independent than the United States. Although the nation imports fewer petroleum products, it must purchase other raw materials on the world market. Copper, bauxite, and iron ore are a few of the imported necessities.

The terrain and geographical size of the nation require that a great deal of its agricultural products be purchased internationally. Hence, Japan is the largest market for U.S. agricultural products. Wheat and soybeans are big imports.

Unlike Americans, Japanese shy away from debt, and the nation's savings are very high when compared to most Yankees. With a focus on putting money aside for a rainy day and an aversion to indebtedness, both Japan and China are strong banking centers, and both nations hold huge amounts of U.S. Treasuries. The U.S. trade imbalance tilts in Asia's favor, and that means that these Eastern nations, especially China, are among America's biggest sources of capital infusion in the form of debt securities. That is, the Japanese and the Chinese are financing a large part of America's financial arrears.

WATCH TOKYO

When New Yorkers are finalizing dinner plans or settling in for a restful evening with the family, traders in Japan are gearing up for a busy day. As the sun is setting on one of our trading days, the ball of fire is mounting the eastern sky and ushering in a new dawn in the Land of the Rising Sun. The Tokyo Exchange opens at 6:00 PM CST (7:00 PM DST) and the action begins. Early risers in the United States may gain insight into the market skirmishes in Tokyo by checking the Nikkei, also known as the Nikkei 225. This is a highly respected and leading Japanese index similar to the Dow Jones Industrial Average. In fact, for many years the index was known as the Nikkei Dow Jones Stock Average. Two hundred and twenty-five of Tokyo's blue chip stocks are listed on the index. Trading on the Tokyo Stock Exchange continues until around 2:00 AM CST (3:00 AM DST).

If there is disturbing economic news anywhere in the world, the traders in Asia will have the first chance to express their sentiment and sell things off. Likewise, if something good occurs, the floor of the Nikkei will ignite with a buying spree. Prices on the Nikkei responded quickly to the capture of Saddam, to the London bombings, to the events of September 11. If an event has implications for the financial markets, Tokyo traders will express their views in the stock market.

By the time the sun makes its way eastward across the sky and illuminates New York, Chicago, Philadelphia, and other western financial centers, Asia has spoken. When stock exchanges in New York open for business, U.S. buyers and sellers are able to consider the wisdom of Asian traders. The entire session in Tokyo is over. In fact, both European and American traders can benefit from having knowledge of the Asian action.

If traders in Europe and the United States agree with the direction of the Nikkei's move, they will join it. If they disagree, they will buck it and chart their own course. Nevertheless, the information and data that can be obtained from the eastern financial centers are not trivial. There are many days when having that information can help one identify a developing trend or pattern. With early insight, you can get on the right side of the market near the start of your day's trading session and reap more profits. Or, if domestic price movements are not in sync with Asia and/or Europe, you can wait, study, and evaluate before putting your money at risk. That will help you avoid unnecessary losses and become a more consistent trader.

Nikkei

Benchmark of stocks traded on the Tokyo Exchange.

225 stocks listed on the index.

　　Opens:　6:00 PM Central Time

　　Closes:　12:15 AM Central Time

Margin requirements vary from brokerage house to brokerage house but should be about $60,000 yen.

　　Price per point:　$500.00 yen

　　Trades in 5-point increments

CHINA JOINS THE GAME

A couple of hours after Tokyo opens for business, the trading floor of the Hong Kong exchange gets busy. The Hang Seng is an index of leading stocks on the Hong Kong stock market. Hong Kong, like Tokyo, is a thriving economic center, and just like the traders in Japan, the Chinese have an opportunity to express their sentiment early in the world's day. When the first share of stock is traded on the Hong Kong exchange on Monday morning, it is still Sunday night in the United States. To be precise, it is about 8:00 PM CST (9:00 PM DST).

If a major economic move is afoot, be it good or bad, the Chinese traders will have an early chance to voice their opinion and move the market up or down. Again, U.S. traders have the benefit of their collective voices.

Some people like to focus on the dissimilarities between people and cultures, but I prefer to focus on the similarities. In many ways, life in Japan or China is very different from that in the United States. The cultures are distinctly different, and so are the political systems, the languages, and many aspects of their economies. However, in spite of these differences,

Asians and Americans share common goals and dreams. On both sides of the Pacific people want good things for their families. They want safety and happiness for their children, and on both continents people work hard to achieve these goals. When it comes to financial matters, investors and traders, regardless of the language they speak, want to maximize profits and minimize risk.

A couple of years ago I had the privilege of meeting an Asian American businessman and trader, Marty Shih. He came to the United States from Taiwan in 1978. Marty's mother worked hard for years in order to send her children here, a place where she believed they would have tremendous opportunities. In fact, Marty explains that after coming to the United States, he went outside each night to gaze upward at the stars because he remembered his mother's description of the United States: "In America the moon is bigger, the sky is bluer, and the grass is greener." Marty just had to keep checking out the truth of those words, and night after night he looked at the moon and sized up its dimensions.

When Marty landed in Los Angeles, he had $500 in his pocket and the goal of creating his own business. He rented a small stand and began selling flowers on a busy street corner. At the close of his first long workday, Marty had sold only one floral bunch for $1.99. But, he was not discouraged—rather, he was encouraged. Encouraged to try harder and find a way to reach his goals. Marty soon had a moped and was speeding through the streets of L.A. personally delivering fresh flowers to his clientele.

With a strong work ethic, an extraordinary degree of intelligence, and an unstoppable determination to succeed, Marty and Helen, his sister, created an American success story. The tiny floral stand soon grew into a floral chain, and Marty's sites expanded. He knew how difficult coming to the United States had been for him, and he understood very personally the unique problems and issues faced by Asian Americans. Therefore, Marty expanded his business lines and added more and more services to help immigrants from the east. Today, Marty heads up an Asian American club that addresses the unique issues that he knows this segment of our population faces. An array of products and services are offered in a friendly environment in which one can communicate in his or her own language and easily obtain help. Marty is a very successful businessman by anyone's standards. He understood that Asian Americans want the same things that the rest of us want and he set out to fill the need and meet the market niche of a particular segment of our population.

Just as Marty's Asian American club addresses unique needs of participants, so do financial markets. Those who need capital and those with excess capital join together for the mutual benefit of each. Asian investors want to increase profits and limit risk, just as do American investors. Therefore, when economic factors or other events indicate that problems are ahead, they react just as American investors do. Hence, their actions are a heads-up for us. When interest rates rise, Asian markets generally respond by taking equity prices down. If fuel is scarce and pricey, Asians worry just as we do and express their anxiety by selling off equities. If corporate earnings are good and inflation is held at bay, their faith in the economy moves prices up. In a global economy with many intersecting and interdependent factors, U.S. traders can learn a lot by taking an occasional look at prices and trends across the Pacific.

Please do not think that the U.S. markets or the European markets merely ditto Asian action in Tokyo and Hong Kong. Each geographical area is unique. Each nation has its own central bank and banking policies, its own GDP and other statistical economic indicators, and there are a number of other huge differences. When traders in the United States see and evaluate the activity of the financial markets in the east, they merge that data with the economic realities on our shores. If the trading direction chosen by Asian investors appears to be right, the move may be accelerated. If not, traders on our side of the world will express their disagreement by heading in the opposite direction or by not joining the party that began in the Land of the Rising Sun.

CHINA: NO LONGER A SLEEPING GIANT

China, with its enormous population of more than 1.2 billion, is very different today from the homeland that Marty left. According to the CIA, in purchasing power parity (PPP), China is the world's second-largest economy, second only to the United States. According to the World Bank, China's GDP grew by whopping 9.9 percent in 2005; the economy is on fire. By almost all accounts, the Chinese economy will grow by about 10 percent in 2006. However, much of that growth is attributable to the tremendous surge in exports—billions and billions of dollars of finished goods leave China each year, and a huge percentage of those exports come to the United States. If the American economy falters, China will feel the pinch, and if China encounters a big bump in the road, the U.S. will suffer more than a little inconvenience.

China provides Americans with tons of high-quality, low-cost goods, and China also supplies a lot of money to finance America's cash shortfall. In fact, America's negative trade balance with China exceeds ten billion dollars a month. The yuan, or Chinese currency, is cheap in relation to the dollar on the international foreign exchange market. This fact keeps down the costs of Chinese exports and means that many Chinese corporations and individuals receive huge amounts of U.S. currency for the goods sold in the United States. To mop them up and keep the yuan low, the Chinese government exchanges somewhere between $10 billion to $20 billion of U.S. currency into yuan each month[*]. That's a heap of cash! In January 2006, the Chinese government announced a policy shift whereby it would seek diversification of its foreign exchange reserves—that is, the U.S. dollar would no longer be the exclusive currency of choice. China appears to be losing some respect for the U.S. dollar, or at least questioning its economic policy regarding greenbacks. If enough U.S. dollars get dumped into the market, our currency prices will tumble. That potential prospect sent gold futures upward when China made the announcement. It is a sensitive subject with enormous connotations.

China and Japan are not alone in holding large amounts of greenbacks. The oil-rich nations of the Mideast have been collecting petro-dollars for decades. With so much conflict in the region, and a great deal of animosity toward the United States in some sections, there has been a great deal of talk about dumping dollars and holding petro-euros. If U.S. dollars flood the foreign exchange market, prices will fall and the consequences for our economy will be disastrous. Hopefully, that scenario will never happen.

Additionally, like Japan, China is a nation of savers. With surplus capital from savings and trade, China holds a huge amount of U.S. Treasuries. As trading ties become stronger, the financial interdependence of the United States and China will continue to grow. Therefore, keeping an eye on China and its financial markets is a good idea for any serious trader.

Hang Seng

The benchmark for stocks trading on the Hong Kong Exchange consists of 33 listed corporations

Open outcry pits: Open at 8:00 PM Central Time

Close at 2:00 AM Central Time

Point value is $50.00 per point

Margin requirements vary depending on brokerage house but should range between $5,000 and $10,000 per contract (intraday). A larger margin is required when holding positions longer than a day.

---

[*]See Keith Bradsher, "China's Exports Climbed Steeply in April," *New York Times*, May 12, 2006; and Fred Bergsten, "Trade: Clash of the Titans," *Newsweek*, International Edition, May 24, 2006.

THE HANG SENG REGISTERS THE ACTION

A couple of hours after the financial markets open in Tokyo, Hong Kong comes to life. The second Asian index that I check each day is the Hang Seng. The Hang Seng China Enterprises Index lists state-owned Chinese companies that are traded on the Hong Kong Stock Exchange. Trading begins in Hong Kong at 8:00 PM CST (9:00 PM DST). That means that before most folks in the United States hit the sheets, Asian traders are out in full force. Just like other markets throughout the world, these markets are operational for about eight hours. Shortly after Europe begins trading around 2:00 AM Central, Hong Kong winds down and the trading pits close.

Similar to the Nikkei in Tokyo, the Hang Seng registers the sentiment of traders in that part of the world. Sometimes the Nikkei and the Hang Seng move in unison and other times they do not. I look for those times when they agree as to a direction, especially if a big move has taken place. That fact tells me that globally, some financial move may be afoot.

HOW I USE THE INFORMATION FROM ASIA

I use information that I gain from Asia in two ways. First, if I am trading the night session, I wait for the stock markets in Tokyo and Hong Kong to open before I place my first trade. The reason that I do so is that these geographical areas reflect the sentiment of millions of traders. When the big exchanges in Tokyo and Hong Kong open, prices may bump up or down on our exchanges in the United States. If Asian activity is strong enough and influential enough, we will feel the effects. I suggest that evening and night traders in the index futures wait for these important trading centers to open and prices to settle for a few minutes before putting money at risk.

The second way that I use Asian data is to get a heads-up for my day. When I check prices, if I see that Asia and China agree, then I look to Europe for further information. I do not monitor prices on the Nikkei and the Hang Seng during their trading sessions. Rather, I want to know closing prices. I am interested in determining whether these Eastern exchanges ended their sessions up or down and whether the move was large or small. A move of 1 percent or greater draws my attention. Those data tend to point me in the right direction when I begin my early morning trading.

In 2000, when I caught the big Nasdaq fall and experienced a very profitable trading day, it was Asia that gave me my first hint that a major undercurrent might be coming my way. Because I had a heads-up, I was able to get prepared and make money. I followed the trend as it crossed Asia and traveled to Europe. I saw momentum grow as the selling moved from continent to continent, and I was able to join the sellers and ride my way to some really nice returns. Asia led the way and I simply followed the trend that started in the Land of the Rising Sun.

I live in Mobile, Alabama, near the Gulf of Mexico. Our area is blessed with some of the most beautiful white sandy beaches in the world. (If you doubt it, just come and see for yourself.) Along the coast of Florida near Pensacola, the warm Gulf waters are crystal clear and brilliantly blue; the sand could not be whiter. However, sometimes a dangerous undertow is lurking beneath the idyllic surface. Swimmers who are unaware of the danger are easily taken by surprise and yanked out to sea. Sadly, a number of visitors drown each season because tourists do not take precautions, heed warnings, and exercise good water-safety practices. Those unaware of the danger are at risk. With a little care, preparation, and education, most of those tragedies could be prevented. As a general rule, people who respect the power of the ocean and know how to protect themselves are able to enjoy the beach and return home safely.

That is also true for the financial markets. Traders who prepare themselves have a better chance of survival. Looking at Asia and gaining as much information as possible from Eastern action helps me get better prepared. When faced with economic reports and financial data, traders on both sides of the Pacific tend to react in the same way. If news is good there will be jubilation and buying, and if it is terrible there will be dread and selling. Therefore, Western traders can learn a great deal by paying a little attention to Asian traders who are plying their trade on the other side of the world.

GET A COMPETITIVE EDGE

Athletes involved in sporting events try to get a competitive edge. If a shoe material or shoe design is believed to help athletes gain a miniscule amount of speed, everyone who is a serious competitor wants it. In bike racing, if a bike made with a better tire design or a lighter material can add a second or two to your speed, that product is the product of choice for all serious racers. Tiny changes in equipment or execution can make the difference between winning or losing the race.

Trading is no different. It is a highly competitive occupation, and serious traders want every trading edge that they can get. Over the years I have met a number of people who have questioned my use of the 24-hour clock and my obsession with checking closing prices on the Hang Seng and the

Nikkei every morning. The skeptics see little to no connection between trading on the Asian exchanges and prices on the Dow Jones or the S&P 500. Obviously, there are many connections. However, I must agree that just because the Nikkei closed up does not necessarily mean that the Dow will also move up during its session. If that were true, it would be great. We could just look at Asia and buy or sell accordingly.

Nevertheless, having knowledge of Asian activity is important. Price movements on the Hang Seng and the Nikkei reflect the views of millions of traders. Therefore, by looking eastward before you begin your day, you can gain a bit of information about global opinion. If a worldwide trend is afoot, you have a chance to see it early and join the party. Personally, I want every edge and bit of help that I can get. I know that watching Asia— the Nikkei in Tokyo and the Hang Seng in Hong Kong—gives me a trading advantage.

> ***Trade Secret #4:   The trading day begins in Asia.***

REVIEW

Because the sun rises in the east and sets in the west, Asia is the first to welcome each new day. For practical purposes, as the world turns, some geographical site on the globe must be the point or demarcation where one day is separated from the next consecutive day. That point is the International Dateline, or the imaginary line that separates the world into the Eastern and Western Hemispheres. That means that Asians are also the first to express their sentiment regarding the world's global markets.

Asia is vast and diverse. Across the continent there are a number of developed economies and a number of others that are undeveloped or underdeveloped. Parts of Southwest Asia are currently experiencing armed conflict, while in East Asia, North Korea's focus on atomic weapons is causing a great deal of concern for the world. In the midst of so much unrest, China, Japan, and Singapore are three of the most economically developed and politically stable nations.

A number of nations on the Asian continent are growing economically, and many of them have thriving financial centers and active financial markets. For my trading purposes, I watch the price action in Japan and Hong

Kong. Specifically, I note the buying and selling on the Nikkei, a stock index located in Tokyo, and I check the Hang Seng, an index situated in Hong Kong. I believe that market sentiment in Asia will be reflected on these indexes. When I begin trading, I want to know if these two financial centers agree as to the direction of a market move. Are equity prices moving up or down in unison in both areas? How did these two indexes close? Were they up or down, and by what percentage? The bigger the Asian market move, the stronger is the indication that a global trend may be afoot. If a trend appears to be emerging, I look westward to Europe to see if the move continues as markets open for business there.

Trading is a competitive field. Individuals who ply their craft in the financial markets of the world are some of the most intelligent and most well-informed businesspeople around. When you execute a trade, you are going head-to-head with them. You should take advantage of every opportunity to get a trading edge. Because of that, before I buy or sell my first equity or futures contract, I get informed about the market action across the Pacific. Sometimes I see no movement of note and the information I gain is not very valuable. But, there are other days when Asia gives me a heads-up. I have an initial idea of market direction. Then, if that first hunch is confirmed, I am better able to make money and consistently stay on the right side of the action. Being aware of Asian trading patterns helps me be a more consistent trader.

 MARKET INSIGHT

The trading day begins in Asia. If any major economic or financial movement is afoot, that movement will be expressed in the financial markets of the East. Specifically, before trading, check the closing prices on the Nikkei and the Hang Seng. If there is a 1 percent or greater change in the index, that movement may hint of a global trend in the making.

CHAPTER 5

Land of the Long Siesta

Europe Joins the Party

O nce Asia steps off the dance floor, Europe steps on. While the sun in shining brightly on the other side of the Pacific, trading is active there. But, as dusk nears and the Hang Seng, Nikkei, and other eastern trading centers are winding down, Europe gets going. Germany is one of the first European markets to welcome the day. Trading on the Dax futures begins at 1:00 AM. Central Time and financial markets in France, Germany, Switzerland, and other parts of Europe open soon after. Europe dominates my second time segment, as shown in Figure 5.1.

I am not now, nor have I ever been, much of a world traveler. However, thanks to the generosity of Uncle Sam, I had a chance to tour Europe in the 1970s. I was in the Air Force and was stationed in Spain. During my off days and leave time, I traveled around quite a bit and learned many valuable lessons about the people and their culture. In fact, although I did not realize it at the time, I also learned a great deal about markets and trading in general.

My first big problem was gaining an understanding of the whole siesta concept in southern Europe. I could never get the midday napping times straight. Inevitably, when I wanted to transact business with the locals, it was time for a siesta and no one was working. The business hours of an establishment seemed to vary from day to day. If a merchant needed a long nap or a big lunch, he just returned to work an hour later. Hence, my first

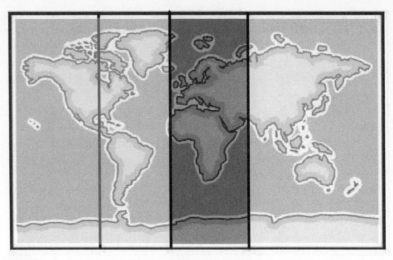

FIGURE 5.1 European trading dominates Time Segment #2. Trading on the German Dax begins at 1:00 AM Central Time.

memory of my stint in Europe is the long siestas and the problems that I had with getting into the swing of the Spanish lifestyle.

Another huge lesson that I learned across the Atlantic was the significance of supply and demand. When I had time or Uncle Sam sent me, I traveled to other parts of Europe. I observed the power of the law of supply and demand in action in a bar in Turkey. I was enjoying a break and visiting the officer's club on the Incirlik Air Base. Everyone was sitting around and talking quietly until a young officer strutted into the bar with a six-pack of Coors in his hands. He had just received the brew from the states and was going to sell it—can by can—to the highest bidder. At this particular time, Coors Beer was not sold in the United States east of the Mississippi, and it certainly was not sold in Turkey. The patrons went wild with excitement as the officer turned trader stood in the center of the room, displayed his merchandise, and opened the bidding. The supply was limited—only a total of six cans of the brewed delicacy to sell. The action was fast and furious as the spirited officers yelled out their bids. Quickly prices escalated, and soon the cans of Coors were selling for about $300 each. That guy was quite a businessman, and his day's earnings proved it. Today he is probably running a Fortune 500 company.

Law of Supply and Demand	
Supply:	Only Six Cans of Coors Beer in Turkey
Demand:	Room of 30 Airmen
Selling Price:	$300.00 per can

Another thing that I learned in Turkey was the importance of a good product line and excellent customer service. In Adana, the bazaars were alive, and along the alleys and winding streets, many traders sold their wares. The U.S. military was well represented, as uniformed men strolled along the byways from stall to stall seeking copper and ornaments to carry back to the United States. Each shopper rummaged through the merchandise trying to ferret out a unique or beautiful product that would impress friends and family members back in the states. The most successful shopkeepers treated their customers like royalty. Tea was served while soft music played in the background. As a southerner, I pride myself in extending a heap of southern hospitality on my clients, but those Turkish merchants had the technique mastered. When I ended a day of shopping in Adana, my cash reserves were lighter, but I felt like a million bucks.

Customer service was king in Adana, Turkey.

Always be prepared—I learned that lesson when I visited a restricted site in Europe. Nuclear weapons were waiting on the base and were ready to be launched, if necessary. It was tense on the base because everyone knew the seriousness of the situation. The Cold War was raging, Germany was divided, the U.S.S.R. was posturing. If a nuclear alert were given, there would be a quick response. I kept my flight suit handy and was prepared to jump into it with a second's warning. When on that particular base, I made certain that I got enough sleep; I stayed alert and took no siestas. Being ready and prepared was my total focus. Luckily, all I ever experienced during those Cold War moments was practicing and preparation. Today, I put great store in those two skills. I believe that being ready or prepared is one of the important characteristics needed to succeed in any field, and that includes trading. Starting a day without the right preparation is a sure way to lose money.

> *Like a Boy Scout, always be prepared.*

Consequently, each day before I begin trading I get prepared. A big part of that preparation process is gathering information about the global markets. In the 1970s, I walked the streets, rode the trains, and sped along the highways gathering information about the culture of various areas of Europe. Today, my focus is on the financial markets, and I get all the information that I need with a click of my computer mouse. Before I make a trade, I learn how Asia and Europe ended their market sessions. If I am trading the Dax or another financial product located in Europe, I check a trading calendar so that I will not fall into a news trap. I do not want to risk money until I am prepared for the obstacles that the market may pose.

EUROPE TAKES CENTER STAGE

Until recently, I had not returned to Europe since Uncle Sam brought me home. However, our neighbors across the Atlantic and their financial markets are very important to me and my trading strategies. As the glow of the afternoon sun sets into Tokyo Bay and workers in Beijing and Shanghai leave their offices and begin enjoying their evening hours, the soft light of the morning sun is dawning in parts of Europe. Commuters pack the Paris metro and Germans board the ubahn and head into Frankfurt, Munich, and Berlin. At 1:00 AM Central Time, trading begins on the Dax. A short time later, around 2:00 AM Central Time, traders begin shouting out their orders on the floor of the Frankfurt Stock Exchange. Also at 2:00 AM Central, the Paris Bourse comes to life; 30 minutes later the London Exchange and the Swiss Exchange light up, and the financial markets across the Atlantic Ocean take center stage.

More than 665 million people live in about 50 different states on the continent of Europe. Germany is home to Europe's biggest national economy. The GDP of this central European nation ranks fifth in the world. Throughout much of the twentieth century, Germany was a powerhouse of industrialization. Defeated by both World War I and World War II, the nation was weakened and divided. However, like Japan, Germany quickly regained its economic agility and has again taken its place among the leading nations of the world. Today Germany is a major exporter to the United States and a significant player in the global marketplace.

Eight stock markets are located in Germany, but the Frankfurt Stock Exchange is by far the largest with over 90 percent of all stocks traded in Germany listed on this exchange. The foremost stock index on the Frankfurt Exchange is the Dax. Like the Dow Jones Industrial Average, 30 blue-chip companies comprise the Dax. Similar to the Nasdaq, the Dax is traded electronically and the trading platform is the Eurex. The currency of Germany and the Dax is the euro. Trading on the index is in half-point increments and the value of each point is about 25 euros. The Germans have been expanding the trading hours of the Dax, and trading currently begins at 1:00 AM Central Time; trading in the Dax Index futures continues until 3:00 PM Central, when the NYSE closes. For many years, trading on the Dax Futures ended at 1:00 PM Central each afternoon. However, often the U.S. financial markets made big moves in the late afternoon hours, and German traders had to make their best guess as to how Chicago and New York would decide to end the day. Not anymore. Now the Dax closes at the same time as the NYSE and only 15 minutes before the CME. Like the Nasdaq, the Dax is a totally electronic exchange.

As I mentioned in the previous chapter, I have watched the Dax for years, but I did not trade it until the disaster of 2001. With exchanges in New York and Chicago closed for about a week, I needed a trading forum and found it in Europe. After September 11, trading the Dax futures became part of my routine. Now, I always monitor and actively trade this index. In fact, I cannot imagine trading the S&P or the Dow and not knowing how the Dax is behaving. Before I trade equities or just about anything, I like to gauge the Dax. Working without checking Dax action is like walking a tightrope with my eyes closed. I do not do it. The Dax is such a large index and it reflects the opinions of a lot of European and global traders.

Dax Futures

Totally Electronic Market.

Trades on the Eurex Exchange through the CME.

   Opens: 1:00 AM Central Time

   Closes: 3:00 PM Central Time

(continued)

Dax Futures *(continued)*

Margin requirements: $11,400.00 euros (intraday); margins will vary slightly depending on the brokerage house.

Trades in .50 point increments

Price per point: 25.00 euros

A novice must beware of the dangers before attempting to trade the Dax. Germans like speed, and sometimes that characteristic seems to surface in their financial markets. When I was in Europe in the early 1970s, I visited Germany. I remember traveling via car on the autobahn and being amazed at the way the Germans dashed from place to place. Then, as now, there was no maximum speed limit, and every driver acted as though he were racing from point A to point B. Did the drivers know of any other option than running their engines at full throttle? It did not appear so. Sometimes the action of the Dax mimics those drivers. You do not want to be on the wrong side of a big market move when the Dax is really racing. The first 30 minutes of trading are generally very active, and I advise everyone except the well trained to stay out during that time. If you like trading futures and you have not looked at the Dax futures, I highly recommend that you do. Even if you do not trade it, you should use that important European Index as an indicator for trading other markets. By doing so, you gain a broader view of global sentiment.

Shortly after trading begins on the Frankfurt Exchange, the Paris Bourse, the London Exchange, and the Swiss Exchange open their doors. The French economy is the third largest in Europe. The Paris Bourse boasts a long history of providing a financial forum for traders. The CAC-40 Index (Compagnie des Agents de Change 40 Index) is the benchmark for tracking the Paris Exchange. As with other major world stock markets, there are also electronic trading opportunities here.

CAC-40: Paris

Trades on the MATIF Exchange.

Opens: 3:00 AM Central Time

Closes: 10:00 AM Central Time

(continued)

CAC-40: Paris *(continued)*

Margin requirements: $2,750.00 euros (intraday), as always, margin requirement differ slightly from broker to broker.

Trades in .50 increments

Price per point is $10.00 euros

The United Kingdom is Europe's second largest economy, and London is home to the London Stock Exchange, where Great Britain's largest companies are traded. The London Exchange traces its history back for centuries, and it is a highly respected global financial leader. A good gauge of London financial sentiment is the FTSE. The FTSE-100 (Financial Times 100 Index) is the most well-known and respected index reflecting trading on the London Exchange. This index tracks the top 100 British companies. The currency of the FTSE is the British pound sterling; Britain has not become an economic member of the European Union. Like the Dax, the FTSE is important to watch because it mirrors the economic attitudes of a great number of European traders.

FTSE: London

Trades at the LIFFE

Opens: 2:00 AM Central Time

Closes: 11:30 AM Central Time

Margin requirements: $3,500.00 British pounds

Trades in 5-point increments

Price per point is 12.5 British pounds;
intraday and will vary with broker.

Another important trading area that becomes active around 2:00 AM Central Time is Zurich. The Switzerland Stock Exchange (SWX) is not enormous in size, but it is big in influence. Long a respected financial center, Switzerland boasts one of Europe's most stable economies. The Swiss Market Index (SMI) consists of 30 of Switzerland's largest stocks and is the benchmark for Swiss equities.

SMI: Swiss

Trades on the Eurex Exchange.

Opens: 1:50 AM Central Time

Closes: 10:30 AM Central Time

Trades in 1-point increments

Price per point is 10 Swiss francs*

*There is a variety of different levels of contracts, so verify price and other data. Also know that the exact margin differs from broker to broker.

Even though my European trading vehicle of choice is the Dax Index futures, I keep up with the action in other areas. I respect the influence and significance of exchanges and indexes in the other important trading centers such as Paris and Zurich. Prices on these indexes reflect the economic and financial health and well being of much of Western Europe, and that means that they affect U.S. prices. Therefore, each day before I put money at risk, I look to see how trading sessions in Europe are going. I want to know if prices in these hubs of trading activity are moving up or down. In the early morning hours, around 4:00 AM Central, if the markets in all of these geographical areas are in agreement as to direction, I perk up. Then I review Asian prices and determine whether their markets closed up or down during the session. If the east and the west are agreeing as to direction, I pay careful attention because I know that a global market trend may be coming my way.

EUROPE RULES WHEN ASIA CLOSES

From the time that markets in Frankfurt, Paris, and London open until traders in New York and Chicago start yelling out their orders in the trading pits on the floor of the NYSE, the CME, and the CBOT, Europe and its markets rule. The futures markets like the S&P 500 and Dow futures are trading but the leaders of the financial marketplace are across the ocean. The Dax carries a big stick, and if the Dax starts traveling up or down, the S&P and other U.S. indexes will almost surely follow. This is especially true if the move is big and support or resistance levels are broken.

When I trade in the early-morning hours, I keep an eye on the Dax. If the Dax is very strong, I will not sell the Dow, Nasdaq, or S&P. The Dax may be sending a message. Many times the Dax has saved me by keeping me out of losing trades. However, if the Dax is strong and the S&P or other index is breaking resistance, I will probably be a buyer. Strength on the Dax confirms the move on the S&P.

I remember a day in early June 2006 when the Dax was exhibiting a great deal of strength. Several times during the early morning the bears tried to take prices down below the open, but they were never able to do so. When U.S. markets opened, the S&P and Dow moved downward and there was a great temptation to short the market. But, I remembered the strength of the Dax and I hesitated to sell. In spite of prices that looked negative, I kept on looking for a chance to buy. After an hour or so, my chance came. A lot of traders fell for the sucker move and went short. They saw U.S. indexes heading down and started selling. Because I was aware of the strength of the German Dax, I did not fall for the move. I waited for prices to start up and joined the winning side. The Dax showed me the way. Many times it has done so.

THE EARLY BIRD GETS THE WORM

Another way that I use global markets is to determine a developing market trend. By 4:00 AM Central Time, the Asian Nikkei and Hang Seng have closed and one can easily check prices and determine whether the sessions closed up or down. Many times the two markets do not agree as to a direction; one finished up and the other down. However, if they are in agreement—that is, they both ended their sessions either up or both down—then I look to Europe. Morgan, my son, gets up early and often checks the action for me. In addition to the Hang Seng and the Nikkei, he looks at the Dax, FTSE, CAC, and SMI prices. If all of those indexes are moving in the same direction and if that direction mimics that of Asia, Morgan gives me a phone call. If all of the major Asian and European indexes are expressing the same sentiment, it is a good signal that a trending day may be coming to the United States.

As a futures trader, I do not care if the move is up or down. If there is a trend in either direction and I can identify it early, I have the chance to make money. The sooner the direction is identified, the sooner the profits can start rolling in. Therefore, if I get a call from Morgan, I get to my trading computer and assess the situation. I probably will place a trade and see if the trend will last. If the move appears weak, I will just probe the market by trading a light position. If the move strengthens, I will add more positions. Sometimes harmonious actions in Asia and Europe point to the day's direction in the United States and sometimes the distant moves mean little to players in our shores. At any rate, by having knowledge that a move may be afoot, I have a chance to catch it, if it continues and fully develops.

USE THE DAX FOR CONFIRMATION

On June 13, 2006, the markets were unusually volatile. During the first 30 minutes of trading, the Dow futures had a high of 10,950 and a low of 10,855—a move of 95 points in only a few minutes. Such a wide range is often the range for an entire session of trading. With so much quick action, I decided to be patient and analyze the situation before I jumped into the fray. In addition to running a trading school, I also operate a traders' chat room. Throughout the trading day, myself and other staff members analyze the index futures and make trade recommendations. Because I know that other people are listening and depending on me for guidance, I try to play it safe. On this particular day, I knew that the markets had been selling off for days and I was looking to the short side, but with the market so volatile, I was not yet certain as to how I should proceed. I did not want to lead my chat room listeners down the wrong path. As I often do, I looked to the Dax for a clue.

It was about 9:30 AM Central Time and the Dow was approaching the key number of 10,950. I told my listeners that I was selling a small Dow position at 10,849 (just below a key support level). I also cautioned them to keep an eye on the Dax futures because the daily low of the Dax was 5,280. If that low was broken, I had confirmation of the move. Our sell stop was hit and we were in the market. The Dax confirmed the play. Then I informed listeners to look for the Dax to break the 5,270 barrier for further confirmation. That price was also broken, and the Dow moved to a low of 10,835. Not a huge distance from our entry—14 points—but plenty of room for me to make a decent profit for my efforts. In a highly volatile and somewhat dangerous market, the Dax served as my security blanket. Had the Dax not broken the 5,280 price, I would not have proceeded with the trade. Over time I have learned to respect the wisdom of those German traders across the Atlantic.

During the early morning hours, before the U.S. day markets open, the Dax often leads the way for the other markets. If the Dax opens and sinks, I will not take a long position on the S&P or Dow. The Dax is too influential in the world marketplace to ignore.

The older I get the less enthusiastic I am about rising early. Therefore, many mornings I do not look at the Dax until around 6:00 AM Central. The 6:00 AM price on this index is important because it corresponds to the

12:30 PM Central price on the S&P 500. That is, at 6:00 AM Central, many European traders are returning from lunch and taking a new look at the markets. If they like the morning move they confirm it and prices accelerate upward; if they disagree with the picture they are seeing, they reverse and things go down. I believe that the 6:00 AM Dax price is a new line in the sand by the bulls and the bears and a new benchmark for me. Therefore, I use this price as a major pivot point for the next 24 hours. The bottom line: Knowing about global markets gives me another indicator or gauge to interpret the action.

When the NYSE and the CME open for business each morning, the world markets have been trading for many hours. Asian exchanges have opened and closed; European exchanges are winding down. Why not use that information? Think of a group of athletes preparing for a racing competition. Those who warm up and get prepared for the challenge that lies ahead have an advantage from the get-go.

Believe me, if traders see a global problem they will sell the Nikkei and Hang Seng. When exchanges in France and London and other European cities open, they will join the selling spree. Likewise, if there is some good news that is expected to favor economic conditions, buyers will step in and voice their confidence. Therefore, knowing global sentiment and using that knowledge to better interpret and anticipate the day's action in New York and other trading centers of the United States makes a lot of sense. Like the runner who is ready for the race, a trader who starts the day by being informed about the global action is ready for the game to begin. Before I begin trading, I always get a global reading. I use that information to help me determine whether to be long, short, or out of the market. When planning my daily strategy, especially my morning strategy, I consider international sentiment.

That is why I also use the Dax so heavily in my trading. If the S&P and Dow are moving up, but the Dax is lagging or falling, I will not buy the other markets. Many times the Dax has saved me from some foolhardy buy or sell. If German traders do not want to come to the party, I also hesitate to join it. Believe me, if a strong bull is stampeding in the United States, the Dax will be heading higher also. If I am considering a long position on the Dow futures, I look to the Dax. If the Dax is strong and breaking through resistance, I will follow through on my move and buy the Dow based on the move of the Dax. However, if the Dax is unable to break resistance and move up, I will likely abandon my buying plan and sit on the sidelines. Figure 5.2 shows how closely the S&P 500 futures and the Dax futures tend to move in unison. These charts depict the action on July 20, 2006.

When the S&P futures take a dramatic move up, so does the Dax. Although the graphs are not mirror images of each other, they are definitely close.

FIGURE 5.2   The close correlation in movements between the S&P 500 futures and the Dax futures. On July 20, 2006, the trading patterns are very similar.

USE THE DAX TO SEE DIVERGENCE

I use the Dax for confirmation of a market trend and I use divergence as a signal of caution. If a trending market appears to be developing, but the Dax is not joining it, I am careful. I view the divergence of the Dax to be a sign that the move lacks strength and is not likely to develop to any profitable degree. Therefore, I shy away it. I do not quickly jump into the action until the Dax and those German players are willing to jump on the bandwagon.

TRADE THE DAX

Over the last few years the Dax has become one of my favorite trading vehicles. Just like the S&P 500 or the Dow, traders can trade the Dax Index futures, and I regularly do so. The Dax is traded at the CME on the Extera Exchange. A Dax contract trades in .50-point increments, and each point is valued around US$25. That amount varies as the price of the euro and the dollar move up and down on the international currency market.

During the first 30 minutes of trading (1:00 to 1:30 AM Central Time) the Dax is generally very active and prices are popping. I use that first 30-minute trading bar as a reference bar and trade off of it. That is, if prices rise above the bar, I consider the move bullish, and if prices break below that reference bar I consider them bearish. When I first started trading the Dax, I was fascinated with it, and I was a very faithful early morning trader. However, I admit that these days I enjoy sleeping. But, many traders like to rise early and play the Dax. It is an exciting market and can be profitable for those who are knowledgeable. I suggest that if you trade the Dax, you pay close attention to the opening price and the first 30 minutes of trading. Watching that open and the high and low of that first bar will help traders stay on the right side of the action.

Another time that I look to trade the Dax is around 6:00 AM Central Time. The Germans are returning from lunch at 6:00 AM Central Time. They have had a midday break and are reevaluating their morning trading direction. They are establishing a new benchmark. Just as the 12:30 PM price is a good pivot price for our markets, so is the 6:00 AM price for the Dax. I use this price point as a gauge for my trading. Above the price and I will be looking to the long side; below it and I will be seeking shorting opportunities. Many times I trade the Dax around 6:00 AM.

Throughout the day, as I am trading U.S. markets, I also watch the Dax. If I see a good setup for trading, I take it. I follow the same time restraints as with trading other markets. That is, I trade in the morning but do not trade the Dax between 10:15 AM and 12:30 PM. I also stay clear of it between 1:30 PM and 2:00 PM Central. I find that those times are not generally good for my breakout trading strategy.

I enjoy trading the Dax, and it has proven profitable for me. I suggest that traders beginning to trade this or any other product be careful. Observe trading for a while before actually putting any money down. Locate support, resistance, and key numbers. Once you are comfortable with the new market and have a feel for how it moves during various times of the day, start trading it, but do so slowly. Always learn to crawl before trying to run.

THE BEAT JUMPS TO THE UNITED STATES

Europe dominates time segment two. Throughout much of this trading timeframe the sun is shining brightly in Paris, Frankfurt, London, and other great European financial centers. Then, as the business day is winding down across the Atlantic, the most active global trading shifts to our shores. At 8:30 AM Central Time, the New York Stock Exchange opens and futures contracts begin changing hands at the Chicago Mercantile Exchange and the Chicago Board of Trade. Now it is America's turn to set the global beat.

> **Trade Secret #5:   Controlling risk while you sleep is the first step toward success**

REVIEW

When I visited Europe several decades ago, it was the long siestas that initially caught my attention; those long naps forced me to pay careful attention to my time schedule when conducting business with the locals. However, today it is the financial markets that demand my consideration. In the early morning hours, Europe takes charge of world trading. The focus of financial activity follows the path of the sun as it moves across the sky from east to west. Initially, as each new day dawns across the Pacific, Asia dominates the trading scene. But, as the ball of fire travels westward, so does the focus of global trading. When the trading floors of the Asian exchanges empty and eastern markets close, activity shifts to Europe, and the financial markets in Germany, London, Paris, and Zurich take center stage.

Beginning with the opening of the Dax futures at 1:00 AM, Europe comes alive. Because Germany has the largest economy in Europe, the Dax, a well-known and highly respected equity index, leads the way during early morning trading. I trade the Dax futures, but I also use the Dax as an indicator of global market sentiment. If I am considering a buy or a sell on the S&P or the Dow, I look to the Dax to determine its strength or weakness. If the Dax confirms my play, I make it. But, if the Dax appears to be disagreeing with my move, I wait and look a little closer. Many times the Dax has been the indicator that has saved me from a foolish early morning play. By avoiding false moves, I am a more consistent trader.

Once the NYSE and the CME and CBOT open in Chicago and New York, action shifts to our shores. However, the Dax futures continue to trade until 3:00 PM. Therefore, I watch that index all day, and it is both a trading platform and a market indicator for me until its close.

The bottom line is that we live in a big world that is connected. Economic or political events in Asia and Europe quickly echo through our financial markets. The sentiment of Asian and European traders is expressed in the Dow, the S&P 500, and the Nasdaq. Just as a doctor uses a thermometer to get an idea about the health of the patient, I use the markets of both Asia and Europe to gauge the trend and possible course of markets in the United States. By doing so, I gain greater consistency and I am able to make more money.

 MARKET INSIGHT

Europe is the center of global trading in the early morning hours. Before trading, check European markets. If they are trending in unison, see if that direction parallels Asia's move. If so, determine the extent of the move. A movement of 1 percent or higher may signal a global trend that may move across the Atlantic to our shores.

CHAPTER 6

The United States Steals the Show

A t 3:00 AM I get rolling—literally. The year is 1971. I'm a college student working a summer job, and each morning, before the sun greets the new day, I drive the 20 miles or so to Macon, Georgia, to pick up my bread truck. When I arrive, the truck is loaded and ready. All I need to do is double-check the cargo. After a quick audit of loaves and rolls, I'm off for my daily rounds. I need to get the show on the road, because my route is in Milledgeville, Georgia, a few miles down the highway. The Piggly Wiggly is one of my best customers, and I want the early morning shoppers to have fresh bread. The freshest bread always sells, and I do not want to miss those opportunities to move my product and make easy money.

The bread truck rolls all day and I carry my palettes of aromatic, yeasty offerings to groceries, convenience stores, and restaurants around the area. Around five in the afternoon, I call it a day and head back to Macon.

Working on the bread truck taught me a lot of important life lessons. I learned to use my time wisely—especially the mornings—so that I could get a jump on the competition. I still do that today. By using the 24-hour trading clock, I get a jump on other traders. When my day begins, I know the sentiment of the Asia and Europe and I use that information to make money in the United States.

During that summer, I also learned to identify my profit centers and focus my greatest efforts there. Piggly Wiggly was my biggest customer. Hundreds of loaves of my bread went off the shelves of that particular grocery each and every day. That meant that money flowed into my pockets at week's end. I understood the importance of taking care of my profit centers, or good customers, to increase my commissions and sweeten my weekly check. Therefore, every morning, my priority was the Piggly Wiggly stores on my route. I considered those sales low-hanging fruit; it was a sure bet that my loaves of bread and pastries would move quickly at the Piggly Wiggly. I concentrated my efforts there.

Today, I still look for low-hanging fruit and I prioritize my time and my analysis on my key profit centers. I do this by using a 24-hour trading clock and having the market information that I need when Wall Street opens. While other traders are trying to determine what to do, I already have my plan and I am ready to execute it. I have identified what I believe to be the most lucrative markets to trade and I am ready to pluck the low-hanging fruit. I know the collective sentiment of traders across the Pacific and the Atlantic and my trading vehicle is ready to roll.

> *Pluck the low-hanging fruit. There is no need to fight the trend.*

NEW YORK AWAKENS

A pink glow spreads across the East River as the sun rises. Soon one of America's biggest cities comes to life, and commuters board the subways and flood the streets, avenues, and highways leading into Manhattan and its financial district. To the west, Chicago is also coming to life. Traders walk into the executive offices of some of the world's biggest commodity clearing firms while pit traders step into their soon-to-be-frantic spaces on the floors of the exchanges. Throughout the trading districts of the United States, the business of the financial markets gets underway. At 8:30 AM Central Time, trading opens on the floor of the New York Stock Exchange, and contracts also start changing hands in the pits of the Chicago Mercantile Exchange, the Chicago Board of Trade, and other trading hubs across America. With the sun shinning brightly on our shores, the eyes of the world focus on Wall Street (see Figure 6.1).

America's critics may find a lot of faults with the red, white, and blue, but the United States still boasts the world's largest and most technologically powerful economy. The average per capita income exceeds $40,000

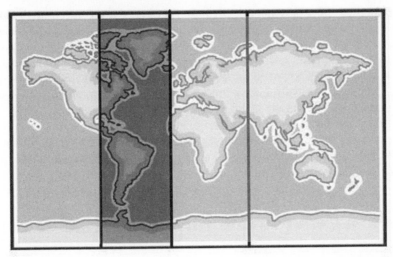

FIGURE 6.1 The United States dominates morning trading action. From 8:30 AM until 12:30 PM Central Time, all eyes are on our shores.

per year. That compares to an estimated $30,400 for Germany, $31,500 for Japan, $10,000 for Mexico, and $6,800 for China (CIA data). Even though manufacturing jobs have been lost to China, Mexico, and other nations, the United States is still leading the world in many technologically driven fields such as aerospace, computers, and medical advances, and our financial markets reflect our strength and remain among the world's largest and most powerful.

Nevertheless, the United States faces many economic challenges. One big issue that must be dealt with is our dependence on foreign oil. The United States imports about two-thirds of the oil that it consumes. That reality obviously leaves us vulnerable to world conditions; when oil supplies are disrupted our prices soar, the economy feels the pinch. Other major issues that our nation must face are the maintenance costs and lack of productivity of an aging population, and our large and ever-growing trade and budget deficits.

Even in the midst of war in the Mideast, some devastating natural disasters, and galloping oil prices, the U.S. economy has remained strong. At the time of this writing (September 2006), the S&P 500, Dow Jones, and Nasdaq-100 continue to trade above their 2006 openings. That is to say, 2006, to date, is still a bullish year. In fact, unless the scene changes toward the end of the year, 2006 has been pretty stupendous. In September the Dow Jones futures approached 1853.00, an all time high for that index, and on October 3, 2006, the DJIA closed above its previous all-time high. It closed at 11,727.34. On that date the index also hit a new intra-day high of 11,758.95. Numbers approaching that height had not been seen since the dot-com bubble burst in 2000. The 2006, yearly open for the S&P 500 Futures was 1255.25 and during September, prices were hitting the 1350.00 level. In November, traders saw the 1400.00 level crossed to the upside on the S&P Futures.

Because the U.S. economy and our financial markets are so formidable and powerful, once the trading pits in New York and Chicago open for business, the world shifts its attention to the United States and our markets lead the way in global trading.

TIME SEGMENT THREE: THE U.S. MORNING

Once the U.S. exchanges open for trading, the international scene shifts to our shores. No financial center in the world merits more respect than Wall Street. Not surprisingly, U.S. stock markets dominate the morning action. The first several hours after New York opens are very active, and prices tend to move in our equity, bond, commodity, and futures markets.

As noon approaches, traders step away from their desks for lunch. When they return, they often reevaluate the morning's action. Therefore, I consider the 12:30 PM timeframe to be one in which the markets tend to reset. By that I mean that traders rethink the morning's move. If they like it, they may push down on the gas and pick up the pace. However, if they disagree with it, prices may shift and move in a contrary direction. The 12:30 PM price is the new benchmark by which I gauge trading for the next 24 hours. After lunch, time segment four begins. It encompasses afternoon trading in the United States, and market movements may be very different from those of the morning.

A SURVEY OF THE LANDSCAPE

The New York Stock Exchange is the oldest stock exchange in the United States, tracing its origins to 1792. In 2006, a merger of three separate institutions—the New York Stock Exchange, Archipelago (ARCA), and the Pacific Exchange (PCX)—created the New York Stock Exchange Group. The NYSE Group operates two exchanges: the NYSE and NYSE ARCA. The latter is a completely electronic stock exchange. In terms of the dollar value traded, the NYSE is one of the largest stock exchanges in the world, and it is also near the top in terms of the number of companies listed.

The Nasdaq is also a major international contender. However, with a global capitalization of more than $20 trillion, the total market capitalization of the companies listed on NYSE is many times that of those on the Nasdaq. Both U.S. and international corporations are listed on the Big Board (a popular term for the NYSE), with trillions of dollars of capitalization in non-U.S. companies. Trading on the NYSE begins at 8:30 AM Central Time (9:30 AM Eastern) and continues until 3:00 PM Central (4:00 Eastern). If you are trading, you must know how the NYSE is doing. New York is too powerful to ignore.

The Nasdaq is another very important exchange. The Nasdaq began operations in 1971, and it is the nation's largest equity electronic exchange. Originally, the Nasdaq was formed to allow electronic opportunities for over-the-counter shares (i.e. shares that were publicly traded but not listed on any other major exchange). Today the Nasdaq is known for its technology stocks. Most high-tech equities are listed on the Nasdaq. Due to its saturation with high techs, the Nasdaq took a dive during the dot-com crisis in 2000. The Nasdaq consists of far more than just high techs, however. More than 3,000 companies, mostly large caps, are listed on the Nasdaq.

The third largest stock exchange in the United States is the American Stock Exchange. In 1998, the Nasdaq merged with the American Exchange. However, both exchanges operate separately. Due to its less onerous listing requirements, the shares of many small to mid-size corporations are traded here. The American Exchange is also one of the world's largest options exchanges, with nearly 2,000 stock options available. Additionally, many exchange traded funds (ETFs) are housed at the American Exchange, including the S&P 500 Spyder and the Dow Jones Diamond. Without question, the United States is home to a number of the biggest and most influential stock exchanges in the world.

INDEXES THAT LEAD THE WAY

The health of the equity markets is reflected in several major indexes, including the Dow Jones Industrial Average, the S&P 500, and the Nasdaq-100. The Dow Jones Industrial Average (DJIA) was first published in 1896 by Charles Dow, then editor of *The Wall Street Journal*. The Dow tracks stock prices for 30 of the nation's largest blue-chip corporations in nine different economic sectors. The Dow is a price-weighted average, which means that larger corporations exert greater influence over the index data than smaller ones. The result of this price-weighted data reporting system is that sometimes the Dow presents misleading numbers. Big corporations have the ability to skew the data. Nevertheless, the Dow continues to be a well-respected reflection of the overall health of equity markets in the United States.

> *The Dow Jones is generally considered to be not only the oldest but also one of the most highly watched equity indexes in the world. It is deemed by millions to be a benchmark for U.S. stock performance and a reflection of the health of the U.S. Economy.*

If one desires to trade the stocks listed on the Dow Jones Industrial Average, that possibility is now available via the Diamond, an exchange traded fund listed on the American Exchange. The symbol for the Diamond is AMEX:DIA. Trading the Diamond is a way to participate in the action of all of the DJIA stocks simultaneously. Theoretically, the returns received on one's investment in the Diamond should be closely correlated to total price movement on the index. Of course there are fees and cost associated with buying and selling the shares.

Another major index is the S&P 500, which tracks stock price action on 500 of the nation's largest publicly traded companies. Corporations listed on the S&P 500 are selected not only for size but also to obtain a good cross-section of the major industrial, manufacturing, financial, and other economic sectors within the U.S. financial system. Due to the breadth of this index, many consider it to be the most reliable benchmark for gauging the health and well-being of the overall economy. Unquestionably, the S&P 500 covers far more ground than the Dow. Like the DJIA, the S&P 500 also offers exchange-traded funds (ETFs). These funds are known as Spyders and are also traded on the American Exchange. The symbol is AMEX:SPY.

Finally, one other often-watched index is the Nasdaq-100. This index tracks 100 of the nation's largest nonfinancial domestic and international public companies that are listed on the Nasdaq Exchange. The Nasdaq-100 is considered to be a good measurement for gauging the health and well being of the technology sector. Again, one has the ability to trade ETFs holding exclusively traded shares. The shares are known as the QQQQ, and these shares are traded on the Nasdaq.

When U.S. markets are trading, the world looks at the price action on the exchanges and the numbers on the indexes that reflect that action. The S&P 500, the DJIA, and the Nasdaq-100 are respected and highly regarded from Dubai to Iceland and everywhere in between.

DERIVATIVES MARKETS

In addition to equity markets, a large and active derivatives market operates in the United States. My focus in this market is both futures and options. The Chicago Mercantile Exchange, founded more than a hundred years ago, is home to the nation's biggest futures exchange. For many years corn, soybeans, and many other commodities and products were traded at the CME. In 1982, the CME expanded its offerings and began trading the S&P 500 Index futures contracts. By means of this derivatives market, one is able to participate in the equity markets' (specifically the S&P 500's) moves. I traded those S&P futures contracts on the first day that they were issued.

A big S&P 500 futures contract trades for $250 per point and trading is in 10-point increments. In 1997, the CME began offering a mini S&P 500 contract. The mini contract, known as an e-mini, trades for one-fifth the size of a big contract, or $50 per point in quarter-point increments.

In 1992, the CME began hosting after-hours trading on its Globex technology. Today trading is available on the Globex almost 24 hours a day. Globex trading begins at 3:30 PM Central and continues until 3:15 PM Central the following day (there is a brief halt in trading during each session for maintenance).

If you were to purchase a futures contract after the Globex session opens, you would be able to hold it until the session closes—almost 24 hours later—with no additional margin requirement. Therefore, I never carry a contract from the day session into the night session. If I want to trade in the evening or early morning hours, I enter the market during Globex trading. In fact, unless there is a technological problem, I always use the Globex for trading the S&P 500 minis. Order execution is faster because no phone or order entry person is required.

In 1996, the CME also added futures contracts to its menu. The big Nasdaq contract (ND) is $100 per point and the mini (NQ) is $10 per contract. The hours of operation for the big contract coincide with those for the S&P futures (i.e., 8:30 AM until 3:15 PM CST), and like the e-mini S&P, the mini opens for after-hours trading on the Globex system at 3:30 PM Central and continues until 3:15 PM Central Time the following day.

Another big trading forum for the derivatives markets is the Chicago Board of Trade. The CBOT claims to be the world's oldest futures and options exchange, and it traces its history to 1848. According to the CBOT, it is the only exchange in the world that continued trading during the 1987 market crash.

A wide array of financial products is traded at the exchange, including precious metals, agricultural products, and the Dow Index futures. I have traded the Dow futures for years and enjoy doing so. A big Dow contract trades in one-point increments, and the price is $10 per point; a mini Dow trades for $5 per point. The mini Dow is one of my favorite day-trading products. Due to the small value of each point, it is a good place for beginning futures traders to gain their wings. Trading in the open outcry pits begins at 7:20 AM CST and ends at 3:15 PM The big Dow is traded in the pit during those hours and traded electronically after hours from 7:15 PM until 7:00 AM CST. Electronic trading on the mini Dow begins at 7:15 PM CST and ends at 4:00 PM CST. Electronic trading opens the doors of our trading centers to the world.

Options are also traded at several exchanges, including the American Exchange (large numbers of stock options are traded here), the Chicago Board Options Exchange (CBOE), and the CBOT.

With a powerful economic engine and so much to offer traders, it is understandable that once U.S. markets open for business, they lead the way in global trading.

S&P 500 Futures Index

Traded at the Chicago Mercantile Exchange (CME).

Outcry pits: Open at 8:30 AM Central Time

Close at 3:13 PM Central Time

Big contract is $250 per point.

Mini contract is $50 per point.

Margin requirement for mini contract varies depending on your broker but should be around $2,500. Greater margin is required for the big contract and for holding positions from session to session.

Mini contract always trades electronically on the Globex system.

Globex trading begins at 3:30 PM Central Monday through Thursday and at 5:00 PM on Sunday.

Dow Jones Futures Index

Traded at the Chicago Board of Trade (CBOT).

Electronic trading begins at 6:15 PM Central Time and continues until 4:00 PM the following day.

Big contracts trade for $10 per point.

Mini contracts trade for $5 per point.

To trade the mini contract, a margin requirement of $2,000 or so is required per contract. If holding positions overnight, a greater margin is necessary.

Nasdaq Index Futures

Traded at the Chicago Mercantile Exchange (CME)

Outcry pits: Open at 8:30 AM Central Time

Close at 3:15 PM Central Time

Big contract is $100 per point.

Mini contract is $10 per point.

Margin requirement for mini contract varies but should be around $2,500. Greater margin is required for the big contract and for holding positions from session to session.

Mini contract always trades electronically on the Globex system.

Globex trading begins at 3:30 PM Central Monday through Thursday and at 5:00 PM on Sunday.

SELECT TRADING TIMES CAREFULLY

Lake Tahoe and the surrounding countryside are beautiful geographical areas. When I was in my twenties, I spent some time in California and Nevada, and I remember riding my Triumph motorcycle along the mountainous roads that winded along the lake. I had some favorite paths and small roads where I especially enjoyed cycling. The scenery was breathtaking year round. In the spring everything was green and lush, and in the fall, browns and oranges painted the landscape. The area looked like a fairyland in the winter. Everything was icy and white. But, I could not see the wintry scene from the seat of my Triumph. Some of the roads and paths that I traveled just a short time before were slick with sheets of ice. They were impassable, or—if passable—extremely dangerous. When I took my mountain rides, I selected my seasons carefully. Safety was my primary concern.

Trading is like riding a motorcycle on those mountainous trails. Some times are safer for taking a ride than other times. When you are trading, you must have liquidity and volatility; that is the only way to make money. Some hours during the day are traditionally better for trading than others. And, some are just plain dangerous. Therefore, I select my times carefully and seek ideal conditions when money making will be possible. Here is how I do it.

THE UNITED STATES IS THE CENTER OF GLOBAL ACTION

When New York comes to life, the financial markets of Asia have closed and markets in Europe are nearing their end. The electronic German Dax is still trading, but the S&P, Dow, and Nasdaq dominate the stage. Generally, the first few minutes of action are very volatile and dangerous. Traders do not yet have a sense of where prices are going; it is impossible to determine a direction. Only the foolhardy jump into the market before it has had at least a few minutes to settle down. I often give it a full 30 minutes before I put any capital at risk. With morning volume high, from around 9:00 AM until 10:15 AM tends to be lucrative for my breakout strategy. Those with good analysis and the ability to realize when the odds of success are in their favor will usually be able to take a position, get some movement from the market, and exit their positions with profits.

As the morning passes, traders identify the direction they believe the market is taking and they place their trades. After several hours of working, their thoughts turn to lunch and volume tends to level off or fall. I consider the time between 10:15 AM until 12:30 PM to be generally slower. If I am in a profitable trade from the morning, I will check to be certain that a protective stop is in place, and then I will busy myself with activities other than trading.

I will not place new trades at this time. Experience has taught me that when I trade during this market lull, I tend to take too many risks and lose too many trades. Therefore, I sit on the sidelines and analyze the data or busy myself with other activities. I always keep a book handy to distract myself so that I will not be lured into a dangerous and slow-trading situation. I spend 90 percent of my time thinking and 10 percent of it trading. That gets me the best results.

U.S. MARKETS DOMINATE THE AFTERNOON

Once traders enjoy their sandwiches and salads, they return to the business of the markets. The afternoon session is like the dawn of a new day. I consider 12:30 PM Central Time to be the start of time segment four. Traders evaluate the morning action and determine whether they agree with it. If they agree, the morning trend will be accelerated, and if they decide that prices are going in the wrong direction, there will be a reversal and the direction of the morning will be shifted.

Many novices look at the price direction from eight until noon and place their trades based on that information. What they do not understand is that the morning movement may not be followed through in the afternoon. For some reason, a new benchmark for the day is formed at 12:30 PM. That is, at that time the bulls and the bears square off again and draw a new line in the sand. I consider that price point to be a pivot price and I use that price for my trading for the next 24 hours. If the market trades above that point in the afternoon, I look to be a buyer. If it trades below that price, I look to be a seller. Of course, I watch far more than that one number. But, if prices are lower than the 12:30 PM price, I will buy only with caution.

Trading between 12:30 PM and 1:00 PM is also important. The price bar formed during that timeframe is noteworthy for me, and I use it as a reference for my afternoon trading. If prices move above the high of trading between 12:30 and 1:00 PM, I look to be long. If prices move below the low of trading during that 30-minute time, I look to be short. I use that trading bar to interpret market sentiment.

For much of the afternoon I stay out of the markets. I will take a trade between 12:30 PM and 1:15 PM Central, if there is one to take. If not, I wait until around 2:30 PM and look at prices again. If I see a strong move, I will take a position and try to hold it until New York closes at 3:00 PM. In fact, if the trend is strong and the boys in Chicago appear to have clearly expressed a market direction, I will try to hold on until 3:13 PM or so in order to get the maximum movement from the trend. However, I will always close out my futures positions on or before 3:15 PM Central Time. Holding them beyond this point will result in a far greater margin requirement. Also, holding positions overnight carries far greater risk. Therefore,

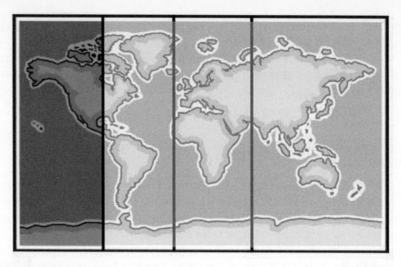

FIGURE 6.2 As the sun moves across the U.S. from New York to California, the U.S. dominates global trading.

I get out of the market and go to the sidelines. If I feel strongly that I see the market's direction and want to reenter the fray, I can always do so during the night or Globex session. No need to incur greater expenses and add to my risk by holding positions overnight.

TAKE ONLY CALCULATED RISK

An essential part of trading is taking risk. The trick to winning is calculating the risk and only taking those trades that have a great probability of success. When I was in college, I liked to play poker. My roommate was the worst poker player in the world. If he was in the game, we knew we had a shot to take home some cash because he was going to make every wrong decision. He did not understand anything about the odds of getting winning hands. He just did not get it.

Another one of the players always counted cards and he was tough to beat. He knew when the odds were working in his favor and when they were not. If he had a losing hand, he did not bet the bank on it. But, when he had a winner—or at least the odds were in his favor—he raised the ante and took home the cash. He took a risk, but it was a calculated risk. I lost more than a few bucks to him.

In order to trade one has to understand the odds of winning and losing and take those trades when the probabilities are great that he is on the right side of the market action. If he is risk averse and never wants to take a chance, he cannot trade. Or, if he has no fear and does not respect risk, he will soon be broke.

Almost everything in life requires that one take a chance. I remember when I met my wife in Oklahoma City. I thought that she was the most beautiful girl I had ever seen. I had a slight problem, however, in that I was dating another person at the time. I decided to take a chance, exit the other relationship, and go for the gold. The risk paid off big, and Paula and I were soon married. I thought the odds in that play were in my favor, and I was right; we've been married for about 25 years, and I think she plans to keep me for a few more.

Remember that with every trade it is important to know the risk involved. If the risk is too great, walk away. Learning to properly interpret key numbers and market indicators, and selecting the right times to trade reduces risk. (Chapter 10, *Golden Keys to Unlocking the Secrets of the Financial Markets* discusses key numbers and market indicators.) If I am trading index futures, at the end of the Globex session (3:15 PM Central Time), I generally call it a day for those contracts. I consider the added risk of carrying the contracts from session to session to be too great. If I want to trade at night, I simply reenter the market during the Globex trading hours.

THE WORLD KEEPS TURNING

As trading comes to an end in Manhattan and traders vacate the trading areas in Chicago, Asian markets are getting ready to open. The NYSE closes at 3:00 PM Central. The S&P 500 Index futures and the Nasdaq Index futures close at 3:15 PM A few minutes later the Dow futures settle out their day's accounts. Trading in the United States is over, and the spotlight moves from our shores.

In China and Japan, the sun will rise soon. Just like the folks in that old Bill Haley tune, traders rock around the clock. When New Yorkers are gazing at the stars, traders in Hong Kong are placing their orders. When folks in Chicago are enjoying their dinners, Asians are busy buying and selling an array of financial products that are actively being traded on their exchanges. The 24-hour trading clock resets as another day's global market action begins.

> *Trade Secret #6:   The German Dax controls direction in the pre-market (early morning trading) in the U.S.*

REVIEW

As the sun rises across the eastern United States, our trading centers in New York, Chicago, and Philadelphia take center stage. With the world's largest and most powerful economy, the United States leads the way as the NYSE, the CME, and the CBOT open for business.

The health of our financial markets is reflected in prices on several internationally respected indexes. The DJIA has been watched and honored by traders around the world for more than a hundred years. Other highly watched indexes include the S&P 500 and the Nasdaq-100. By monitoring these indexes one is able to evaluate price action.

The NYSE opens at 8:30 AM Central, 9:30 Eastern, and America is at the center of global trading. During the first couple of hours of trading, there is generally a great deal of volume coming into the market and prices react with a healthy amount of volatility. That makes this a good time to trade. Then, as traders tire and turn their focus on lunch and a midday respite, volume leaves the market. Most wise traders should, too. Trading in a market with low volume is too dangerous. A few big traders can skew the indicators and draw one into a risky trade. Therefore, after the early morning flurry is over and the market settles down, do not rush into a trade but rather, wait patiently until traders finish lunch and return to their trading desks.

I use the 12:30 PM price on the S&P futures as a benchmark for afternoon trading. If prices rise above that price, I look for an opportunity to buy; if they sink below it, I anticipate a selling point. I often enter a position between 1:00 PM and 1:15 PM If the numbers and indicators support a play, I take it. Otherwise, I read a book, send an e-mail, call a friend, or do something else, but I do not enter a trade until the market nears its end. I look at prices again around 2:30 PM Central Time. If a direction can be identified, I move with it. Many times one is able to identify a direction and stay with this trade until the close.

Once New York and Chicago traders shut down their trading platforms and head for home, the global markets are quiet for a couple of hours. But, only for a couple of hours; soon the Nikkei in Tokyo and the Hang Seng in Hong Kong will open. A couple of hours later, the German Dax, the French CAC, the London FTSE, and other European exchanges will open their doors and trading will begin again.

 MARKET INSIGHT

Once U.S. financial markets open, the eyes of the world are focused on us. Nevertheless, the Dax futures are still trading and can be used as an indicator for determining market direction.

CHAPTER 7

Short-Term Strategies around the World

Y ou do not have to trade a foreign index or put your money into an emerging market like India or China to take advantage of international opportunities. In this age of information and technology, every financial market is a global market because every market is influenced by world trends and events. In that way, the world's financial centers are intrinsically connected to each other. Because I live in the United States, most of my trading involves financial products that are traded here. When I consider my short-term strategies, most of them revolve around the futures and equities markets. Therefore, I will explain how I approach my trading in these two specific areas.

All traders are global traders—whether they know it or not.

STOCKS AND HOW I PLAY THEM FOR THE SHORT TERM

If you want to make an equity play, the first step must be to identify a stock to trade. There are thousands of equities out there. So, how do you select a few, or even one, of them to buy or sell? I choose stocks that I know. That is, I want a company or a product that I have heard about. Geof Smith, our chief instructor, at DTI, our trading school in Mobile, Alabama became interested in Bed Bath & Beyond because he noticed that it was one of his wife's favorite places to shop. When he balanced his bank statement and saw all those canceled checks to the store, he determined that the company was worth looking into. His initial analysis must have been good because Geof has experienced a high rate of success with trading that particular company. Likewise, if a restaurant chain is very popular and you like its menu, perhaps the company might be worth investigating—or a clothing business, or anything else that is popular and has a good product line. Remember that if you like the product, perhaps other folks agree with you. Check it out.

The single biggest no-no in trading is buying stocks based on the recommendation of friends or some Web site or newsletter. Never pick a stock posted on any trading bulletin board as a top pick or because some friend made money trading it. By the time the stock is posted on the board or the friend gets around to offering the tip, the trading opportunity is probably over. Therefore, you should start with what you know. Pick a popular company and start watching it. Making your own selections may take more time and involve a little work, but in the long run it will be worth it. You will feel comfortable with the decision because you will know the rationale behind your stock play.

After I do a little homework and make my initial selection, I look at several other factors. Before I trade a stock, it must meet certain criteria. First, it must have an average true range (ATR) of at least $1.00. That is, during the course of a daily trading session, prices must generally move up or down at least that much. If it does not, there will be too few short-term opportunities with that particular product. One can find the average range of most equities by visiting www.barchart.com or by using DTI's proprietary software, the Stock Box. The second essential criterion for a short-term stock is liquidity. At least two to three million shares of the stock must trade each day. That is the absolute minimum. If a trading product does not have liquidity, you may be unable to get into or out of it quickly. If there are millions of buyers and sellers, that problem is solved. To check liquidity, get the average daily volume. Again, you can obtain this information from www.barchart.com.

Another important criterion is *beta*. Beta is a statistical volatility measure. It reflects how a stock ranks in volatility when compared to the overall market. By definition, the market has a beta of 1.0. Therefore, stocks with a beta lower than 1.0 have less volatility than the overall market. Stocks with a beta of 2.0 have twice as much volatility as the overall market. For my trading strategy, I want a beta of at least 2.0. Because greater volatility can translate into greater risk, a stock's beta is also considered to be a measure of the potential danger or risk of the stock. That is, stocks with high betas are generally believed to be riskier than stocks with low betas. However, when you are trading short-term—and by that, I mean intraday trading—you must have volatility in order to make money. A stock with a low beta will probably offer too few short-term, money-making chances. But, if you make the right play, a stock with a high beta will allow you to execute your trade and take some profits off the table quickly.

Next, I consider the market sector of the stock. Is the sector bullish or bearish? If the sector is bullish, is the particular stock also moving up in price? If not, why not? Is there some specific problem or issue with this particular stock? If the stock is not trending with the sector in general, I suggest staying clear of it. It is never wise to buck the trend. Find a stock that is marching to the step of the other stocks in the sector.

Once I identify some stocks that meet these criteria, I look to see how they are trading in relation to the broader market. As a general rule, a stock must be moving with the overall market trend. That is, if the Dow Jones Industrial Average is bullish and the stock is listed on the index, I expect it to also be bullish. If it is not, I find another one. Again, why go against the trend? That is generally an unwise move.

In determining the market's direction, I look at indexes like the S&P 500 and Dow, and I also look at the German Dax. Asia is not trading during our day session in the United States, and most of Europe closes toward the start of our session, but the Dax futures trade until 3:00 PM Central Time. The Dax futures do not close until the NYSE ends its session. Therefore, when I check market direction, I look at the Dax. I want to know how German traders are feeling. Are they bullish or bearish? For me, the Dax futures index is an important indicator of market sentiment.

Although I generally trade stocks that are in step with the general market, I must note that there are some exceptions to this *go with the trend* rule. Some stocks historically move in a pattern that is contrary to the S&P or the Dow. For example, when oil prices rise, stocks tend to move down, but stocks in oil and oil services generally get bullish. So, the major indexes may go lower when news of higher oil prices breaks, but Halliburton and similar stocks will likely rise. Therefore, if trading stocks in the oil sector, I may buy shares of stock while selling futures contracts in the S&P 500. I know that this particular sector may move in a reverse pattern to the major equity indexes.

Finally, before I trade a stock, I want to know its personality. Every stock has some things that are peculiar to it. For example, if it is a retail stock it may tend to sag in the summer months and pick back up as winter and Christmas near. Or, it may be a stock that is very active during the first hour of trading and then it dies for most of the remainder of the session. Or, it may tend to hit a particular price point and then roll over, settle down, and start moving again. Look at the stock. Study it and learn its particular personality. In that way you will be better able to take advantage of its flukes to make money.

You should enjoy and like trading the stocks you select. But, you must never marry a stock. You can't buy a stock and stick with it through thick and thin. If the stock is no longer a winner, do not trade it. Sometimes people feel that a stock is just too good to abandon and they refuse to sell when the time is right. One should find a stock that trades well and trade it. However, when it stops paying, it is time to move on to greener pastures. Take Microsoft (MSFT): It was a great stock to trade from 1985 all the way to 2000. Then it stagnated and, in my opinion, it hasn't been worth trading since. For the last four years or so, it has stayed within a seven-point range. It tends to move between $22 and $29. I used to trade MSFT regularly. I loved it. But when it stopped paying, we had to part ways.

Checklist for Intraday Stock Trading

1. Know something about the company and the product.

2. The daily average true range (ATR) must be at least $1.00.

3. Liquidity must be at least two to three million shares per day.

4. Volatility or beta of at least 2.0.

5. The stock should be trending with its sector.

6. The stock must be moving in agreement with the general market trend, unless it is a stock that traditionally moves in a reverse pattern to the broad market.

7. Know the stock's particular personality.

8. Become familiar with a stock, but never marry it.

MY STRATEGY

Now that I have identified stocks with good betas, good liquidity, and a nice daily trading range, and I know them and am comfortable with them, I'm ready to trade. Once New York opens, I watch prices for the first 30 minutes.

I note the high and the low of trading during that time. That opening 30-minute price bar (formed between 8:30 and 9:00 AM Central Time) becomes my reference bar for my morning stock trading. If prices break above that first bar, there will often be some follow-through and prices will go higher. If prices go lower than the bottom of the bar, there is a good chance that they will go lower still. One must remember that in order to trade stocks for the short term, the volatility, liquidity, and beta must be right.

I confess that I do not check with barchart or any other site each day to get the average true range or to obtain the average number of shares traded or the beta or for some of the other important stock characteristics. Instead, I use my Stock Box software and let it do the work for me. Of course, it cannot determine the personality of a stock, but it is able to handle all of the statistical criteria. However, without software, it is possible to get the information you need manually and select a stock to trade. The process is just harder and takes more time. I prefer doing it the easy way.

EXAMPLES OF SHORT-TERM STOCK TRADING

I often make short-term stock plays. As a rule, I look for breakout moves during the right times during the day. I want the market to be awake and moving so that I can get paid. On July 19, 2006, I followed this procedure and identified several stocks that fit my criteria. Figure 7.1 graphically shows how the Southern Copper Corporation (PCU) shares responded when prices broke above the top of the first 30-minute trading bar. The top of the first half-hour of trading was $87.50. I always round up to the next nickel and add a penny to obtain my purchase price. Per my method, the stock was a buy at $87.51. In 15 minutes, a dollar of profit could have been made. On this particular day, this stock was a buy, but had the bottom of the bar been broken, a sell might have been executed. Note that the Stock Box gives both a long and a short position. It depends on the market to decide which one is triggered.

When I execute a transaction, I know where my profit target will be. I determine this by using the average true range (ATR). If the ATR of a stock is $2.00 and the stock has a low of $50.50 and a high of $50.75, I know that it has a potential, if it stays within the average range and keeps moving up, of reaching a high of $52.50 or a low of $48.75. Therefore, if I am long, I will take my profits before the $52.50 price is hit. Again, I do not do this calculation. I let the software do it for me. The program tweaks the data and adds in another variable, so the numbers given by the program and those obtained by a manual calculation are not exactly the same. But, they are generally very close.

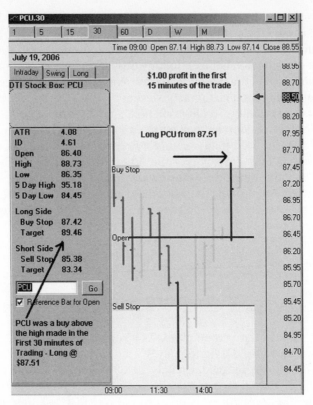

FIGURE 7.1   On July 19, 2006, Southern Copper Corporation (PCU) offered a great opportunity for a short-term play.

PCU has an average true range of $4.08. Because I am going long, I need to know the anticipated top of the current day's market in order to get my profit target. I take the low of $86.35 and add $4.08 (the ATR). Therefore, my profit target is $90.43. (That is the maximum that I should expect from this stock in one day.) The profit target on the Stock Box is $87.51. The Stock Box gives a more conservative recommendation, and its exit is in front of the total ATR move. Those traders lucky enough to find PCU made a nice quick profit on this date.

Let's look at another example. On July 18, 2006, Best Buy (BBY) was a good short-term play. First, I check to be certain that the average true range is greater than $1.00. The ATR of Best Buy is $1.88, so I can continue to step two. I check liquidity and again this stock fits the bill. This is a highly liquid equity. I know the beta is adequate for my trading. Now, I check those first 30 minutes of trading. The high is $45.17 and the low is $44.50. The short side play is triggered. I take the low of the bar, bump down a nickel, and move down one additional penny. That is the place to position a sell stop—$44.44. My profit target is $43.25. The Stock Box target is $43.59. (Again, the Stock Box may give a target that is more conservative than the manual calculation.) I obtain this number by taking the high of $45.17 and subtracting the ATR of $1.88. That gives me a target of $43.59. This trade takes longer than the bullish PCU trade, but before lunch, those who sold BBY got paid, as shown in Figure 7.2.

Let's look at one final example. On July 18, 2006, Google (GOOG) experienced a nice fall. With an ATR greater than $10, Google easily fits the volatility criterion. Google is also highly liquid so there is no problem

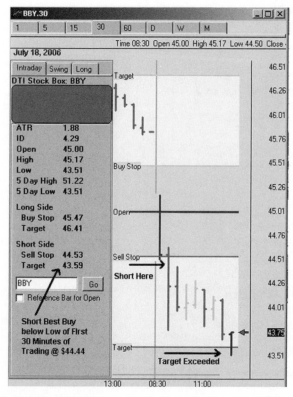

FIGURE 7.2 On July 18, 2006, my profit target for Best Buy (BBU) was more than met.

there. With a low on the reference bar of $406.72, our entry point was $406.69. Google quickly moved down and paid, as shown in Figure 7.3.

I trade stocks often, and I follow this procedure for my short-term plays. Check liquidity, verify volatility, get the trading range within the first 30 minutes and do the other essential homework, and you are ready to go.

When I trade stocks, I generally trade in multiples of three. For example, I often trade 3,000 shares. When I make .25 or .30 per share, I exit at least a third of my positions. Then when I have made .50 or so, I exit another third. Then I hold the remaining third to reach my final profit target and maximize my trade. Many traders use an all or nothing approach. When they enter a trade, they have a profit target set. All positions are liquidated at the profit target. That strategy works great if the desired price is hit, but if it is not reached, the trader may suffer a huge loss. By scaling out of

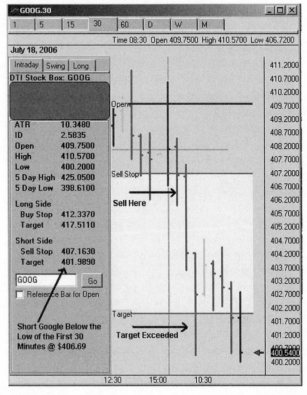

FIGURE 7.3 Google (GOOG) offered a good shorting play at $406.69 and paid quickly.

some of my positions with profits, I reduce the risk of the trade in two ways: I have progressively fewer contracts and that means less exposure and I have guaranteed myself that some portion of the trade yields profits. Those profits help off-set any losses that may be suffered if the market shifts. My experience is that too often, traders using an all-or-nothing approach will get nothing.

INDEX FUTURES

Index futures are another way to participate in equities trading. As a rule, I trade futures every day. However, they are derivative products and have some unique characteristics that one should know before trading them. First, a future is a derivative because its value is derived from an underlying product. The price of an S&P Index futures contract is derived from or based on the S&P 500. Likewise, that of the Dow is derived from or based on the Dow Jones, and the Nasdaq futures on the Nasdaq-100.

One of the aspects of futures contracts that has great appeal for me is the leverage. To trade futures you must have a margin account. With futures the margin is large. For example, the approximate value of one e-mini S&P 500 futures contract is about $70,000 (based on current prices). The margin required to trade one contract varies from brokerage house to brokerage house. But many houses allow investors to trade a contract for as little as $600 to $2,500. That means that for a small amount of "good faith" money it is possible to control a lot of asset value. Note that those margin or "good faith" costs are for intraday trading only. Also, margin requirements not only differ from brokerage house to brokerage house, but they change from time to time. If there is a market crash or significant price correction, margin requirements get higher—much higher.

Another interesting aspect of futures is the tax advantages that it offers. Thanks to some federal legislation that was passed some years back, if you hold a futures contract for one minute or one year, 60 percent of profits are deemed to be long-term and 40 percent are short-term for federal tax purposes. That rule helps me when I settle my bill with Uncle Sam. Check with your CPA to determine the tax advantages or disadvantages that trading futures may offer you.

It is possible to trade the e-mini intraday from 3:30 PM Central Time to 3:15 PM Central Time the following day; that time frame is deemed to be one day. I know that may seem odd to the uninitiated, but that is the way it works. Holding a contract from 3:30 PM on Monday until 3:15 PM on Tuesday constitutes one trading session. However, if you hold the contract between 3:15 PM and 3:30 PM on the same day, it is considered overnight trading, and a much larger margin is required.

I like the leverage offered by futures. However, having such large leverage is a double-edged sword. For those with skills and knowledge, it offers the opportunity to use those assets to make more money. For the unskilled and uneducated, it can lead to real disaster. Since the account is leveraged, you can easily lose more than you have in your account. If that happens, there will be a margin call from the brokerage house demanding that the adequate margin requirements be met immediately. Not having the cash to meet the margin call can create a serious problem. It could require you to liquidate other assets or resort to some other means of raising the necessary cash. Therefore, I suggest that you never trade futures or other highly leveraged instruments without first getting a good education. The Chicago Board of Trade (CBOT) and the Chicago Mercantile (CME) offer many educational opportunities. And, of course, so do I and others in the field.

By now you should know that I like the index futures and I do a lot of short-term trading in that market. I have been trading the S&P 500 Index futures since 1982. My trading strategy involves time of day, key numbers, and market indicators.

DECIDE WHICH CONTRACT TO TRADE

Just as with stocks, if you are trading index futures like the S&P 500 or Dow, you must first determine which particular index you will trade. There are a couple of things that must be considered before determining the contract or contracts to trade. First, you must learn about the contract. Where does it trade? The S&P and Nasdaq index futures trade on the CME. The Dow is traded at the CBOT. The Dax is traded through the Eurex, and the Nikkei is also traded through the CME system. What are the trading hours? If your schedule allows or demands that you trade when most New York markets are closed, perhaps a foreign index like the Dax or Nikkei may be best. I suggest that beginners select an index and work to master it. Then they may expand their scope and take other indexes to harness. What are the margin requirements? Check with several brokers; margins may vary from brokerage house to brokerage house. Margin requirements for Asian and European products will generally be higher than those for U.S. products. Check with a broker. Determine the trading price per point for each product before trading it. I suggest that those new to futures consider the mini-Dow. It trades for $5 per point. Start off small and trade only one or two contracts. Put in stops and limit risk. In that way, you may be able to get a feel for futures.

I started trading index futures with the big S&P and it trades for $250.00 per point. Now I also trade the mini contract that trades for $50 per point in .25 point increments. You must select the contract that meets your requirements and time and monetary constraints. Then master it. Once that contract is under control, look at another one. I regularly trade the Dow, S&P, Nasdaq, and Dax Index futures. After studying the market, I determine which one is likely to pay, and that is where I lay my money down. Traders must always be careful and use protective stops and *never* take risks (large or small) that they cannot afford to take.

PICKING A MARKET

I trade several futures indexes on a regular basis. How then do I decide which one I will trade at a particular time? If the general market is bullish and I want to be a buyer, I select the index that is exhibiting the most strength. Inversely, if I am looking to sell and the general market is bearish, I locate the weakest player and put my money there. It just makes sense to do that because the odds of getting paid and getting paid quickly will be increased.

TRADING FUTURES: THE BASICS

Trading futures is about more than just reading the tape or understanding the numbers and the data during different times of day. I look for breakout moves. I want to execute my trade, get in the market, and get paid within minutes. If I have not been paid on at least a portion of my positions within two minutes or so, I carefully evaluate the situation to determine whether I am on the winning team. Even though the Nasdaq, the Dow, the S&P 500, and the Dax are the index futures that I trade most often, I sometimes trade gold, bonds, crude oil, or some other futures product.

The essential elements of my strategy are time, key numbers, and market indicators. First, I only trade during certain times during the day. For many years, I traded constantly. I executed a zillion trades and never stopped to calculate the fees and costs of associated with that strategy. In addition to the monetary expense of trading, there is also an emotional expense. Believe me; constantly trading takes a huge amount of emotional capital. Also, trading is an odds game. Every time you enter the market, you assume a risk. Therefore, one of the easiest ways to increase accuracy is to decrease the amount of times you trade. You must only trade when the time is right and all factors are in place for success. I have some trading times that are almost sacred to me, and I rarely trade outside of them. Here is a snapshot of some of my favorite trading times:

Sunday Globex session:	5:00–5:30 PM Central Time (observation only)
Monday–Thursday Globex:	3:30–4:00 PM Central Time (observation only
	1:30 AM Central Time (after first 30 minutes of Dax trading
	4:30 AM Central Time (after European news)
	6:00–6:30 AM Central Time (Dax Trading)
Monday–Friday day session in U. S.:	9:00–10:15 AM Central Time
	12:30–1:15 PM Central Time
	2:30–2:45 PM Central Time

I have a few cardinal rules about certain times during the day. I never go short between 12:30 and 1:00 PM Central Time. I have been taken too many times by selling the market during this time. For some reason, the market often gives a sell signal and then turns around and rallies. Therefore, during this time I either go long or stay out.

Another one of my big-time rules is that I do not trade when news is breaking. Economic news is often reported at 7:30 AM or 9:00 AM Central. If I am in the market, I put in tight stops or get out. And, if I am out of the market I stay out until the news clears. It generally takes two or three minutes for the news to exert its effect on the markets and then pass away. News generally has an immediate but short-term effect on prices. They may jump wildly and give a buy or sell signal, but in just a couple of minutes things settle down. Then you are better able to determine the true sentiment of the market.

If I see a trading opportunity during my ideal trading times, I take it. If I am unable to identify a good play, I let it pass and stay on the sidelines. I keep my powder dry until I see the whites of their eyes. I do not want to waste my capital until the target is in sight.

Trade only when the time is right.

Another vital element to trading futures is key numbers. Traders must know the points of support and resistance in the market, and that means that they must be familiar with the key numbers. Key numbers are those stopping points at which the market may reverse or accelerate. Chapter 10 is devoted to key numbers and market indicators, but I cannot discuss futures trading without saying something about the numbers. As a general rule, you should wait for resistance to be broken before you become a buyer and you should wait for support to be crossed to the downside before you are a seller. Otherwise, a trade may be halted by the forces of the market and the trade will not pay.

As traders, we may have short memories, but the financial markets do not. The price point where the bears were stopped yesterday or the high that the bulls were unable to move above last week are important, and the market remembers them. These price points, along with other important numbers, will be likely stopping points or pivots for the market. Some of the most important key numbers that I watch are the yearly open, monthly opens, weekly opens, daily opens, and daily highs and lows. I also note the 12:30 PM price on the S&P and the 6:00 AM price on the Dax. Throughout the day when I am trading I keep an eye on these price points and use them to stay on the right side of the action. I could not trade without knowing and using key numbers.

Finally, I use market indicators. I look at the NYSE Tick, the NYSE issues, and the Nasdaq issues. I also check the TTICK, my proprietary indicator. If I am buying, I want these indicators to be strong and getting stronger. If I am selling, I want them to be weak and getting weaker. Again, all of these indicators and how to read them are discussed in depth in Chapter 10. Therefore, I will not go into that here. Remember that in order to trade futures successful, three things must be working in your favor: Time, key numbers, and market indicators.

> *Good traders are like highly skilled marksmen. They identify their target, aim carefully, and only execute the shot when they believe they will hit the target dead center on the bull's eye.*

Regardless of what you trade, risk management must be your primary concern. Never take a trade unless the risk is known and you are willing and able to assume that risk. If you handle the risk first and only then consider the profits, you can win.

For short-term trading I generally use either the equity or the futures market. I select a stock that I am familiar with and do some homework. I want to know the ATR of the stock. Its ATR must be at least $1.00. I also want to know the liquidity; at least two to three million shares must trade each day. What is the volatility, or beta? I want a beta of at least 2.0. Then I look at the sector. The stock must be trending in the same direction as the sector. How is the stock trading in comparison to the general market? I generally look for stocks that are trending with the market. Why try to go against the trend? I also determine the personality of the particular stock. When is it most active? What are its particular trading patterns or unique traits? Once I find a stock that meets all of my criteria, I tend to trade it often. However, be careful not to marry a stock. Never think that the agreement is "until death do us part." Trade it when it is profitable to do so and leave it when it is not. There are many stocks that meet my criteria. If one of my favorites falls out of favor, I simply select another one.

In addition to equity markets, I also trade index futures for short-term profits. Before trading these products, be sure you understand and are able to assume the unique risks. These are leveraged products. For that reason, however, there is the possibility to make a lot of money here. You can trade the S&P or Dow or venture into foreign products like the CAC-40 in Paris or the Dax in Germany. There are many opportunities in futures. In fact, not only can you trade index futures, but you can also trade gold, oil, and bond futures, and many others.

Futures may also offer some unique tax advantages, check with your CPA about the 60 percent/40 percent rule. If you hold a futures contract for one minute or one year, 60 percent of the profits are long-term gains.

Once I select the contract that I will trade, I look for the index that is going my way. That is, if I am shorting the market, I want the index that is the weakest. If I am a bull, I look for the strongest index. I only trade if three things are in my favor: time, key numbers, and market indicators. My ideal times to trade domestic products are 9:00 AM to 10:15 AM Central Time, 12:30 to 1:13 PM Central Time, and 2:30 to 2:45 PM Central Time. I generally only enter new positions during these times. That is because I use a breakout method of trading, and the markets are, as a rule, more liquid and more volatile during these times. That gives me the chance to get in, make money, and get out quickly.

In addition to time, I also rely on key numbers. The market remembers certain price points and repeatedly returns to them. The points at which the bulls charged today may be an important number tomorrow. Or, the place where the bears were able to take control this week may be a critical point in the market next week. Therefore, keep up with important numerical data such as the yearly open, monthly opens, weekly opens, daily opens, and highs and lows in the market. Those numbers or points will be important and they will be areas where support and resistance will be drawn.

Finally, I rely on important market indicators like the NYSE Tick, the NYSE and Nasdaq issues, my TTICK, and the TRIN. I use these to help me stay on the right side of the market. (Chapter 10 goes in greater depth on both key numbers and market indicators.)

Always remember that the most important part of any trade is risk. Know the risk of every trade, and only assume that risk if it is acceptable to you.

 MARKET INSIGHT

Before trading a stock short term, check for liquidity (at least 2,000,000 shares traded per day), volatility (at least a beta of 2.0), and the average daily trading range (at least $1.00).

CHAPTER 8

Swing Trading Strategies across Time Zones

I enjoy short-term intraday trading. Over the years I have been able to make money with that particular play. I have the ability to successfully execute single-day trades like those described in Chapter 7 because my strategy works most of the time, and I have a time schedule that allows me to implement it. With my work routine, I have the flexibility to transact most of my trades during the daylight hours; I have the luxury of checking prices and having my orders executed—from 8:30 AM until 3:15 PM. As a professional trader, I arrange my appointments and activities around the market's agenda. I know that certain times during the day the financial markets are more likely to pay, so I avoid scheduling activities that take me away from my computer screen and my trading platform during those times.

When I buy or sell S&P futures contracts at 9:00 AM, or stocks at 10:00 AM, I know that if I have analyzed the market correctly, I should be able to profitably exit a portion of my positions within minutes, maybe even seconds. That is because I look for breakout moves; if my entry point is correct, my timing is right, and the market responds as I anticipate, I will get paid quickly. Therefore, intraday or short-term trading is one of my strong areas.

However, I do not exclusively trade intraday. I also swing trade some markets, holding positions for days or, in rare cases, weeks or months. However, as a rule, I do not hold index futures positions overnight, and any financial product that I carry for days or weeks is carefully monitored; there is always a protective stop in place.

Not everyone has the ability to trade during the day session. Many of my students are professionals in other fields and are holding down very demanding jobs. For the bulk of the daily trading session in the United States, they may be seeing patients or developing a shopping center or a condo. Nevertheless, they enjoy trading and find the time to do it. The 24-hour global marketplace expands their opportunities and allows them to design an agenda and a plan that works for them. To assist traders wishing to trade after-hours, DTI offers telephone assistance. Just log onto our website for details.

In addition to time restraints, not everyone wants to limit transactions to exclusively intraday action. Many traders may want to try a longer-range approach that allows them to hold positions across time zones and for days or even weeks. They are simply more comfortable with a wider trading window. Therefore, here are a few ideas to explore.

SWING TRADING GOLD

During late 2005 and early 2006, gold became a popular commodity. Gold prices rose significantly and broke 25-year highs. Gold is a traditional inflationary hedge, and with prices rising and the Fed raising interest rates, many traders obviously believed gold offered some safety. Gold is also considered to be a shelter during times of crisis. Since it is an international currency, many nervous traders and investors believe that investments in gold offer some degree of financial protection. Regardless of whether those beliefs are true or not, as shown in Figure 8.1, gold prices unquestionably moved upward recently when the world faced many unsettling problems: rising oil prices, unrest in the Mideast, tribal fighting in Nigeria, uranium enrichment in Iran, and fears of atomic bombs in North Korea. Wow, that is a list of global woes! No wonder traders were looking for a safe haven!

Like thousands of others, I, too, have been trading gold. When I do, I generally trade gold futures. Gold futures are traded in the pits at the Commercial Exchange (COMEX) and are traded electronically at the Chicago Board of Trade (CBOT). Electronic trading in the gold futures begins at 6:16 PM Central Time. Trading begins one minute after the Dow futures opens. For 45 minutes the gold market is trading but major stock markets around the globe are closed. New York has shut down for the day and Asia has not yet opened its exchanges. During the summer months, trading does not begin in Tokyo until 7:00 PM Central. So, for 45 minutes I watch and wait. Once Tokyo opens, I determine whether gold has a direction, just as I do with futures trading, I look for a breakout move. If I am able to iden-

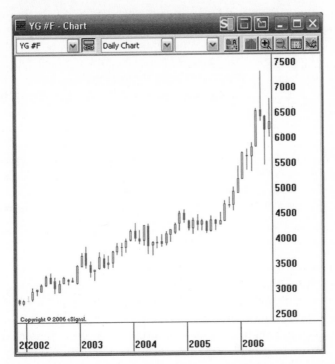

FIGURE 8.1 A monthly chart of gold futures. Note the bullish move of gold in 2005 and 2006. It is no wonder that many traders turned to gold. (*Source*: Copyright 2006-DTN ProphetX.)

tify a direction, I trade. That is, if Asians are buying gold and sending prices up, I buy; and if they are selling and moving prices down, I go short.

Determining the point for protective stop placement is critical to making a good trade. If a stop is too tight, it will likely be hit and money lost. If it is too loose, the risk is too great and excessive amounts of money will be at risk. The goal is to give the trade enough room to work while also exiting the trade if you are wrong. Therefore, I use one of two methods to determining my stop placement.

First, I may use the high and low of trading between 12:30 and 1:00 PM Central Time as a gauge. My rationale is that I consider this timeframe very important for the markets. Each day at this time traders tend to establish a new benchmark for afternoon and evening action. Traders return from lunch and rethink the morning's direction. That is, they evaluate the movement of the markets in the morning and either confirm it or reverse it. Because I use the high and low of this 30-minute trading bar as a guage for my after-hours trading, I refer to it as a reference bar. It is the new line drawn in the sand by the bulls and the bears. If prices rise above the high of the bar, it is a good sign for the bulls. If they sink below the low of the bar, the bears are celebrating. If I am swing trading gold and I am short, I place my protective stop just above the high of that reference bar. If I am long gold, I do the reverse and place my stop just below the bottom of that bar.

> *Determining the point for protective stop placement is critical to making a good trade. If a stop is too tight, it will likely be hit and money lost. If it is too lax, the risk is too great and excessive amounts of money may be given up unnecessarily.*

Another way to determine stop placement is by using the high and low of the first 30 minutes of night trading. I note the high and the low during the first 30 minutes of Globex action. Then I use this bar for reference or guidance. If bulls pull prices across the top of the bar, they are showing their strength and I am more bullish. If the bears succeed in holding prices down below the bottom of the bar, they are in charge and I join the family of bears. Therefore, I use this bar as a reference or gauge to measure the strength of the opposing sides. If I am long, my protective stop is placed just below the low of that opening bar. If I am short, I place my stop just above the top of the bar.

An hour after the stock markets open for trading in Japan, equity markets in China open. Prices on the Hang Seng register the action. If prices continue to move my way, I hang with the trade. When Europe opens around 1:00 or 2:00 AM, prices will likely get moving again. If economic news is released, gold will really react. For some reason, the gold market is especially news sensitive. Economic news is often released at 7:30 AM Central, so gold may bounce around at that time. To obtain a news calendar, you can visit www.barrons.com or www.dtitrader.com.

New York opens at 8:30 AM, and the gold pits at exchanges in the United States open an hour later. Then gold starts moving again. From 10:30 until 11:00 AM, gold tends to be very active and volume and volatility are great. During the afternoon gold generally settles down for a couple of hours. Trading pits in New York and Chicago close—including the gold pits. However, at 6:16 PM, electronic trading on gold futures opens and the action begins anew. Then gold traders are off again, rocking anew to another market session.

FIGURE 8.2 The weekly movement of gold. The gold bulls took a dip in June, but prices soon started moving up again. (*Source*: Copyright 2006-DTN ProphetX)

As the market trades, if the direction of my play is confirmed by the global markets, I stay with the trade and adjust my stop. That is, if I am profitable, I move my stop closer to the market's trading price and reduce my risk or lock in profits. Once a new reference bar is formed between 12:30 PM and 1:00 PM Central Time, I use it for stop adjustment. Or, I use the high and low of the last 24-hour trading session as a bar of reference or gauge. If I am long, I put my protection just below the bottom of the bar. If I am short, I put my protection just above the high of the bar. Sometimes, if the market lets me, I stay with this trade for days or weeks. I just keep adjusting my stop daily and locking in profits.

On May 20, 2006, one of my students took this particular trade. He bought some gold futures contracts at 568.60. He placed his protective stop at 564.00, just below the low of the first 30 minutes of trading. Prices headed up and hit 573.40. It was a nice trade for him. Figure 8.2 depicts the weekly gold rush. As the year has progressed, gold has dipped down from its highs. However, gold opened the year trading around $500.00. At the time of this writing it is October and the market is still well above that price. That means that the bulls are winning the annual game and until gold falls below its opening price, I am bullish gold.

SWING TRADING STOCKS

Most traders hold stocks for the long term. There are several reasons they do this: They believe in the buy-and-hold strategy, or they have day jobs and cannot do a great deal of intraday buying and selling. Traders who buy stocks and hold them for a significant period of time need to keep an eye on them. It is unwise for any trader to put money at risk and then just walk away.

Sometimes I swing trade stocks and hold them for weeks or even months. However, I always have stops in place and I monitor the situation. Under certain conditions I may hedge a stock position with an option. I never just buy and forget the purchase. The market is too dangerous for that approach. And, if equity prices on one of the major indexes like the S&P 500 or the Dow drops 10 percent during any eight week time period, I am probably going to exit the trade and exit the equity markets entirely— at least with any long positions—until prices start moving up again. I have no desire to go down with a market *Titanic*.

When I trade stocks, I generally place my trades between 8:30 and 10:30 AM. I use the same general approach for selecting stocks that I explained in Chapter 7. That is, I want stocks with an average daily range of at least $1.00. I want good liquidity of at least two to three million shares a day. A high beta of at least 2.0 is important. I also want the stock to be performing well in both its sector and the overall economy. Then I get to know the stock and its personality. What are its unique traits? Once I feel comfortable with a stock, I'm ready for the trading to begin.

When I am in the market, I put an initial protective stop below the previous day's low or above the previous day's high. As with all of my trades, I look for entry points at times when I anticipate a breakout move. If I have succeeded in my analysis, I exit a portion of my positions quickly with some small profits. In that way, even if there is a reversal in the move, I have made some money to cover any potential loss in my remaining positions. For example, if I purchase 3,000 shares (I like to trade in multiples of three), I will exit 1,000 of them with a profit of .25 or .50. Then I move my stop on my remaining positions to $1.00 below the trading price. When prices rise and I am able to exit another 1,000 shares with profit of .75 to $1.00 per share, I take the play. Now I adjust my stop on the remaining

1,000 shares to break even, or maybe even lock in some profits. At this point I cannot lose money on the trade. I am playing with the market's money. By taking profits early on some positions, I have protected myself from any financial loss on the remaining shares. As the market moves in my favor, I adjust my stop and trail prices. Everything now is just gravy.

If I am still in the trade and making money when New York closes, I know that I will have to hold my position until the following morning. No equity markets offer electronic trading during the night. Therefore, I make certain that I have a protective stop in place. I use the high and low of the day's trading to get my stop placement. I know that if I am long, the low of the day's session should not be broken if the bulls continue to be in charge. If the day's low is crossed, the bears may be moving prices down, and I do not want to go along for the ride.

Using stops for protection does not mean that you will necessarily be removed from the market at your selected exit point. Let me explain how protective stops will work in the stock market. Assume that you are long a stock that is currently trading at $52.75. There is a protective stop or stop market order at $50.00. The company reports earnings after the market closes, and the company has done far worse than expected. Prices fall dramatically. Remember, there is a stop market order waiting to exit the trade at $50.00, but when the market opens the next morning the stock is trading at $40 a share. The market just blew right through the order. Once the market opens, that stop market order immediately becomes a market order and the position is liquidated at the $40 price.

Just be aware that a protective stop may not always offer full protection. However, it offers some protection. If that particular stock continued to move down and hit $20, you would be thrilled that you departed at the $40 price. Therefore, I do not recommend trading without a protective stop.

Determine risk tolerance before entering a trade. I do not want to risk more than 5 to 7 percent of the purchase price on any trade. For example, if I purchase a $70 stock, I want to keep losses around $3.50 to $5.00 per share. I often limit losses to a dollar a share. By adjusting my protective stop based on the high or low of the previous day's trading, I am often able to hold equity positions for days or weeks. Each morning, I readjust my stop and keep locking in my profits.

For any trader, the most difficult decision that must be made is deciding when to cut his losses and run. As long as the trade is working, the decision-making process is relatively simple and not too dangerous. Just decide where to take profits and how tightly to place protective stops. But, the problem arises when the trade is not going the way that you planned. That is why you need to decide in advance how much you will lose on any trade. If the market takes that money, let the trade go. Do not just stay with a losing trade and keep adding up losses. Every trader makes mistakes and takes bad trades. If a trade does not pay, exit. Cut and run as soon as possible and move on. There will be thousands of good trades. Wait and take one of them. The market will be there tomorrow.

SWING TRADING FUTURES

Index futures are open virtually 24 hours a day. That is one of their big advantages. Therefore, traders have access to the futures markets around the clock, and it is easier to fit trading into a schedule that would otherwise not allow intraday trading. For some traders, that may offer too many trading opportunities. The temptation to over trade is great. Beginners may want to buy and sell constantly. They must learn moderation and self-control. When I acquired my first Globex terminal, I felt compelled to constantly trade. I started trading during the night, the early morning, all day, the afternoon, and the evening. I traded around the clock, and consequently, I was exhausted. Not only does the pace of continuously trading drain physical energy, it drains emotional energy. I soon learned that I had to pick trading times with care. It is not necessary to take every trade. In contrast to my tendency to jump into and out of the market very quickly, many traders want to hold positions for longer periods of time. The futures markets offer them a chance to do that, too.

Many folks stay clear of futures because the risk scares them off. Although trading futures may be risky, there are also some advantages. The leverage allows you to make maximum use of your investment dollars and your skills. Also, many traders like the virtually 24-hour accessibility of the index futures. However, holding a position overnight requires a far greater account balance, and one who holds a position and does not manage it assumes a far greater risk. With that said, many traders prefer to swing trade the S&P futures or some other futures contract, so I want to address how one may execute such an approach.

As with any trade, identify the direction of the market. If indicators and prices are moving up, you want to be a buyer. The opposite is, of course, also true. Do not fight the market's trend. Once in the market, if you hope to hold your position intraday, you must put a stop that is at least as great as the daily range of the index. Or, if you intend to be a long-term player, you must identify major longer-term support and resistance areas and place your protection just above or below those. For example, the S&P futures opened in January 2006 at 1255.25. Therefore, that price is a major pivot point throughout the year. In fact, I consider that price to be the year's most important pivot. If you bought the index in April or May and intended to hold it for days or weeks, an obvious protective stop placement point (for a long position) is just below the yearly opening price. If the bears succeed in taking prices down below that point, I do not want to be long and you probably do not want to be either. The yearly opening price is so important that once that price is broken to the downside, prices may sink. Just as I placed my protective stop just below the yearly open when I was long, I place it just above that number if I am short. If the bulls take prices above that annual opening, they may be strong enough to head for the moon. Therefore, as a short, I want to exit my position, because I may well be on the wrong team.

Many futures traders enjoy swing trading, and it can pay. However, if you are holding futures positions for days or weeks, you must be careful: Know your risk and use protective stops. I also suggest that you carefully monitor your positions and exit the market if prices, indicators, and economic data move strongly against you. Also, if you are fortunate enough to be on the right side of the action, as prices move in your favor, you should move protective stops toward current prices in order to lock in profits and limit risk.

SWING TRADING OPTIONS

I have traded options for decades. Options are financial products that offer the buyer the opportunity but not the obligation to buy or sell an underlying asset for a set price (the strike price) on or before a set date (expiration). A call option gives the buyer the right to buy the asset if it rises to the strike price. A put option gives the buyer the right to sell the asset if it moves down to the strike price. Therefore, traders who anticipate that a stock will rise in price will purchase call options. Conversely, those who believe that the price of the stock will fall purchase put options. Each option gives the buyer the right to control 100 shares of stock. For the right to control the shares, the buyer of the option must pay the seller a fee or premium.

> *The premium is the price per share that a buyer of an option must pay the seller. It is the cost that the buyer is required to pay for having control of the underlying asset if the strike price is hit on or prior to the expiration date.*

I often trade options. I especially enjoy trading the exchange traded funds like the Nasdaq QQQQ, the Dow Jones Diamond (DIA), and the S&P 500 Spyder (SPY). These funds consist of holdings in every stock listed on the exchange. The shares are traded like stocks and one is able to either trade the funds or shares outright or trade them using options. I often do the latter. The Diamond and the Spyder are traded on the American Exchange; the QQQQ is traded on the Nasdaq. My favorite exchange traded fund is the Dow Diamond. I like it because it has a good intraday trading range. That is, the volatility is generally greater than that of other similar funds.

Before trading options, know the risk. Ask your broker for the *Options Risk Disclosure* booklet. Always evaluate the risk of any trade or investment and only take those that you are comfortable with and can afford.

BUSBY'S THREE-DAY LONG OPTION PLAN

Over the years I have developed some rules regarding options trading. They are simple and straightforward:

1. I only risk 50 percent of my initial premium. That is, if my premium per share is $3.00, I will never risk more than $1.50. Therefore, at all times I know my maximum exposure.

2. Liquidate the entire position in three days. The rationale for this action is that the biggest enemy of long options is time decay.

3. Only choose options that are near the strike price. They must be within a dollar of the strike price.

4. Make sure that the option has a minimum of 30 days until expiration.

5. Liquidate 50 percent of the position at any time during the three-day period if you are profitable by 25 percent.

The strike price is the price per share at which the option purchaser can buy or sell his underlying shares. If you own a call option, you may buy the underlying stock at the strike price. If you own a put option, you may sell the shares of the underlying stock when the strike price is hit.

There are a few simple rules to keep in mind about options. When the stock market is bullish, you want to buy stocks and buy calls or sell puts. When the stock market is bearish, you want to sell stocks and buy puts or sell calls. The following chart may be helpful.

Long Stocks:	*Short Stocks:*
Buy call options.	*Buy put options.*
Sell put options.	*Sell call options*

Trade Secret #6: If you trade options, keep it simple. Liquidate long options quickly to avoid time decay. Be certain that short options are out of the money and there are no more than 45 days until expiration.

REVIEW

Due to personal preference or work schedules, some traders do not trade intraday; they prefer to swing trade and may hold positions for days, weeks, or even months. I, too, enjoy swing trading, but I do so only under certain conditions. First, I select my product carefully. Gold and the precious metals markets lend themselves to swing trading because they tend to take a direction and follow it for a period of time. Oil and petroleum is another commodity that I swing trade.

With gold and precious metals, a good beginning point for a protective stop is above the high or below the low of the day's 12:30 to 1:00 PM trading bar, or above or below the previous day's prices.

I do not swing trade futures contracts very often, but many traders do. Those market players who cannot enter and exit positions throughout the day may like the flexibility of the index futures because they operate virtually 24 hours a day. However, the risks are greater, and so are the margin requirements.

If you are holding futures overnight, you must be careful to identify support and resistance levels and use those points for stop placement. One of the biggest levels of support and resistance in this market is the yearly opening price. Other important areas of strength or weakness will be the monthly, weekly, and daily opens and weekly and monthly highs and lows. Remember to always use stops and keep an eye on the trade. Swing trading futures is generally a little too rich for my blood.

One may also swing trade stocks but should never risk more than 5 to 7 percent of the purchase price on any trade. Often I only risk a dollar per share. Never buy a stock and hold it through thick and thin. If it is a loser, let it go and pick a winner. Like all traders, swing traders must manage their money and limit losses if they want to stay in the game.

One of my favorite swing trading avenues is options. You can trade stock options, but I also like trading options in exchange traded funds. My favorite fund to trade is the Dow Jones Diamond. It has greater volatility than the Spyder or the QQQQ, and that characteristic allows me the chance to make more money.

Regardless of the product you trade, you must limit risk and always monitor your trade. A trader must never take any market position unless he or she knows the risk involved and is willing and able to assume them.

 MARKET INSIGHT

One of the most important aspects of swing trading is protective stop placement.

CHAPTER 9

Approaches to Long-Term Trading

Financial publications generally tout their stock picks. Especially during December or January, they print those eye-grabbing headlines directing readers to articles about "The Top Ten Stocks to Own" or "The Must-Have Stocks to Add to Your Portfolio." The stock-picking game is a lot of fun; I like to play it myself. However, by the time the holiday bells ring in December, some of the picks that looked so good in January have generally lost their luster. During the course of the year, some of them did well and others did not. After all, no one has a crystal ball, and much can happen during the course of a year.

Therefore, a better strategy is to approach the markets without any bias or preconceived notions. You should never adopt someone else's list of stocks and simply phone your broker to make the purchase. Maybe the stocks on the "best picks" list were once good equities to own, but now the economic picture has changed. Or, perhaps those stocks are not the right stocks for your particular portfolio.

Although I do a good bit of short-term, intraday trading, I also make some long-term plays. I like to reevaluate my equity positions when each year starts. Here is the general strategy that I use. I identify 10 high performers by studying stock performance during the last quarter of the previous year. Then, as odd as it might seem, I eliminate those stocks from my list. So, after identifying the stocks in the top 10 percent for the final quarter of 2006, I scratch them from my list for 2007. The reason is simple—experience has taught me that many of these stocks have exhausted their upward momentum.

One good historical example is eBay. In 2004, eBay was flying high and I loved it. I regularly traded it, and it proved to be very profitable for me. When 2004 came to an end, eBay was in the top 10 percent of stocks during the final quarter. Then 2005 began. Per my parameters, I did not trade eBay in 2005, and eBay proved to be a marginal performer. I scratched Apple from my list for 2006 because Apple was in the top 10 percent in 2005. Maybe a stock will continue its upward climb, but I will not be climbing with it. I will bet on another rising star for my long-term plays.

Now that the top 10 percent of performers from 2005 are eliminated, I focus on the losers. I eliminate the bottom 50 percent of performers during the final quarter of the year. That leaves me a nice list of stocks to trade.

Once I have my stock trading universe, I follow the same procedure previously outlined. That is, I select stocks with liquidity (two to three million shares traded per day). I want some price movement in the stock, and I focus on equities that have an average true range of at least $1.00. I like volatility, because that is the only way that I can get paid. So, a beta of 2 or better is good for me. I also check to see that the stock is in a bullish sector and that the sector is in sync with a bullish market. I study the stock's personality and identify its particular trading patterns. Now, I am ready to select the stocks that I want to buy.

Each year I track the stocks I plan to trade. I begin my yearly tracking process by recording the yearly opening price. That is the place where the first big battle of the year between the bulls and the bears will be waged. The bulls will struggle to pull the price higher while the bears will do their best to push it down. After recording the yearly opening price, I track its monthly opening. From month to month, I want to know if prices are moving up or down. I use these monthly prices to form a trend line. In addition to tracking the monthly opening prices, I also track each weekly open. By following this simple procedure, I can look at my trend line and get a good idea of the overall health of that particular stock.

Now I use the numbers that I gathered. I will not buy a stock unless it rises above the yearly open. I may sell it, but I will not buy it—at least not on a long-term basis. If a stock is following an upward path, I will check its progress. In relation to the last month or two, how is it doing? On a weekly basis, are the bulls winning the battle? If so, it may well be one of my plays.

As with other products, I look at resistance. I do not want to go long just before a strong resistance level. I wait for resistance to be broken before I risk any capital. If this month's opening price is $52.75, I will wait to be sure that the market is strong enough to get above it before I lay my money down. I know that the monthly open will be a point where resistance will be strong. If it is too strong, the bears may be able to take charge and move prices down. Another big resistance level will be the yearly high. If the stock is trading close to that level, let the bulls get it over that level of big resistance before taking a long position.

When I make a stock purchase, I always know my stop placement and my profit target. I determine my profit target by viewing a chart of the stock and identifying the points of resistance over a three- to six-month period. As prices rise to the next strong resistance level, I will probably take at least some profits. Then I will adjust my stop closer to the current trading price to reduce my risk and lock in some cash. As the stock trades in my favor, I will continue to lighten my load by taking out more profits. As long as the stock keeps paying me, I will probably stay with it, but as each new resistance level is broken, I will tighten my stop.

I identify my stop placement in a similar manner. I look at a monthly chart for a three- to six-month period. I note the areas of key support. I place my stop just below the first big support level. As prices move up, I adjust the stop placement accordingly. I may stay with the stock for months. It just depends on its movement and whether it is paying me.

NEVER ADOPT A "BUY IT AND FORGET IT" STRATEGY

Regardless of what you trade, it is never a good idea to make an investment and fail to track it. Check the market on a daily basis and look at equity holdings. If you respect your money and want to keep it, you need to take some personal responsibility for your assets and follow prices.

EXCHANGE TRADED FUNDS

Exchange traded funds (ETFs) may also be good long-term plays. Each of the major indexes has a fund. These are actually stocks that are much like a mutual fund. The QQQQ is an index stock for the Nasdaq. It is traded on the Nasdaq exchange. The Spyder is an index stock for the S&P 500 and it is traded on the American Exchange. The Diamond is an index stock for the Dow Jones. It, too, is traded on the American Exchange. I am partial to the Diamond because it is generally very volatile, and I like that characteristic.

Exchange traded funds have a number of advantages over common stock. First, they are less news sensitive. If a trader owns IBM and IBM reports bad earnings, or he owns XYZ and the CEO goes to jail, the stock price sinks. But, with ETFs, the problem is minimized because the stock is a combination of all stocks on the index. Just because one of the holdings in the fund goes south, does not mean that the entire fund will take a dive. That aspect of ETFs offers some protection.

TRADING OPTIONS

Another approach you might wish to consider is selling a covered call. Assume that you want to hold a long stock position, but also want to make some cash on the play. If the stock is not paying a dividend, you are out of luck. However, there is another approach you may consider. You can try to keep the stock while letting it generate some income by selling a covered call. Here is how it works. You own a stock position. You sell a call that is out of the money. That means that the agreed strike price or price at which you will be forced to sell the stock is above the current trading price. You receive a premium for the option sale. If the stock reaches the strike price, you must sell at the agreed price, but you still make money on the rising stock price. You also make money on the sale of the option. If the strike price is not hit, you have the premium and you still have the stock.

Call Option

Selling a covered call option is an option strategy whereby one is long stock and writes an option against the shares on a one-to-one basis.

Here is how the play may work. Assume that you own shares in the Board of Trade (BOT) and you want to hold onto your position. The shares are trading at $120 per share. You sell a $130 call. It is a near-month call so you do not have a great deal of time before expiration. Assume it is July and the call expires in August. If the strike price is not reached, the option expires, and is worthless to the buyer. You pocket the premium of $130 (100 shares at $1.30). Now you have the premium and the stock. If the strike price is hit, you must sell the shares at $130. That means that you have made a profit of $10 per share and have also received a premium for the option. One of my friends and students, Russ, holds a position in XLU, a utility exchange traded fund. Russ has used this strategy a number of times and has experienced great success with it. Translation: Russ has made a good bit of money selling covered calls.

One of the secrets to executing this strategy is trading only near-term options. You are literally banking on the fact that the strike price will not be reached. Therefore, time decay is working in your favor. You do not want to sell a covered call more than 45 days out; the greater the time, the greater the risk that the strike price may be reached.

If executed correctly in the right market conditions, this strategy is a good way for you to really have your cake and eat it, too. Always know the risk of any trade before taking it. Ask your broker about the specific risk of trading options.

TRADING MUTUAL FUNDS CAN BE ANOTHER GOOD LONG-TERM PLAY

I like to buy and hold mutual fund positions. Let me explain my approach. I identify the top-10 performing mutual funds for the previous year. Then I eliminate the top two performers. Then I allocate 80 percent of my mutual fund account balance to the remaining eight funds. At the end of the first quarter, I close out the worst three funds. I allocate that money to the top five of my remaining funds. At the end of the second quarter, I reallocate again. I close the worst two funds and add those monies to the top three funds. My profit goal is 10 percent on any given fund. If I have achieved that goal at the end of the second quarter, I either close out the fund profitably or exit half of my funds to lock in the 10 percent profit. At the end of the third quarter, I eliminate the worst performer of my remaining three funds and ride the funds that I have left to the end of the year. At that time, I go to cash. When the New Year begins, I start the process all over again.

REVIEW

There are many ways to make money in the financial markets. I prefer to make a lot of short-term plays, but some traders are more comfortable with a buy-and-hold strategy. If the broad market is bullish, I too take some long positions and hold them for a period of time. If you wish to be a long-term player, you should select your stocks carefully. I evaluate stock prices at the end of each year. I make a list of stocks that I will trade in the upcoming year. I strike the last year's performers that are in the top 10 percent; many of them have run out of steam. Then, I also eliminate the bottom 50 percent. I do not want to risk buying a stock that has historically performed so poorly. The remaining stocks compose my universe of potential stocks for my upcoming year's trading.

Now I consider other factors such as liquidity, volatility, beta, and how the movements of the stock correspond to price movements of the major indexes like the S&P 500 or the Dow Jones. The charting patterns of a great number of stocks exhibit a close price correlation. That is, when prices on the S&P 500 Index rise or fall, so does the stock price. I like to trade these stocks because the S&P futures can guide my path. You can easily do some investigating and identify some of these stocks.

I use the yearly and monthly opening prices for stocks as key numbers for my purchases. I will not go long on a stock that is trading below its yearly open. I also want the stock to be bullish on a month-to-month basis. The yearly and month opening prices for the stock are key numbers that can be used for determining stop/loss placement.

Even with my long-term plays, if a stock moves up in price and offers me an opportunity to take some good profits off the table, I will do so with a portion of my position. As prices rise, I will also move my protective stop closer to the market price and lock in profits while reducing risk.

If you own a stock position and want to make a little cash off of it, you may want to consider selling a covered call. The strategy requires that you sell a near-term call with the expectation that it will expire out of the money. Then you will have the ability to keep the shares and also pocket a premium for the sale of the call.

I also trade ETFs like the Diamond and the QQQQ. These funds are traded like stock but have less risk in that they are composed of all of the stocks on a particular index. Also, they are less news sensitive than one individual stock.

Trading mutual funds is yet another way to make a long-term play. As with stocks, I generally go to cash at the end of the year and reevaluate my specific strategy for the next year. I find the top10 best-performing mutual funds. I eliminate the top two and distribute 80 percent of my cash in the remaining eight. At the end of the first quarter, I close the worst three and put that money in the best five funds. At the end of the second quarter I repeat the process. My goal on this entire play is a profit of 10 percent. If that goal is reached on any single fund, I will close it and take the money to the bank, or at least exit half of the position. I keep following the process of selecting the cream of the crop. At the end of the year I again go to cash, reassess, and start all over again.

Regardless of the trading strategy that you use, you must always watch your money and take personal responsibility for it. Even if you have a financial advisor or manager, you should keep your eyes open so that your assets can be protected and grown.

 MARKET INSIGHT

Always keep an eye on a stock's yearly opening price. That price will be an important number throughout the year and can be used for determining anticipated support and resistance.

CHAPTER 10

Golden Keys to Unlocking the Secrets of the Financial Markets

Beating Wall Street is tough. Institutional investors and other wealthy and well-resourced traders have a lot of advantages. For example, they have the ability to get the best research that money can buy. Many have teams of analysts that review both technical and fundamental analyses in an attempt to identify winning opportunities. In addition, many of these big players have deep pockets that allow them to easily withstand a market dip or small correction. The little guy sitting at his kitchen table in Kalamazoo may be financially devastated by that same small dip or correction. That, however, does not mean that the market is the sole domain of the wealthy. It means that the little guys must be savvy and educated if they want to win. Not only must they know how to read the tape and stay on the right side of the market most of the time, but they also have to practice good money management and always limit risk. With that said, I want to explain the basic parameters of most of my trades.

When I select a trade, I do so based on three factors: time of day, key numbers, and market indicators. I have already explained the significance of time. Entering the market when there is no liquidity or movement equals price stagnation. For successful trading, prices must move so that you can gain a profit. Therefore, selecting an optimum trading time is essential if you are to make money. During the trading day, I trade in the mornings after the exchanges in New York and Chicago open their trading pits. I stop trading in late morning as traders begin thinking about lunch, and I have a short trading window after the lunch break and another one when the U.S. exchanges are nearing their close. If I trade in the evening, night, or early morning, I wait until Asia has voiced its opinion. In the morning hours, I wait for the Dax futures to trade for at least 30 minutes so that I have a clue as to the direction of European markets. By selecting optimum trading times I automatically increase my changes of success (by looking for breakout moves and by not overtrading). I know that if I select the right entry point and the right market direction, I should be able to pick up some fast profits.

Other than time, there are two critical aspects of profitable trading: key numbers and market indicators. These three are the golden keys referred to in the title. If you master them, you can open the doors to profitability. This chapter will focus on the two not yet detailed: key numbers and market indicators.

Golden Keys

- Time
- Key numbers
- Market indicators

KEY NUMBERS

Knowing the indicators to watch and reading them correctly is a big part of trading; it is one of the golden keys. Another essential element is key numbers. I cannot emphasize enough the importance of knowing the numbers in a particular index or stock that will be important for that trading product. Key numbers are critical to my trading method. I could not and would not trade without them. I would feel lost at sea—in the middle of the ocean—without a compass.

Yearly Opening Prices

The biggest and most important key number is the yearly opening price for any stock, index, or commodity that you are trading. That opening price is the line in the sand between the bulls and the bears. As the days and weeks of the year pass, if prices are above that yearly open, the bulls are winning the annual game; if prices fall below that yearly opening price, the bears are in charge. It may seem like a simple concept, but that one bit of information has saved me so many times.

Yearly Opening Prices for 2006	
S&P 500 futures	1,255.25
Dow futures	10,780.00
Nasdaq futures	1,659.00
Dax futures	5,448.00
IBM	82.45
MSFT	26.25

Once I know the yearly open, I have a sense of the overall sentiment of the market. I know if there is a bullish or a bearish cloud hanging over it. If I am considering taking a contrary position that is not a short-term and intraday one, I think twice. I double-check my data and question myself. At least I am challenged to prove to myself the wisdom of my move.

Monthly Opening Prices

Second in importance to the yearly opening prices, I note the monthly opening prices. In February, are prices higher or lower than the yearly open? In March, is the opening price higher than it was in February? Or, is it lower? Are both February and March higher or lower than that all-important yearly opening price?

I track these numbers on a trend line and I add to the line with each successive monthly open. In this way, I always have a broad or big picture view of the market in my head at all times (see Figure 10.1). That information is valuable and helps me stay on the right side of the action.

Weekly Opening Prices

As each Monday morning ushers in a new week, take note of the weekly opening price for the stocks, bonds, indexes, and other items that you are trading.

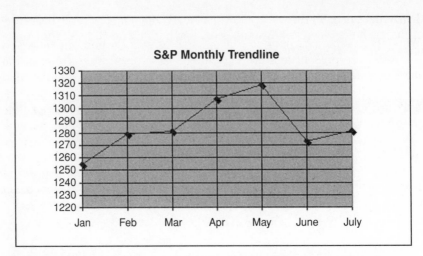

FIGURE 10.1 A monthly trendline chart. Opening prices for each month are visually expressed.

Chart this data, as in Figure 10.2. Then consider the data in the context of the year. How are the bulls doing? The bears? In thinking about the month's trading direction, are the bulls or the bears winning the monthly battle? Having this intermediate view is very important. On a more short-term basis you are able to get a clearer view and anticipate what to expect.

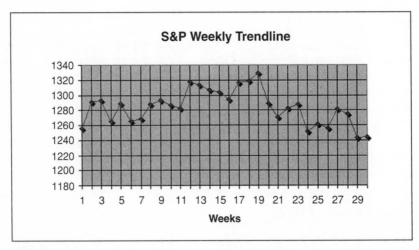

FIGURE 10.2 A weekly trendline chart. Opening prices for each week are noted on the graph. A trendline is formed by connecting those prices.

Daily Opening Prices

When the trading pits open in Chicago and New York, both the bulls and the bears are present and are determined to express their views in the day's trading action. The daily opening price is the line drawn in the sand between the two contenders. If prices move above the opening price, the bulls are stronger than the bears. If the bears are able to pull prices below the open, they are the most formidable. Therefore, watch that opening price. It is a simple thing to do, but by doing it, you are able to have an immediate view of the collective sentiment of most traders.

Figure 10.3 shows the bulls charging. The horizontal line across the bottom of the chart is the opening price. The bulls took charge of the Nasdaq futures on this date and just kept charging up. The opening price each day

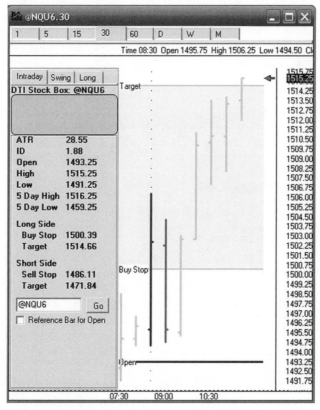

FIGURE 10.3 The bulls charging as they pull prices above the opening price. The opening price is very important in determining which team is winning the daily battle.

is the initial line drawn in the sand by the bulls and the bears. Bulls work to move things higher and bears try to pull them down. The bulls are clearly winning the battle.

Figure 10.4 is a chart of Murphy Oil prices. The horizontal line in the middle shows the opening price. Initially the bulls were strong enough to stay above the open for a few minutes. Then the bears gained control and prices sank below the open.

Other Daily Key Numbers

There are other numbers that I consider to be important during the course of any trading day. In addition to the daily open, I also want to know the previous day's close and the opening of last night's Globex or night session on the S&P futures. I also check for the high and the low of the S&P 500 futures during the night session. I know that those price points served as support and resistance during the night session, and they may do so again during the day's session. Therefore, I want to know what they are and want to be aware of their potential importance. If I am going long early in the day's session, I may want to wait until the Globex high has been crossed.

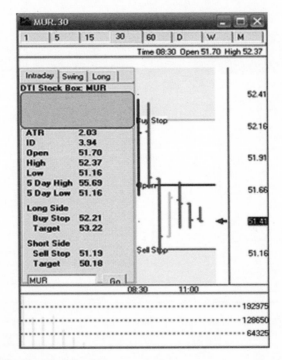

FIGURE 10.4 Murphy Oil prices.

Otherwise, that point may again serve as resistance and my play may be tackled by the bears.

Most stock exchanges are open for business about eight hours a day. Traders work for several hours, take a lunch break, and then get back to business. Therefore, I consider the U.S. trading session to be like two sessions. That is, there is a morning session that goes from the time the exchanges open until lunchtime. Then traders leave their stations and fill the restaurants and cafes of Manhattan and the Chicago Loop. When they return to business, they often shift the market. The direction of the morning is not necessarily the direction of the afternoon. Just because the bulls were powerful between the hours of 8:30 and 10:30 AM does not mean that they will continue to be so. Therefore, I look at the price bar formed between 12:30 and 1:00 PM Central Time to get a new gauge of market action. That is the newest line in the sand. If the bulls pull prices above that bar of reference, I will be looking to the long side. If the bears are strong enough to pull them down, I will be on the lookout for a point at which to be a seller. Therefore, the 12:30 price on the S&P 500 is a key number for me. Also, the trading bar that is formed between 12:30 and 1:00 PM Central Time is a big reference bar that I watch to gauge short-term trading. Figure 10.5 depicts a sell-off of the e-mini S&P futures. Reference Bar 4 was the line drawn in the sand by the bulls and the bears. The bears won this battle.

FIGURE 10.5   E-mini S&P futures selling from Reference Bar 4.

Historical Key Numbers

In addition to the market-generated numbers, there are some key numbers in each index or stock that are noteworthy. For example, the century points are very important. Consider the Nasdaq. Anytime prices cross the 1,500 or the 1,400 price point, expect traders to respond. If prices are moving down and the bears are able to cross that century point, they are showing strength, and things will likely fall farther. The reverse is also true.

Another example can be seen in the Dow futures. At the time of this writing, the Dow has just posted an all-time high. Prices on the Dow futures soared well above the 11,900 mark. That new high, as well as any new high or low, reached in the future will become a significant key number for the market.

In the Dow futures, each 25-point increment tends to be important. For example, expect 00, 25, 50, and 75 to be significant. That means that in the current market (early October 2006) 11,000, 11,925, 11,950, and 11,975 will all be important price points. When I buy or sell, I want the market to have crossed those points by at least five points before I make a trade. Therefore, in a bullish market I would consider a buy at 11,931, 11,956, or 11,981. To the short side, I would consider a sell at 10, 919, 10,944, or 10,969. I know that support and resistance can be expected at those key numbers, so I use that information to try to get the most optimum placement for my entry.

Will those numbers always be points of support and resistance? Of course not. But, observation and experience have taught me that they are important, so I pay attention to them. That does not mean that I only make trades based on these numbers. I merge my key number data with other key number information and indicator data. Then I decide whether I will be long, short, or out of the market. If I decide to trade, then I determine my entry point.

Each stock, index, and financial product has its own key numbers. It does not matter whether the financial product is traded on an exchange in Asia or an exchange in the United States. There are key numbers that are important to it. In order to locate them, you must watch that particular market or product trade and locate those price points where support and resistance come into play. Then, you can use that information to improve your trading.

FILTER OUT EXTRANEOUS DATA BY LOOKING AT THE RIGHT INDICATORS

Computers open so many doors. They allow traders to receive a wealth of information that was once unavailable to them. With just a few clicks of your mouse you can travel hundreds, maybe even thousands, of miles away and view dozens of charts, graphs, and other pictorially presented bits of information. You can also gain corporate information and learn about corporate management, assets, markets, profits and losses, cost ratios, and much more. However, is all of that information needed? Information may be good, but too much information is deadly. Getting too many numbers and statistics leads to confusion and malaise. To avoid an information overload, you must know where to focus your attention and be able to filter out the noise to get a clear view of market action. A trader must carefully select the indicators that are most helpful and use those indicators effectively.

Over the years I have come to rely on a few major gauges that keep me on the right side of things. I read these indicators every day and believe them to be so important that I have incorporated them into my RoadMap software. When I glance at my RoadMap, the color-coded printout tells me if the indicator is bullish, bearish, or noncommittal. I use both this statistical data and well-known index futures to guide my trading and lead the way. I suggest that serious traders obtain some type of program that has the ability to present the necessary information in an easy-to-read and straightforward manner.

USE INDEX FUTURES AS PREDICTORS

In theory, futures markets predict the direction of the cash markets. At the end of the quarterly contract expiration, the S&P 500 futures contract should be trading at or near the price of the S&P 500 stock average, at least theoretically. If futures are moving up, the cash markets should follow and if they are moving down the cash market should also be heading lower. That is true for commodities also. For example, if our nation's corn crop is devastated by a drought resulting in a corn shortage, we would expect prices to rise not only in the supermarket but also in the corn futures markets in Chicago. It works the same way in the stock market. If economic factors are favorable for stock prices to rise, we expect stocks listed on the major indexes like the S&P 500 or the Dow Jones to rise. Stock prices in the futures markets or derivatives markets should also move up as they reflect those optimum economic conditions. Therefore, index futures may be used as indicators for making trading decisions. I trade futures, but even those who do not, may use the S&P futures or Dow futures as a gauge to predict stock performance.

There are four major index futures that I watch on a daily basis. I never trade without knowing what is happening on the S&P 500 futures, and the Dow, Nasdaq, and Dax futures. If the futures markets are trending either up or down, the cash markets should also be trending in that same direction. And, in theory, the futures should be leading the way. Furthermore, if a trend is significant, all of the futures stock indexes will be moving in the same direction. If there is a laggard, beware because the move may be short lived. For example, if the S&P 500 futures, the Dow futures, and the Dax futures are all moving up, but the Nasdaq futures refuse to join the party, double-check your analysis before taking a long position. Often, if there is one lagging index, it is a warning signal that the move lacks strength and prices may be near their correction or reversal point.

I use a piece of software, the *Stock Box*, to help me identify entry points for equities. Look at the action on July 24, 2006 (see Figures 10.6 to 10.9). The S&P futures opened at 1,274.50, the Nasdaq futures at 1,549.50, the Dow futures at 11,165.00, and the Dax futures at 5,708.00. As buyers stepped into the market, prices on all indexes rose, and by 10:00 AM Central Time the S&P was breaking above 1,282.00, the Dow was crossing 11,231.00, and the other index futures were also exhibiting strength. Note how the stocks below were also moving. Traders who identified the upward momentum in the index futures were able to use that data to purchase some equities and also benefit from the move. A look at the price movements of the Dow futures (Figure 10.6), Nasdaq futures (Figure 10.7), S&P futures (Figure 10.8), and Dax futures (Figure 10.9) on July 24, 2006, illustrates how these major index futures tend to travel together.

The point is that the index futures predict, in theory, the prices of the equity markets. Therefore, they may be used as indications to trade equities and other markets. I use them for that purpose every single day.

FIGURE 10.6 A chart of the Dow futures on July 24, 2006.

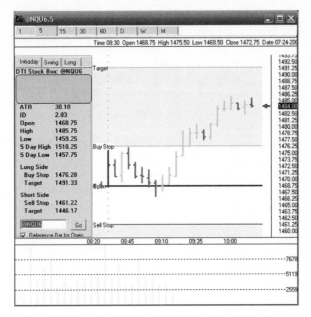

FIGURE 10.7   A chart of the Nasdaq futures during the same timeframe on July 24, 2006.

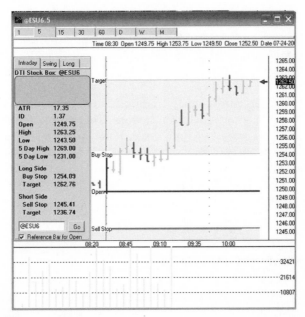

FIGURE 10.8   A chart of S&P futures during the same time of day on July 24, 2006.

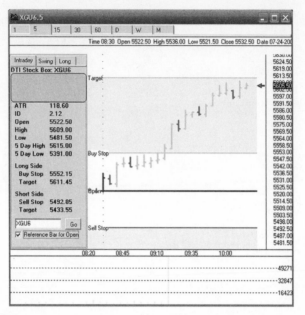

FIGURE 10.9   A chart of the Dax futures reflecting similar price movements on July 24, 2006. Often, the major index futures move together. Many stocks also mimic their movements. Therefore, the futures are useful indicators for trading both futures and equities.

To further demonstrate the point, look at the price movements of stock in The Chicago Board of Trade (BOT) and Intercontinental Exchange (ICE) on July 24, 2006. Figures 10.10 and 10.11 mirror the pattern of those of the futures.

Futures markets are unique. Trading futures involves risks that are not encountered in some stock transactions. Therefore, trading futures is clearly not for everyone, and I am not recommending that readers begin trading futures. Certainly no one should do so without proper education and adequate financial resources. However, even if you do not trade futures, you can use the index futures as indicators or gauges to predict market direction and improve your trading accuracy.

STATISTICAL INDICATORS

In addition to keeping an eye on the index futures, I also monitor certain statistical data. In particular, I track the NYSE Tick, the TRIN or Arms Index, the issues on both the NYSE and the Nasdaq, and I also use my own

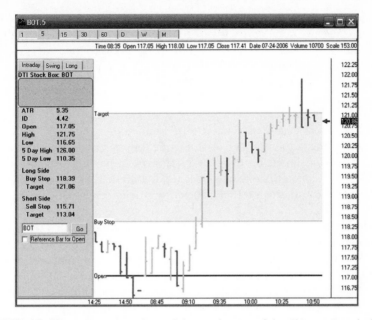

FIGURE 10.10 A 30-minute chart of the stock price of the Chicago Board of Trade on July 24, 2006.

FIGURE 10.11 A 30-minute chart of the stock price of the InterContinental Exchange on July 24, 2006.

proprietary indicator, the TTICK. I am able to track this information easily because I use my RoadMap software to do it for me. Again, you do not have to use the RoadMap, but you need some program to follow, interpret, and present data in an easy to use and understandable format.

The NYSE Tick

One of the most widely used short-term indicators is the NYSE Tick. This indicator reflects the number of stocks ticking up as compared with the number ticking down on the NYSE. That is, a reading of +500 means 500 more stocks on the exchange are ticking up than are ticking down. A reading of −700 indicates that 700 more stocks are ticking down than are ticking up.

Reading the Tick is easy. Numbers hovering around zero tend to fall in a neutral zone. That is, they carry very little weight and are generally insignificant. However, once the readings get strong, either positively or negatively, you should pay attention. I consider readings of 500 to be noteworthy. For example, I consider 500 and higher to be bullish and −500 and lower to be bearish.

In addition to signaling buying and selling opportunities, the NYSE Tick may also warn of overbought and oversold situations. When readings become too strong, a correction or reversal may be on the way. If the market is very strong or very weak, the correction may be short lived and prices may soon continue on their established course. But, if the market is not very strong, the reversal may shift prices, and the daily direction may change. For example, if the Tick soars to 1,200, there is a glut of buyers and the market cannot sustain this level of activity for very long. There will be a price reversal, either momentary or for a longer period of time. Therefore, if you are long and the Tick gets too hot, you should lighten your load or exit your positions profitably. You do not want to enter the market when the Tick is too high. Wait for prices to settle, and then, if the Tick and other indicators remain strong, look to become a buyer.

The NYSE Tick is one indicator that I always watch. Even though it is a NYSE indicator, one may be sure that if a significant number of stocks on the NYSE are trending in one direction, other exchanges are experiencing the same move. Therefore, if the Tick is running very negative, I will not be a buyer. I will wait for the Tick to be on my side before I risk my money. Likewise, if the Tick is posting high numbers above 500, I will not be a seller. I will wait for the stocks listed on the New York Exchange to favor my play. By keeping an eye on the NYSE Tick, you increase your chances for success. Look at the 1,200 + NYSE Tick reading in Figure 10.12. Also, note the upward movement of IBM in Figure 10.13 as the tick races upward.

FIGURE 10.12   A one-minute chart of the action on the NYSE Tick. On this particular day, the equity markets are very bullish and the NYSE Tick is registering a high of over 1,200.

FIGURE 10.13   IBM has a bullish upward pattern as the NYSE Tick is soaring above 1,200. IBM is only one example of stocks that are moving higher as the NYSE Tick races above the 1,000 mark.

Issues

Two additional indicators that I always track are the net advance/decline issues on both the NYSE and the Nasdaq. These indicators offer a broad view of market sentiment. The numerical data reflect the number of issues listed on the New York Exchange that are ticking up, as opposed to those ticking down based on the previous day's close. For example, if the net issues are 995, that means that 995 stocks on the New York Stock Exchange are trading above their previous day's closing price. Likewise, if 995 stocks are trading below their previous day's closing price, the reading will be –995. Like the NYSE Tick, I consider readings of +500 to –500 to be in the noise zone. That is, readings in that area are not particularly pronounced. However, once the issues rise higher than +500 or sink lower than –500, the market is expressing an opinion as to direction. When readings soar higher than 1,000 in either direction, they are very strong. This indicator differs from the NYSE tick in that the data offer a slightly longer view because they are based on the previous day's closing price and not just the latest tick. However, it is still a short-term indicator.

In addition to watching the NYSE net issues, I gauge the net issues on the Nasdaq. The indicator represents the identical data noted above but on the Nasdaq, and it is equally important to my trading decisions. For example, if the net issues are 1,500 or so on both the NYSE and the Nasdaq, stocks trading on both exchanges are very bullish and prices will be moving accordingly. I suggest that before you trade, you always look at net issues. I would never trade during the day's session without knowing that information. Figure 10.14 charts a negative or bearish reading on the Nasdaq issues (–293). Figure 10.15 shows how Intel is trading as the Nasdaq issues move down. Intel is a bear's play.

The TRIN

Another statistical indicator that cuts through the noise is the Arms Index or TRIN. In the late 1960s, Richard Arms, a master of technical analysis, developed the TRIN, or Short-Term Trading Index. The TRIN measures advances and declines and adds volume to the mix. It is a contrarian indicator that is used by thousands of traders to determine the strength and breadth of market momentum. The TRIN is a ratio of ratios and is calculated as follows:

$$\frac{\text{Advancing issues/Declining issues}}{\text{Advancing volume/Declining Volume}}$$

Because volume is an inherent part of the calculation, the TRIN gauges supply and demand (how many traders want to buy or sell?). The TRIN may be used for intraday trading or for longer-term moves. Most traders

FIGURE 10.14 Nasdaq issues are −293. That means that 293 stocks listed on the exchange are trading lower than their previous day's close.

FIGURE 10.15 Intel was one of the stocks in negative territory. Its price movement on this day mimics the movement of the issues on the Nasdaq.

consider a TRIN reading of 1.0 to be a neutral reading. That is, no market sentiment is expressed. High readings indicate negative market sentiment and low readings register more bullish sentiment. A TRIN of 2.0 is very negative and 3.0 may signal a near reversal or correction. That is, an over-sold situation may exist. Such a high reading is akin to a 1,000 reading on the NYSE Tick. Very low readings indicate a bullish sentiment. I consider a reading of 0.5 or higher to be very strong. Because the TRIN is a lagging indicator, I rely more on the NYSE Tick and the net issues for most of my short-term decisions. However, it is a good idea to check the TRIN before entering positions. If the TRIN is too high, you may not want to jump in on the sell or short side. Perhaps things will be cooling off a little and prices will be undergoing a brief or sustained correction. The same is, of course, also true for a bullish move. If the TRIN looks too inviting, it may be sig-naling a brief or sustained downward move. Perhaps the best opportuni-ties for market entry are yet to come (see Figure 10.16).

In Figure 10.17, the TRIN is moving down, a negative or bearish sign.

The TTICK

I cannot discuss statistical indicators without mentioning the TTICK. The TTICK is a proprietary indicator that I designed several years ago. The TTICK is used by my students to get a market edge. The indicator is based on data

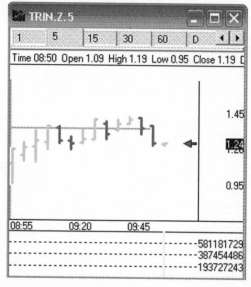

FIGURE 10.16   A TRIN chart. Remember that the TRIN is an inverse indicator. As the TRIN moves down, the S&P futures move up.

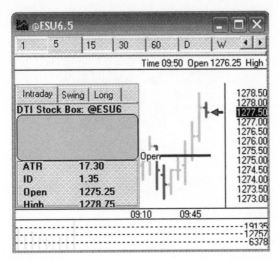

FIGURE 10.17   Note that the S&P futures are moving up as the TRIN is moving down.

from both the index futures and the NYSE. The data are then merged and reflected in a numerical indicator. Readings between +5.0 and –5.0 are deemed to be in the noise zone and are generally ignored. Readings higher than +5.0 tend to be bullish and those lower than –5.0 tend to be bearish. Readings of +10 are very bearish. TTICK reading may go as high as +30 or –30 but that is very rare. As a general rule, once the TTICK reaches a +20 or –20 range, I consider the market potentially overbought or oversold and I will either lighten my load and take my profits or exit my positions altogether and go to the sidelines.

The TTICK is a simple indicator that I use every day, and I believe that it gives me a little bit of a trading edge. One big advantage of the TTICK is that it is available 24 hours a day. The NYSE Tick only works when that exchange is open. Figure 10.18 depicts a TTICK chart reflecting a very bullish reading of 13.53. Figure 10.19 tracks the upward movement of Cadbury Schweppes (CSG) at the same time that the TTICK is racing.

Momentum or Volume Indicators

As Richard Arms realized when he designed the TRIN, volume is a very important trading element because it reveals the strength and breadth of a market move. How many traders are joining the team? Observing volume and correctly reading it is very helpful. There are a number of ways to monitor volume. One of the ways that I use this information is to trade only during times when volume is traditionally strong. That is the reason I

FIGURE 10.18   On this day the market is very bullish. The TTICK is registering 13.53.

trade in the center of the morning trading session, just after traders return from lunch, and near the market's close. Experience has taught me that volume is generally good during those times. The TRIN is another way to determine volume, because volume is part of the formula. However, the TRIN is not a straightforward volume indicator because other data are also included in the mix.

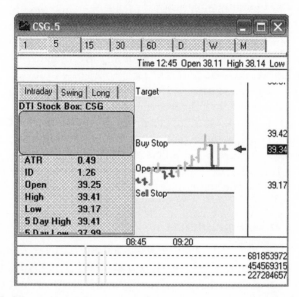

FIGURE 10.19   The TTICK as it is soaring. Note that Cadbury Schwepps is also very bullish.

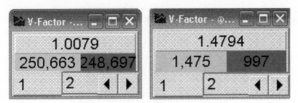

FIGURE 10.20 A V-Factor reading. The V-Factor reports the ratio of buyers to sellers.

My favorite volume indicator is a proprietary one, the V-Factor. With this indicator I am able to see the buying and selling coming into the market. I use the V-Factor for any of the major stock indexes like the Dow or Nasdaq, and I can reset it at important times during the day. Before I trade I check the V-Factor to determine whether I am considering joining the most popular team. If I am going long, I want buyers to outnumber sellers. If I am selling, I want the bears to be prowling in full force. The V-Factor numerically reflects buyers to sellers in actual numbers and as a ratio (see Figure 10.20). If the V-Factor is 2.0 or higher, that indicates that twice as many sellers as buyers have entered that particular market during that particular timeframe. A reading of 0.5 or lower reflects the entry of twice as many buyers as sellers. By resetting the V-Factor before every anticipated trading opportunity, I am able to get a clear view of the immediate volume in the index that I am planning to trade (see Figure 10.21).

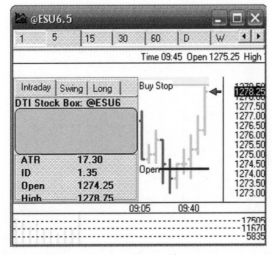

FIGURE 10.21 How the S&P futures respond to the added volume. With more buyers than sellers, prices naturally move up.

MARKET-SPECIFIC INDICATORS TO WATCH

Some economic situations require traders to watch particular market segments or areas to gain clues as to the overall direction of stocks. This section looks at a few of them.

Petroleum

In late 2005 and early 2006, oil prices were soaring. Each Wednesday the Energy Information Administration (EIA), the statistical arm of the Department of Energy, releases its petroleum status report. The report documents both domestic and foreign petroleum inventories. That report has been issued for many years, yet I had never noticed it or paid much attention to it until those oil prices started heading through the roof. Industry needs fuel. In fact, American consumers need it, too. The United States is the world's largest consumer of oil. Therefore, with stock prices noticeably responding to each successive EIA report, I began to pay close attention to those weekly announcements.

During times when oil prices are dominating the news, I also carefully watch the price of crude and also prices in the oil services industry. I know that if both crude oil and oil services stocks are sharply rising, the odds are great that stock prices in the industrial and manufacturing sectors are falling. This relationship is graphically expressed in Figures 10.22 and 10.23. Therefore, during times when folks have the oil jitters, I use crude and oil services as contrarian indicators.

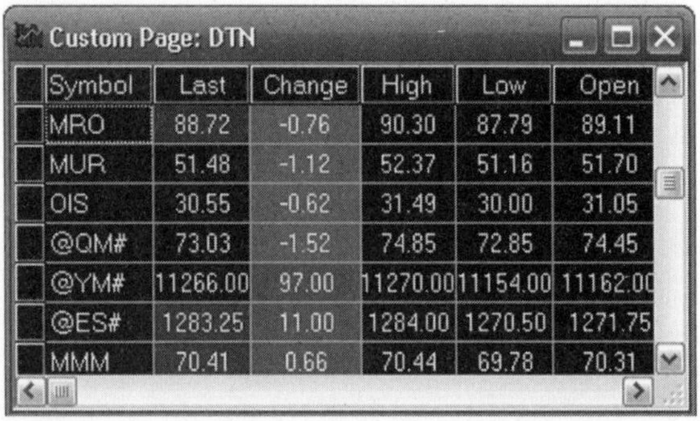

Symbol	Last	Change	High	Low	Open
MRO	88.72	-0.76	90.30	87.79	89.11
MUR	51.48	-1.12	52.37	51.16	51.70
OIS	30.55	-0.62	31.49	30.00	31.05
@QM#	73.03	-1.52	74.85	72.85	74.45
@YM#	11266.00	97.00	11270.00	11154.00	11162.00
@ES#	1283.25	11.00	1284.00	1270.50	1271.75
MMM	70.41	0.66	70.44	69.78	70.31

FIGURE 10.22 A portion of a Quote Page. The four stock quotes at the top are oil services companies. The bottom quotes are index futures. Note that as prices for oil services move down, index futures move up.

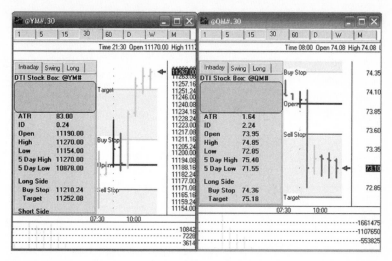

FIGURE 10.23 A side-by-side comparison of the Dow futures and Crude futures. The Dow futures on the left are moving up as the crude futures on the right are moving down. Often there is an inverse relationship between fuel prices and equity prices.

Gold and Precious Metals

Another area that often signals broad market moves is the gold or precious metals markets. Traditionally, traders seek safety in gold, silver, platinum, and valuable metals. Gold is an international currency and it is often bought when traders fear either inflation or unstable and dangerous market conditions caused by geopolitical crisis or some other manmade or natural disaster. Because emotion plays a huge role in determining market prices, if a large number of traders and investors are seeking safety in gold, it is an indication that confidence has been lost in other types of market investments and probably in the U.S. dollar. Therefore, if gold prices rise too sharply, stocks, currency, and bonds may all take a hit (see Figure 10.24).

Most of the time, I do not constantly watch gold prices. However, if there is a major geopolitical threat or some other serious negative cloud looming over the markets, I check gold. I also correlate that price with the price of silver. If the two precious metals markets are in agreement, I know something is afoot. If they are rising sharply, I know that the broad-based stock markets will have a very difficult time moving up. Generally, in those cases I am a bear, and I ride prices lower.

Depending on specific conditions, there may be times when other market sectors are very important to Wall Street. For example, if there were a nationwide drought, agricultural prices might become very important indi-

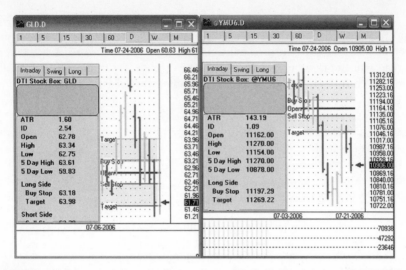

FIGURE 10.24 A side-by-side comparison of GLD (gold) and Dow futures. As gold prices move down in the chart on the left, prices on the Dow futures move up. Again, an inverse relationship is depicted.

cators. Or, if bond yields are very high, the bond market might be an inverse indicator for stocks. During times when there is some unusual or exceptional activity in the market, pay attention and use the information that can be gleaned from that particular situation.

> *Trade Secret #7:   Opening prices are the deciding factor in determining a trend.*

REVIEW

We live in the Information Age. There is a tremendous amount of data available, and anyone with a computer and Internet access can obtain it. The challenge for traders is not to get information, but to get the right information. Therefore, you must filter out the noise and focus your attention on numbers and statistics that paint the true picture of Wall Street sentiment.

I rely on a few time-tested and simple indicators. First, I use the index futures to predict the direction of the cash markets and other futures markets. By their nature, futures markets are designed to foretell the direction of the equity prices upon which they are based. By that I mean that the S&P 500 futures theoretically should predict the average trading price for the stocks trading on the S&P 500 when the quarterly contract expires. Therefore, I always watch the S&P 500 futures, the Dow futures, the Nasdaq futures, and the Dax futures. If those four indicators are all trending in the same direction, the prices on the cash markets will likely follow. Likewise, if the index futures are giving mixed signals, I stay out. For example, if the S&P and Dax are charging higher, but the Dow and the Nasdaq are dragging their feet, I know that the move lacks strength and I will not be suckered into it.

In addition to the index futures, I also use some statistical indicators. I would never trade without checking the NYSE Tick and the NYSE and Nasdaq issues. Those indicators give a good short-term view of market action. If the NYSE Tick is registering numbers of 500 or higher, I will be looking to the long side. If it is reflecting negative numbers greater than –500, I will be seeking shorting opportunities. The NYSE Tick reflects the number of stocks on the NYSE that are ticking up as opposed to those ticking down since the last tick. Another important indicator is the net issues. This indicator numerically expresses the number of issues or stocks trading up as opposed to those trading down; the reference point is the previous day's close. I always watch the net issues on both the NYSE and the Nasdaq. In addition to these two very popular and frequently used indicators, I also use my proprietary TTICK. The TTICK gathers data from the futures markets and the cash markets and merges them. The numerical feedback is a number that is plus or minus 30. Simply stated: The higher the number, the more bullish; the lower the number, the more bearish. Unlike the NYSE Tick, the TTICK reports data 24 hours a day.

Volume is also an extremely important trading factor. Volume measures the momentum that is coming into the market on either the buy or the sell side. Therefore, I highly suggest that you have a method of gauging volume and that you pay close attention to it. I use my own volume indicator known as the V-Factor. It is not essential that you use the same indicator that I use; however, it is essential that serious traders keep track of volume and stay out of the market when volume is low. Volume is a measure of the depth and breadth of a market move.

Finally, when specific market conditions indicate, I focus on market sectors that are demanding attention. For example, if oil is dominating the news and prices are rising in a noteworthy and potentially destructive fashion, I watch crude and petroleum prices because I know that Wall Street is watching and stock prices will fall if oil prices get too unwieldy. Likewise, if there are serious geopolitical problems or devastating natural disasters, I will check gold prices. I know that gold will be a barometer of market sentiment.

Another vital part of successful global trading is key numbers. Every financial product that is traded has numbers or price points that serve as support, resistance, and pivots for that product. As a general rule, the yearly opening price is the single most important number or price. Other important numbers include the monthly open, the weekly open, and the daily open. For short-term trading I also use the 12:30 PM Central Time price, the Globex or evening opening price, and the high and low of evening trading. Using these numbers helps me stay on the right side of the market and keeps me from falling for plays that will not play.

You must select the market indicators that you will rely on carefully. You want information, but not unnecessary or unreliable information. You must also know key numbers and how to use them. These essential elements of trading—along with timing—are the golden keys that will open the doors to profitable trading.

 MARKET INSIGHTS

- Know key numbers and how to use them.
- Use the index futures and statistical indicators to gauge sentiment in the cash markets and other futures markets.

CHAPTER 11

Managing Risk in Global Markets

E very trader, regardless of the product that he trades or the hours that he trades, has to manage risk. Remember Black Monday in 1987 or the crash of the high-tech bubble in 2000? Those events caused bad things to happen to thousands of good traders. What would happen if the market crashed again? What if some terrorist cell succeeded in a deadly and strategic attack in the United States and a large geographical area or vital economic center was affected? In fact, the attack does not have to be targeted at the United States. In our global economy, a serious crisis or event across the Atlantic or Pacific will have dire effects on the world's financial markets. What would happen to your portfolio? How soundly would you be sleeping in the aftermath? The best way to protect yourself is to be an educated investor.

Trading in the global markets is risky. However, on both a short-term and a long-term basis there are things that you can do to protect yourself. Expanding your playing field and understanding how to trade 24 hours a day adds opportunities and allows for greater flexibility both on a regular basis and in times of crisis. With that in mind, I offer the following strategies that may be helpful.

A word of caution: Every trader and investor is unique. Asset levels, risk tolerance, and a wide array of factors determine the trading approach that you should take. Therefore, it is not my intent to offer a "one-size-fits-all" plan. Before taking any action, you must be familiar with all of the risks and ramifications including tax liabilities that you may incur. Those lacking a full understanding of all aspects of any investing strategy should consult a professional to be fully advised of all consequences and risks involved.

STRATEGIES FOR PROTECTING YOUR LONG-TERM ASSETS

Diversify

One of the most basic steps that you can take to protect your assets is to diversify them. As the old adage goes, don't put all of your eggs in one basket. If the bulk of your assets are in technology stocks and the sector goes south, so does the value of the whole portfolio. Get balance within your equity holdings; do not rely on the success of any single sector to safeguard and grow your wealth. And, do not just diversify equities. To the extent that your assets allow, balance the whole account with various financial products. If possible, a portion of your holdings should be in bonds or a bond fund. Bonds, at least under certain conditions, tend to move inversely to equities. If your equity account is ailing, your bonds should be doing better and balancing your losses.

Most of the traders that I know have at least a portion of their wealth in real estate. Investments in real property are another avenue that you might wish to explore. However, with interest rates rising, the real estate market will likely experience a slow down. The particular manner in which you diversify depends on the value of your assets, your comfort zone with various products, and your specific financial needs and plan. At the time of this writing, my personal definition of diversification is cash and profitable stocks. The big idea is that in order to protect yourself from global financial risk, one basic step is to diversify.

Be a Hands-on Manager

Many people like to give the responsibility for managing their money to someone else. It is easier to have Mr. X take care of everything. If the advisor of choice is very good, maybe all will turn out well. But, beware! No one is as concerned about your money as yourself. The person who made the funds has the biggest interest in conserving and growing them. Handing over the portfolio to an "expert" might be convenient but unwise. At least, not unless you also keep track of it and hold the manager accountable. Never trust that someone else will have your best interests at heart and always make the right moves. That is not to say that experts may not be helpful, and there are times when many people need advice. Just remember who the money belongs to and whose final responsibility it is to manage it. If you do not keep an eye on your own assets, the day may come when there are no assets to watch. That is the beauty of educating yourself about the financial markets. Education translates to power; the power to look out for yourself and your interests.

Use Stop/Loss Orders

If equity prices drop 10 percent during any eight-week period, beware. A serious market correction or crash may be afoot. Should that happen, make certain that you have firm stop/loss orders in place that will take you out of your equity positions if the deterioration continues. When prices fall that far that fast, it creates structural problems for the market. This is especially true with leveraged instruments such as futures and leveraged equities. With equities, the margin requirement is 50 percent (for patterned day traders, only 25 percent) and with futures, it is only about 5 percent (maybe even less). Take, for example, an S&P e-mini contract. The value of the contract is about $70,000, but if you carry the position overnight, a good-faith margin of only about $3,000 to $4,000 is required. If a trader buys one contract at 1,250 and the market falls to 1,125, the loss on that contract is $6,250. Remember that only $3,000 to $4,000 secures the contract. Therefore, the brokerage house must issue a margin call or liquidate the position. Additional selling will be forced on the market at a time when buyers are already scarce. The effect of this selling will not only be reflected in the futures markets, but will also effect the equity markets as traders are forced to sell positions to cover margin calls. This selling will accelerate the downward momentum and force prices even lower. Also, remember that if prices fall that far that fast there will be an emotional response; the mass of investors will not rely on rational analysis but panic.

Once the markets enter a crisis mode, it may be too late to take protective action. Prepare in advance. Look at your portfolio and determine the amount of loss you can afford to suffer. If the market heads south at a neck-breaking speed, how far can you afford to travel with it? Once equity markets drop 10 percent in eight weeks, some traders (this one included) will seriously be considering whether to hold any equity positions. However, for a variety of reasons, many traders do not want to liquidate holdings. Therefore, you should use firm stop/loss orders to prevent a devastation of your portfolio. As noted earlier, you are not guaranteed to be filled at your stop price. However, at least a stop/loss order should offer some cover and some protection.

After the market has dropped 10 percent in eight weeks, you can adjust stop/loss orders so that you are no more than 10 to 15 percent below market prices. If the equity markets continue to struggle, you should consider tightening stops by 3 percent a month. In this way, you can limit the bleeding. No one likes losing money, but at least with stop/loss orders in place, the extent of your exposure should be limited.

STRATEGIES FOR MANAGING CRISIS SITUATIONS

Purchasing Gold or Precious Metals

Gold is the traditional inflationary hedge, and historically it has been considered a safe haven in time of crisis. In the not-so-distant past, faced with soaring oil prices, geopolitical crisis, steady interest rate increases, and fears of inflation, gold prices have posted a 26-year high. Not since the 1980s has the market seen prices like those that have been seen in 2006. Should equity markets go into a free fall, you might want to purchase gold or precious metals.

Gold is an international currency meriting respect around the globe. Having a core position in gold should significantly reduce risk during times of market turmoil. There are several ways to purchase gold. You may, of course, buy gold and stockpile it, but few investors want to take that course.

You may also purchase shares of stock in gold mining corporations. With a little research, the interested investor can find a number of gold stocks to consider. However, you must be aware of mine-specific risk. That is, if you invest in mine AB, and the mine AB floods or is unproductive for some other reason, gold prices may be shooting out the roof, but the investment will be in the cellar.

One way to avoid this risk is to invest in a well-managed gold mutual fund. No gold stock or mutual fund recommendations are made here; explore the possibilities and do your homework. You may also purchase gold futures. Gold futures are traded electronically at the Chicago Board of Trade (CBOT). Futures are not for everyone, as they are highly leveraged instruments and you need training and experience before jumping head-long into this arena. However, gold futures may offer just the right hedge for some portfolios.

Another gold trading avenue is exchange traded gold funds. Finally, there are exchange traded gold shares like GLD or IAU, where each share is equal to 1/10 of an ounce of gold. Gold is actually purchased and stored. If you own ten shares, you own an ounce of gold, but you do not have to be concerned with holding the metal and storing it. The informed investor has many ways to enter the gold market. Regardless of the manner in which gold is held, short of investing in an unproductive mine or a poorly managed fund or corporation, gold should offer protection from market storms.

Using Index Futures as a Hedge

If a crisis hits the market, another possibility is to hedge an equity position with an index position. For example, assume you are holding a diversified portfolio of shares with a value of approximately $180,000. Also assume that the portfolio has volatility closely correlated to the S&P 500. (Many stocks mimic the movement of the S&P or other well-known index.) Once you identify the correlation, sell the appropriate number of index contracts to offset long equity holdings.

Futures contracts on the S&P and Nasdaq are traded at the Chicago Mercantile Exchange (CME) and Dow futures are traded at the Chicago Board of Trade (CBOT). Both large and mini contracts are offered. The Big S&P trades for $250 per point, the mini S&P trades at $50 per point. The Big Nasdaq goes for $100 per point, the mini for $10. Finally, the Big Dow trades for $10 per point and the mini for $5.

Here is how the strategy might work on one individual stock. Assume that you own 1,000 shares of stock, and for every five points of S&P movement, the stock price changes by approximately $1.00. You can sell four e-mini S&P futures contracts and mitigate the position. For example, if the stock moves down five points, your equity account decreases by $1,000. However, the four short S&P positions are making money as the market drops. When the S&P Index futures drop by five points, you have recouped $1,000.

Again, futures are not for everyone. They have particular risks but the rewards can also be large. Education is essential before trading them. Being an educated and informed trader is the key to being a successful trader. Also, a margin account and a trading platform are required, so you must be prepared before a crisis hits.

Hedging with a LEAP

The Chicago Board Options Exchange (CBOE) defines a LEAP (Long-term Equity Anticipation Security) as a long-dated put or call option on common stock or ADRs. These options allow the holder the right to purchase a call or sell a put (for a specified number of stock shares) at a predetermined price until the expiration date of the option. With LEAPS, the expiration date may be three years in the future.

In a down market, I recommend strictly a long DELTA approach to options. That is, only buy calls or buy puts. Options and LEAPS may allow you to hold your equity positions while also protecting your downside. For example, assume that you are holding a portfolio worth $200,000. You could buy October 2007 Dow Jones or S&P LEAP puts with a strike price approximately 7 percent below current market prices. If the market drops severely, the LEAPS will go up in value offering protection for the dropping equities.

The cost of the LEAP is the purchase price and the commission, and that is the risk that you face. In case of a strong market downturn, that would be a small price to pay for some portfolio insurance.

These are only a few strategies that you might want to use to get protection for your portfolio should the markets head south. Investigate the range of possibilities available to you and be prepared to act in case Iran or South Korea or some terrorist organization aims torpedoes at your portfolio. The bottom line is, you must educate yourself and be prepared. You never know when that education and preparation will really pay off.

ESSENTIAL STEP: DEVELOP AN ACTION PLAN

What if the market crashed tomorrow? Would you be prepared? Play the what-if game. What if Osama Bin Laden were captured? How would your portfolio suffer? What if there is an oil crisis and fuel is unavailable? What will happen on Wall Street and across America? What if equity prices drop by 10 percent? Or, 50 percent? Do you have any plan in place to protect yourself?

The most important thing that you can do to protect yourself from a market meltdown is to be prepared. You must think in advance and develop a strategy. If you are going to execute any of the above trading tactics, you must have the right kind of account, the right trading platform, and the education to know how to use them. Once disaster hits it is too late. Therefore, you must investigate possibilities and opportunities now.

STRATEGIES FOR MANAGING RISK WHILE DAY TRADING

As a trader, I take risks every day. However, I take calculated risks and put the odds on my side. Years ago I traded like a cowboy. I threw caution to the wind and took unnecessary risks, and I lived to regret it. I paid far too little attention to the dangers of the market and spent my time dreaming about the pot of gold that waited for me at the end of the rainbow. I managed to do well for a number of years by using that approach. Then there was October 19, 1987, and my life flipped upside down. All of those great trades that I had made meant nothing. All of those profits that were acquired during the course of many, many trades and several years were gone in a day. I had fearlessly faced the traders of Wall Street and I lost everything because I took an all or nothing approach—and I got nothing.

I realized that if I wanted to continue to trade the global markets, I had to change my style. I had to be smart and avoid unnecessary risk. If I could not or would not do that, I had to give up trading. That sobering reality fundamentally changed the way that I do business. Today I analyze the risk involved in every trade first; only if the risk is acceptable do I consider making the trade. To stay in the day trading game for the long term, do the following:

Protect Your Trading Account

Simply stated, I trade to make money. Just as the profits from the shop down the street provide the proprietor with his income, my trading account and my market skills and acumen bring home the bacon for my family. When I put my hard-earned cash on the line and take a market risk, it is not a game; it is a serious venture. Consequently, I manage my account like any good businessman manages his business's capital. I watch every penny and I am careful to take steps to protect my assets. Otherwise, money that is made on one trade or investment is lost in the next one.

You must keep up with both your profits and your losses. If losses get too great during any week, day, or session, you must stop trading. Something is wrong. One or more of several things is happening: The strategy is not working, the strategy is not being executed properly, or the market is too unpredictable. In any case, wise traders get out of the market and go to the sidelines until they analyze the situation and rectify it.

Worry about Risk First, and Only Then Consider the Rewards

The risk involved in a trade must be your primary concern. Forget about the rewards. If the risk is managed and controlled, the rewards will come. Putting risk management first seems so simple, but it is not. I learned it the hard way. When I consider making a trade I calculate the risk involved. Only if I am able and willing to take the risk, will I make the trade. The markets offer many good trading opportunities; why take bad ones? You must wait and be patient, and winning trades will come.

Calculate the Risk of Every Trade

If you do not know the risk involved in a trade, you should not take it. Therefore, before clicking the mouse, calculate the risk. Here is how I do it. I determine my entry price and my stop/loss placement. The stop/loss placement is the point at which you place a protective stop to pull out of the market if you are wrong. There are several ways to determine stop/loss placement. The first and most inefficient way is arbitrarily. Determine the amount of loss that you are willing to endure and place a stop at that point. For example, on an equity position, if you are only willing to lose $1.00 per share, place a stop-loss order $1.00 below the point of entry. Assuming that the system works correctly, you know the maximum risk to which you are exposed, because when the loss is suffered, the order is executed and the trader is removed from the market. An arbitrary stop is not ideal, but it is better than no protective stop at all.

A better way to determine your true risk is to use key numbers and charts to identify support and resistance levels. *Support* is the point at which prices have difficulty falling below because buyers step in and pull prices upward. *Resistance* is the point at which prices have difficulty rising above because sellers step in and push prices down. If you are selling or shorting the market, a protective stop or stop/loss order should be placed just above resistance. If enough buyers come into the market and the bulls are strong enough to break resistance, you want to be removed from the position, because staying in is just too risky. Likewise, if you are a buyer and long in the market, you want your protective stop or stop/loss order to be just below support. If the bears are strong enough to break support, a further sell-off may be in the cards and a prudent trader does not want to be along for the ride.

Therefore, to calculate the risk involved in a trade, determine the price of entry and establish the point where a protective stop should be placed. What is the price difference in those two points? That is the risk of the trade.

For example, assume you are trading the S&P futures in 2006 and the index is currently trading at 1,258. You want to buy some contracts and are considering a buy at the market. How do you determine the risk involved in the trade? First, in 2006, the S&P futures opened at 1,255. That was a huge key number because the annual opening price of any index or equity is an important number for that product. Therefore, major support should step into the market at, or close to, the 1,255 level. If I was long and the market fell below that level, I knew I might be in big trouble. Therefore, in this example, I put my protective stop at or just below the 1,255. When I make the trade, I know that my exposure is about three points, or $150 for each mini contract that I am trading.

An example of the risk of an equity position can be calculated in a similar manner. For example, if a stock is selling for $57 per share and the yearly high is $60, you know that major resistance will be encountered at the yearly high. Assume that for some reason you want to short the stock— some bad corporate news or some other factor encourages a sell. Therefore, if you short the stock at $56, you know that the ultimate risk is $4 per share. If the yearly open is crossed to the high side, you do not want to be short. If that risk is acceptable, you can take the trade. Otherwise, you should wait for better odds and opportunities.

Use Protective Stops

Never trade without a stop. Develop the habit of putting a protective stop into the market at the same time that you enter a trade. That way, if you are wrong, you do not simply sit in a daze and watch your money go down the drain.

Many traders think that a mental stop is all that is necessary. Nothing could be farther from the truth. Once the trade backfires, traders start rationalizing. "Just give it a few more minutes and prices will shift. I know I'm right about this one." Traders hate to suffer losses and admit defeat. Therefore, many hang on to losers far too long. That is why it is critical that before entering a trade you identify the point where you will exit if things do not go your way. Put a hard stop in the market and do not move it.

Another reason that this is important is that the market is mesmerizing. When you watch it, the ups and downs of the prices are almost hypnotic. It becomes far too easy to watch and wait instead of acting. Before you know it, you are hoping, wishing, and praying that the market will shift and reduce your losses. Avoid this scenario by always using a protective stop.

Manage Every Trade

Any experienced trader knows that the secret to success is managing your money. It only takes one bad trade to take a week, a month, or a year's profit away. When a trade is working and profits are rolling in, anyone can make money. It is the losing trades that separate the real winning traders from the losers, because the way that you manage your losses will determine success or failure.

Keep losses low. That is easy to say and hard to do. One of the ways that I do it is to manage every trade. Years ago I took an all-or-nothing approach. That is, I put all of my eggs in one basket and either all of them were good or all of them were rotten. A lot of gray hairs and experience later, I have changed my approach. Now I trade in multiples and phase out of both my winners and my losers. Here is how I do it.

First, before I enter a trade I identify several points: The entry price, the profit targets, and the protective stop placement. All of these prices are determined by looking at charts and key numbers. For a review of key numbers and how to find them, refer back to Chapter 10.

Generally, I trade in increments of three. That is, I buy or sell 3, 6, 9, 300, or 3,000 shares or contracts of the items that I trade. Then I quickly exit one-third or so of the positions after my first profit target is reach. When my second profit target is hit, I exit another third or so of my positions. In that way I have picked up some quick profits, reduced my overall risk, and pocketed some cash to offset the downside of the positions that I am holding.

If the market is trending, I have the chance to follow the trend and potentially reap some nice profits with my remaining positions. If the market shifts or a major level of support or resistance is hit, I may exit all of the position and take my profits. If the move looks as though it will continue, I can follow it and adjust my stop/loss order to lock in profits and protect myself from major losses. By using this technique, I limit my exposure, reduce my risk, and manage the trade.

What if the trade goes against me and profit targets are not reached? Just as I phase out of profits, I phase out of losses. For example, if I enter a trade and it immediately goes against me and the indicators shift, I start protecting myself. I exit a portion of my positions, maybe as much as half. Then I watch and assess the situation for a few minutes. If further deterioration occurs, I may exit all of my position, even if the stop/loss point has not been reached. If I keep my losses low, I can make them up with another good trade. But, if I allow them to become huge, it will take many trades and maybe many days to recoup excessive losses. Therefore, I manage every trade. I keep my eyes on each one and exit quickly if it is a loser.

Often I make money even when I am wrong. For example, I buy some S&P futures contracts thinking that prices are going to rise several points, but they do not. However, if they rise enough to allow me to reach my first or second profit target, and then turn against me, I quickly exit my remaining positions and still put money in the bank. Managing the trade is the secret.

I never just sit like a bump on a log and watch my money vanish in the wind. I keep my eye on the indicators like the NYSE Tick and the NYSE and Nasdaq advance/decline lines. If the market appears to be shifting and threatening my position, I take necessary action to protect myself and my money.

Guard against Overnight Risk

I trade a lot of futures contracts. Futures markets are a microcosm of other markets. Consider equities and the S&P futures. The Index futures predict where equity prices on the S&P 500 are going. That is, if the S&P Index futures is heading up, there is a good chance that the equities that form the cash index are also moving up. Or, if gold futures are rising or falling, gold prices are probably moving in the same direction. Therefore, by trading the index futures, I am, in essence, able to trade a slice of the equity pie.

I like trading the index futures such as the S&P 500, the Dow, and the Dax. I also trade commodity futures like gold and silver or crude oil. Often, when I tell people that I trade futures, they look at me in disbelief. "That is too dangerous for me," they say. I admit that futures are risky, but so are equities, options, bonds, and every other trading product. Many investors are raised on the buy-and-hold theory. Buy good equities and just hold them forever. That approach is risky, also.

As a young Air Force office, I made my first stock purchase. I bought 100 shares of Eastern Airlines and 100 shares of Pan Am. For those old enough to remember, those companies were highly regarded corporations, and I thought that my chances for making money were excellent. I used the buy-and-hold strategy. Sadly, due to a number of factors, both companies went belly up. I lost everything that I had invested in them. Visitors to my office see the Eastern Airlines certificate hanging on my wall. That is all that it is good for today, a wall decoration. In that particular case, the traditional wisdom did not work for me.

Our world is a dangerous place, and at any time, day or night, something may happen that results in a financial crisis. The brokerage houses understand the risk of the buy-and-hold strategy and express their understanding in their pricing structure. Take, for example, the pricing structure for trading futures. If you do not hold a position overnight, a lower margin is required. But, if the trade is being held for days, the margin required is more than doubled. The level of danger increases as the time span for holding the product is increased, and the brokerage houses understand this.

As a general rule, I do not hold many positions overnight—certainly not futures contracts. If I am trading at night, I buy or sell once the night session has begun. Then, when the day's session comes to a close, I exit my position. If I have some equities that I am carrying for a longer time, I have stops in place and I monitor them closely. Never buy or sell and then forget about it. The market is too potentially dangerous for that approach. If you have a financial manager, ask him or her how your portfolio is protected in case of overnight disaster.

MANAGE THE BUSINESS AND THE MONEY IN A TRADING ACCOUNT

I am a professional trader. The income that I make pays the mortgage and has sent the kids to college. My trading business is my livelihood, and I must manage it just like the proprietor down the street manages his restaurant. That means that I must have a business plan, and I must follow it. Also, I must practice good money management.

If you do not have a business plan for your trading company, you should formulate one now. Essential parts of the plan include the amount of investment involved, time requirements, the inherent risk, the products that you will trade, costs of equipment and training, and profit targets. All of these factors must be evaluated and you should write out the plan for your trading business and follow the plan. You would not open a department store or launch an Internet company without a business plan. Likewise, you should not start a trading business without planning and preparation. Having a plan is just the beginning; following the plan is critical.

Once the business is operating, you must manage your financial resources. That means that with every trade, losses must be limited. It also means that during every trading session the purse strings must be drawn pretty tight. With any single trade, how much are you willing to lose? My rule of thumb is that I never lose more than one-third of the average daily range of a stock or a futures contract during any single trade. For example, at the time of this writing, the average daily range of the S&P futures is about 16 points. Therefore, under no circumstances would I risk more than about 5 points per contract on any trade. In fact, that would be a huge loss for me in that market, and I would probably exit my positions way before that point. But, if you are a big risk taker, at least draw the line when the market moves against you by a third of the daily range.

With a stock, a 10 percent loss is generally the absolute maximum that I will incur. Again, that is a big loss for me, and generally I cut the bleeding sooner than that.

Another strategy that I use is to establish a tilt number or amount that is the most that I will lose in a session or a week. I consider my account balance and my risk tolerance. Then I set my number. For example, say that I set my tilt number at $5,000 loss for any trading session. Some folks may set their tilt number at $1,000 or $500 and others may go far higher than $5,000. Your tilt number is personal. It depends on the depth of your pockets and the fortitude of your stomach. The bottom line is—how much loss will interfere with a good night's sleep? Once that amount is reached during a trade, a trading session, or a week, stop and take a breather. Analyze the market and your approach to it. What is going wrong? What changes need to be made? Take a break for a few days and clear your head. Once you have evaluated and assessed the situation, you can begin trading. However, you should begin slowly and regain your skills.

Remember, the trade of a lifetime can come but if your trading account is empty, you cannot participate. You must guard your trading capital like the Feds guard Fort Knox.

REVIEW

The financial markets are dangerous places. Even on a good day, if you act foolishly, you can lose a lot of money. However, if you manage risk and take steps to protect your assets, you can do so. Some traders are long-term traders and hold their positions over time. Good advice for those traders is to diversify and be a hands-on manager. You should never give total control of your assets to anyone. Always know account balances and performance records. Hold the professionals accountable. Also, use stop/loss order to limit the degree of your exposure in a down market.

Additional strategies that long-term players may wish to consider in case of a market crash or crisis are: purchasing a core position of gold or precious metals, getting prepared to hedge with index futures, or a LEAP, and developing a strategy to execute in case the global financial markets go south.

On a daily or short-term basis, traders must remember to use stop/loss orders with every trade. Never place a trade without simultaneously placing a protective stop that will limit the bleeding if you are mistaken. Worry about risk first and then reward. If you manage risk, the rewards will come. Know the risk in a trade before taking it. If the risk is too great, pass up the trade. Wait for better opportunities. Once in a trade, manage it.

Phase out profits when targets are reached. In that way you put money in the bank and reduce risk. You must never sit idly by and watch your account drain in an "all or nothing" approach. Those who do so will likely get nothing. If a trade is a loser, exit it quickly. Finally, guard against overnight risk. Know that the markets operate 24 hours a day and while you are sleeping, bad things can happen. Therefore, you cannot afford to leave your assets unprotected.

Finally, you must guard and protect your account balance. A trader needs working capital, and that capital is your trading account. Never risk suffering losses that are so great that your business is closed. That means that you must not lose too much on any single trade or during any trading session. You must keep tabs on your money by establishing a tilt number or maximum amount of loss that you can incur. Once that tilt number is hit, you have to shut down the trading platform and walk away. For some reason you are off of your game, and the sooner you realize it and respond appropriately, the better.

Trading is a risky profession. However, if you act prudently and prepare to handle losses when they occur, you can succeed.

 MARKET INSIGHT

To be successful, a trader must manage every trade. Working capital is essential to trading, so a winning trader takes whatever steps are necessary to protect capital and preserve assets.

CHAPTER 12

Consistency, Consistency, Consistency

"When I turn on my computer and see the prices popping, I trade. If I take the time out of my busy day to watch the numbers, I feel obligated to buy or sell something. At least that is the way I used to act. I felt compelled to place an order every time I took a look at the market. Far too often, I ended up losing money in the deal." That was the way one of my students expressed his experience with trading. Intellectually, Reid knew how to be successful. He understood the significance of time, key numbers, and market indicators, but when it came to practicing what he knew, he fell short and often had to pay for the chance to play.

The single most important trait of a successful trader is discipline and control. Most traders have the same problem that Reid had. When they watch the skirmishes on Wall Street, they feel coerced or forced to trade. Like a gigantic vacuum, the market seems to suck the wary trader into the action. If a trade is not made, it seems as though time has been wasted. However, trades executed without proper analysis and without market support are far too often the wrong trades. Over time Reid has learned one important lesson that is saving him money: Don't trade for the sake of trading. Choose your trades with care. As Reid recently expressed it, "The market will always be there. I know that if I do not see a chance for a trade today, I will see one tomorrow. That is the way the market works; it is my responsibility to have the patience and the wisdom to wait for the right set-up."

Consistency is a major problem for almost every trader. When I travel to seminars and financial events, people always tell me that if they were

187

able to even out their trading they could meet their goals. Most folks can make some winning trades, but the novice makes far more losers than winners. Also, most beginners earn a little money from their good trades and lose a great deal of money with their bad ones. That is because they do not exercise good money management, and they do not understand the significance of controlling risk.

One fact is certain: If you execute trades tomorrow just like you executed them today, you will likely get the same result—that is, inconsistent outcomes. Therefore, to improve your trading, you have to develop new strategies and implement them day after day and trade after trade.

This chapter highlights some ideas that have made me more consistent. Remember, strategies must be implemented correctly and unswervingly to achieve the right results.

USE GLOBAL INFORMATION

Traders who engage the bulls and the bears without taking advantage of the knowledge that can be obtained from global financial markets are like NASCAR drivers racing through the course blindfolded. If a racer tries that, the odds are good that he will end up somewhere other than the winner's circle.

Remember that financial markets in New York and Chicago may only be open eight hours a day, but the world's markets are virtually always open. At almost every hour, day or night, traders are actively making deals and stocks, bonds, and other products are changing hands. Trading in Tokyo or Zurich may seem far away, but the market action across the globe affects prices for financial products in the United States. Therefore, gaining information about markets around the world gives traders an edge. When the NYSE or the CME opens, if you have a panoramic view of world sentiment, you are in a better position to analyze and get on the right side of the battle.

The good news is that when the trading pits open in the United States, there is a great deal of global information already available to the knowledgeable trader. Asian trading sessions have ended and Europe has been trading for hours. Use that information. Check the Nikkei, the Hang Seng. Did the session close up or down? What about Europe? Look at the FTSE-100, the CAC-40, the Dax, and the SSMI. If the major indexes in Europe and Asia are all trading above their opening prices, I will hesitate to take a large short position until I see the numbers and the indicators that support it. I will be sure that the data are on my side before I go against the wisdom of the rest of the world.

True, just because prices across the Pacific or Atlantic are up does not mean that U.S. prices will necessarily rise. They may not. However, if a trader is considering a short position and the rest of the world is bullish, it means that a caution flag has been waved and a prudent trader will take heed.

Trading is a highly competitive business. Some of the sharpest tacks in the box are making money in the equity or futures markets. Those who want to succeed need to use every opportunity available to them to be as prepared and knowledgeable as possible. Surgeons would never operate without the right tools; lawyers do not argue cases without reading the law and developing their arguments. Likewise, traders should not put their money at risk before they analyze the market and find support for their positions. The global markets are a significant part of the data that should be included in the analysis of a trade. If occasionally those additional global numbers can keep you from jumping into a losing trade, the time spent reading them has been worthwhile. I believe that by using the Dax, the Nikkei, and the Hang Seng, and other global markets, my trading has become more consistent. Using the 24-hour trading clock gives me a market edge.

> *Use Asian and European trading to get and stay on the right side of the action.*

CONSISTENCY REQUIRES A PLAN

"What is your trading strategy or plan?" That was my question to Brian, a young man who spoke with me about his trading aspirations.

"Strategy? Plan? I guess I don't really have one. I just watch the prices and look for opportunities."

When I saw Brian a month or two later he had lost $30,000 and was out of the trading game. He had hoped to become a professional trader, but the lack of preparation destroyed his dreams. Brian told me that he had made some really good trades. However, all too often those bonanza sessions were followed by days when he lost even more than he had earned on his big winners. He just could not become consistent.

I was not surprised to learn that Brian's trading efforts failed so quickly. It was obvious: He was doomed to fail because he did not prepare to succeed. When I speak with potential traders across the United States, I am amazed that so many of them do not understand that successful trading requires a plan or strategy. Far too many novices believe that they are so intelligent and so savvy that they will intuitively know how to trade. That belief is, of course, ridiculous. All winning traders do not use the same strategy or approach, but all of them use some proven method. Some of the smartest and best-educated people in the world spend their days (and nights) trading. Guessing and hoping are not sufficient when playing their game. Those without a well-formulated approach are fodder for the pros. Flying by the seat of your pants won't cut it. Reacting one way to financial numbers on Monday and another way on Tuesday will definitely result in inconsistent results.

The strategy or plan must be as detailed as possible. How much will you risk? How many shares or contracts will be traded? When will you trade? What will you trade? How will you determine entry, exit, and profit targets? To what extent will you rely on fundamentals? Technicals? All of these questions and others must be answered before you put real money on the line. Any trading strategy should include a plan for when you will trade and how much you will trade.

Trading Times

Decide when you will trade. Day? Night? Only during certain times during the day or on particular days? I trade breakout moves. Therefore, my strategy works best when volume is high and there is enough volatility for me to make money quickly. I know from experience and observation that there are certain times during the day that are better for executing my strategy than other times. For example, during the morning hours between 9:00 AM and 10:15 AM Central Time, my method tends to have greater odds of succeeding. Other optimum times for me are between 1:00 PM and 1:15 PM Central and between 2:15 PM and 2:45 PM Central. Therefore, I limit my market entries during the day's session to these times. If I am already in a trade and have money in the bank, I may hold positions for hours, but I do not execute new orders unless the time is right.

Traders who have no time schedule will not be consistently profitable. They will be in and out of the market throughout the day and their profit and loss numbers will reflect this unpredictable behavior.

Trading Size

How many contracts or shares will be traded? Some traders take on a very large position in some trades and a small position in others. Far too often they choose to load the boat with the losers and travel light with the winners. The fact is that you cannot determine to a certainty whether a trade will work. Therefore, analyze each trade carefully. Only take a trade if you feel confident in the trade. Not all of those will be winners, but at least the analysis has been done and the numbers and data favor the position. If you want to achieve greater consistency, I suggest trading the same number of contracts or shares each time. As you become a better and more consistent trader, you can increase your positions and in that way boost profits.

CONSISTENCY REQUIRES FOLLOWING THE PLAN

"I know it is risky to trade during lunchtime when volume is low, but the numbers looked too good. Everything was pressing higher so I bought some shares. Then the market shifted and I ended up losing a lot of money." At the end of the day, I often speak with students about the trades they have made. If they have suffered losses, they identify the particular trading rule that they have broken and try to rationalize it. Truth is, many times if they had adhered to their own rules the loss would have been minimized or completely avoided.

You should design or select your trading strategy with great care. Then, once you have a proven strategy, follow it. Don't deviate on a whim. When watching the market, the tape goes up and down; it is too easy to become hypnotized by it. If you cannot resist the lure of the market, walk away from it. Sure, sometimes it is possible to take that extra risk and pick up a few bucks, but far too often impulse trades backfire like an old car burping on its gas. If you want to become a consistent trader, you must be disciplined. Trade only when the time and numbers are right. If you cannot observe the market without jumping into it, you should walk away or close your trading platform. Why bother to design a strategy if you are not going to follow it?

Trading because of a whim or out of panic are reflected in two key strategic errors: trying to trade your way out of a loss, and overtrading. When you deviate from your plan and make these errors, you are digging yourself a bigger hole.

Never Try to Trade Out of a Loss

One of the most dangerous times to trade is when you have just suffered a big loss. Then you think, "I want my money back." That becomes the mindset and the focus. Analysis, deliberation, and care go out the window, unnecessary risk is taken, and hasty trades are executed. When you endure a major loss, just walk away. Clear your mind and consider what caused the loss. Under no circumstances should you immediately enter the market and execute another trade in an effort to get your money back.

Remember that when losses are small, you can quickly recoup and move back into the winner's circle. But, if the hole gets deeper and deeper, it soon becomes cavernous. Quickly you can lose so much money that you cannot get it back. Remember that the markets never sleep. They operate day after day and night after night. If a winning trade is not identified now, maybe there will be one tonight or in the morning. No need to rush into anything until the time, the numbers, and the analysis are right. There will always be another winning trade; you just have to wait for it.

Do Not Overtrade

The biggest mistake that most traders make is overtrading. Like Reid, the trader who felt the need to trade every time he looked at the market, many traders believe that the more they trade the more they increase their chances of success. Actually, the reverse is true. The more times you enter the market, the more often you put your financial resources at risk. Therefore, one of the simplest and easiest things that you can do to achieve greater consistency and reduce losses is to trade less. Only trade when the right set-up is present. Do not negotiate. If the set-up is not right—do not trade.

At the most you should place two or three trades in any given day. I have seen days when I placed dozens of trades. Most of those days did not end happily for me. Remember that trading is not free. There is a commission and other costs associated with buying and selling stocks or anything else. Therefore, if you overtrade, you can make some winning trades, but once expenses are deducted there may be no profits. Resist the urge to play for fun. Remember that the name of the game is making money, and the best way to achieve that goal is to limit your trading to the best opportunities.

Do not overtrade.

STAY IN THE COMFORT ZONE

Successful trading involves numbers, not money. That is a hard concept for beginners to grasp. Do not misunderstand the message. Money matters, and you want to keep losses low. However, once a trade has been analyzed and the risk of the trade correctly calculated, you must determine whether you will take the trade or not. If the risk is too great and you cannot or do not want to take it, walk away. If the trade is taken, do not abandon the ship just because the market moves against you and you are down a few pennies. If the numbers still say the trade is right, stick with it until a key number is broken and the market proves that the trade is wrong.

Most trading platforms have a profit/loss box on them. It is easy for beginners to focus on a monetary loss rather than the numbers. Prices bobble up and down and a trade that will be ultimately successful may show a loss for a few minutes. That is the guile of the market. Exit when the market says the play is wrong. Stay focused on the key numbers and the indicators.

Before executing a trade, identify key points like support, resistance, protective stop placement, and profit targets. Then watch those numbers and use them in conjunction with market indicators like the NYSE Tick and the NYSE Advance/Decline line or TRIN to evaluate whether the trade is working. Just because the market bobbles slightly against the trade and a loss appears on the trading platform does not mean that the trade is, indeed, a loser.

I think that the best way to trade the numbers is to stay in your financial comfort zone. Never take risks that you cannot afford. When you do so, your anxiety level rises and your focus is no longer clear. Understand the risks involved in every trade, and once the risk is accepted, give the trade a chance to work. Use the market's numbers and indicators to identify the time to take profits or eject from an impending disaster.

DON'T RISK MORE THAN TWO-THIRDS OF YOUR WINNINGS IN THE AFTERNOON

Many traders make money in the morning and give it back in the afternoon. There is one simple way to prevent this from happening. Do not risk more than two-thirds of the morning's profits after 12:00 PM. Draw a line in the sand and do not cross it. If morning trades tend to be more successful than afternoon trades, perhaps you should close the trading platform around noon and take your profits to the bank. Remember that you never *have* to

trade. Every time a trade is made, money is put at risk. Even when you analyze carefully and check and double-check all of the charts and numbers,
you may still be wrong. Therefore, if you have earned a nice profit in the
morning, keep it. If you continue to trade, you should never risk more than
two-thirds of those hard-earned dollars after lunch.

DISCARD BIAS

"Will the S&P trade up or down today?" I stand in front of the class and eye-
ball my students waiting for an answer. A few brave souls venture a guess.
That, of course, is the problem. In fact, when New York opens, no one knows
what will happen. Each day when trading begins in the pits, the air is heavy
with anticipation—the bulls expect a rally and the bears look for a sell-off.
Because traders carefully watch the market, it is just natural that they have
a bullish or a bearish bias. Nevertheless, as all traders must admit, your
market prediction is often incorrect; no one can accurately foretell how
Wall Street will behave. Therefore, to increase your chances of being consistently profitable, you must disregard your opinion and keep bias in
check. The numbers will tell the story and lead the way.

To trade successfully, you need to have an accurate long-term,
intermediate-term, and short-term picture of the market in your mind at all
times. Then, you compare your bias or opinion with the real numbers and
determine whether the numbers support or refute your bias. In this way,
you can better determine the true trend and stay on the right side of it. To
get a long-term view, begin by taking one simple step—record the yearly
opening price for every stock, index, commodity, or trading vehicle that
may be traded during the year. Refer to it constantly. As the days, weeks,
and months pass, it is important to know whether the price is above or
below the yearly open.

For example, in 2006, the S&P futures opened at 1,255.50. Throughout
the year as the index traded above that price, 1,255 was a key level of support; as it traded below it, the 1,255 price point became a critical level of
resistance. When I saw the market below its opening price, I understood
that the long-term picture supported more of a bearish sentiment; the farther below the opening price, the more bearish the view. The opposite was
also correct. That is, above 1,255, I knew the bulls were winning the yearly
battle, and the level above 1,255 indicated the degree of strength that they
possessed.

After looking at the big picture, focus on the intermediate view. Record
the monthly opening prices for the securities or derivatives that you are
trading. Note how the market is trading from month to month. Use the

monthly opening prices to create a trend line that will graphically depict the true bias of the market. Is the monthly open above or below the yearly open? Is this month's open above or below last month's open? Are the bulls or the bears winning the game on an intermediate basis?

Finally, focus on the short-term picture by considering the day's opening price in the context of the long-term and intermediate-term view. When the market opened today, was the price above or below the yearly opening price? Was it below or above the monthly opening price? Compare it to yesterday's open and the weekly open. How about the rest of the world? How did Asia and Europe trade last night? What was the global sentiment? In this way, you always have a snapshot of the market's action in mind and a gauge with which to measure current market activity.

This is the bottom line: You cannot trade on the basis of your opinion or your bias. To win the trading game, you have to trade the numbers. When prices are below the monthly open and below the yearly open, the bears are flexing their muscles and buyers better beware. The reverse is also true. Furthermore, it does not matter what you think about market direction; it is what you do that counts. You must not pull the trigger until the numbers support your play. If the long-term, intermediate-term, and short-term picture are bullish and you are a bear, get out of the cave and survey the landscape, because it may be time to grow some horns. Likewise, if the numbers are negative, going short may be the way to play.

It is okay to have an opinion. However, when it comes to trading, trade the numbers and not the opinion. Having a market bias is just part of being a trader. However, to be a consistently good trader let the numbers and the indicators lead the way.

GET EMOTIONAL BALANCE

Emotional control can make or break your trading. Many traders mistakenly believe that all they need to succeed is a cognitive breakthrough—the discovery of some numerical relationship or more reliable statistical indicator that will push their trading over the top. Like knights in search of the Holy Grail, they study charts, numbers, and patterns. Yet for many, that quest is just not enough.

As an experienced trader with almost three decades of trading under my belt, I believe that the reason many traders fail is simple: They are not emotionally prepared to win. Technically they know how to trade, but emotionally, they are unable to succeed. In other words, their lack of emotional control undermines their trading and guarantees their failure. The psychological aspects of trading are tremendous. One resource that has been helpful to me is an old classic by Napoleon Hill, *Think and Grow Rich*. I enjoy listening to the tapes and I think they help me stay in a positive frame of mind.

Do not misunderstand my message. It is important to comprehend the structure of the market and have a successful trading strategy. Obviously, if you have no knowledge of the marketplace and no trading method, your chances of success are slim to none. A prerequisite to success is knowledge and skill. However, the most knowledgeable market guru cannot win unless he is able to hold his emotions in check.

Trading is emotionally charged. Greed and fear are powerful. If not controlled, they will defeat the greatest intellect. Therefore, you must keep emotions balanced so that the intellect is able to play the game successfully. Here are a few simple strategies to help keep emotions in check and increase your odds of success:

Strategy One: Set Realistic Goals

Don't get greedy. During the process of teaching students to trade, I have the opportunity to speak with many aspiring traders. The vast majority of beginners expect the market to make them rich quick. Even some novices think that they will make thousands of dollars a day! Such unrealistic expectations ensure failure. If you expect a fortune from every trade, your focus is on profit at all costs. Regardless of your skill level, this is a formula for disaster. Set realistic goals for your trading that are based on your skill and level of experience.

Strategy Two: Relish Small Gains

The trading game is played by some of the smartest and savviest minds in the world. Therefore, making even a modest profit is no small feat. Remember that consistent small profits quickly add up. For example, if you average a profit of just $50 per day, in 52 weeks you have earned $13,000. As skills grow, so should daily and yearly profit totals.

To keep focused on consistently profitable trading, use a calendar and record daily trading outcomes. At my trading school, DTI, students strive to stay in "Green Circle Country." Each day we mark our calendar. If we are profitable, the calendar gets a green circle. If we have suffered a loss, the day is filled with a red circle. Sometimes we do not trade, and that is noted with a yellow circle. Our goal is to cover our calendar with many green circles. Note that even a single dollar of success merits a green circle. In this way, our focus is not on a "get rich quick" scheme, but rather, on consistently profitable trading that will pay off big in the long run.

Greed is put in perspective as the focus is placed on trading for the long term. Students take great pride in a calendar filled with green circles.

Strategy Number Three: Respect Risk

Trading is risky. Therefore, in every trade the major focus must be risk control. With every trade it is essential that you know your maximum exposure. What are the risks involved with the trade? If the risks are too great, don't take the trade.

Before clicking the mouse, identify three critical points: the point of entry, the profit target, and the emergency exit point (the point at which you know you are wrong). In this way, you know the risks you face, and some of the fear is reduced. Remember that if you consider risk first, the profits will come. When a trade is too fearful and the potential loss is too great, step away from the trade. There is generally a close correlation between risk and reward. To make a huge profit on each trade, you must assume a huge risk—a risk that you probably should not take.

Strategy Number Four: Accept Loss Gracefully

You will make losing trades. That is a fact. Even the best traders lose money sometimes. No one likes to lose. In fact, the process is painful. However, you must learn to deal with it. Understand that during the course of a trading career, you will make thousands of trades. Put the loss in perspective— the losing trade is just one loser among thousands of winners. Refuse to be defeated by a losing trade or a losing week. Move on with greater determination. The markets will be there tomorrow.

Strategy Number Five: Learn from Mistakes

Turn your lemons into lemonade. When you suffer a loss, analyze it and benefit from it. What went wrong? Was there a fundamental mistake in analysis? Was there an execution error? Maybe timing was off, or some other factor was not adequately considered. Work to identify the error and avoid it in the future.

One simple way to learn from your daily trading experiences is to record them. Keep a trading diary and write down every trade. Then study the trades and learn from them. Analyze the good as well as the bad. If a profit was made, could even more have been made? If a loss was suffered, how could the loss have been avoided? Take each trade in stride with one goal in mind: to become a better trader.

The psychological and emotional aspects of trading cannot be over-
stated. If greed is allowed to run wild or fear gains the upper hand, the
trader will be the ultimate loser. You cannot be a consistent trader until
you control your emotions.

> *Emotional balance is critical to successful trading.*

REVIEW

Gaining consistency with your trading is a challenge that most traders deal
with on a daily basis. Over the course of many years of trading I have developed some techniques and strategies that help me stay more balanced and
more profitable. First, I use global information to help me analyze the markets and decide whether to be long, short, or out. When my day begins, I
check major indexes in Asia and Europe to determine market sentiment
across the Atlantic and the Pacific. Did the rest of the world express a
strong opinion of the world's financial direction? If so, I consider that view
and take it into account when making my trading decisions. Doing so gives
me vital information and helps me stay out of losing trades.

You cannot be a consistent trader unless you have a plan or strategy.
There are different ways to trade and a variety of trading vehicles. Everyone
does not have the same plan. However, every winning trader follows a plan.
Before launching a trading career, you must determine what you will trade,
when you will trade, how much you will risk, how much you will invest in
your trading business, and a number of other issues. Once the plan is
developed, it must be tested. If it is a proven strategy, it must be executed
consistently. You cannot use one plan on Monday and another on Tuesday.
Obviously, doing so will yield inconsistent results.

Trading involves losing. Sometimes every trader makes mistakes or
suffers loss due to the markets' wrath. Learn to accept loss gracefully and
never try to trade yourself out of a hole. If you are not careful, you will
dig the hole deeper and become entrapped in it. The market will be there
tomorrow and next week. Wait for a clear head and a winning set-up before
more money is put at risk.

Never overtrade. Every time a trade is executed, there is a chance of loss. Select your trades carefully and only take those trades that favor victory. Two or three trades a day should be your maximum.

Stay in your financial comfort zone. Do not risk money that you cannot afford to lose. Doing so is a sure way to end your trading career. If you are too focused on every dollar, you cannot keep your eye on the ball and remain consistent.

Psychological factors play a huge role in trading. You cannot trade successfully if you do not have emotional balance. Every trader knows the fear/greed dilemma. Making money is the name of the game, but getting greedy leads to disaster. Therefore, a few strategies can help you stay on the high road: Set realistic goals, relish small gains, respect risk, accept loss gracefully, and learn from your mistakes. In that way, you can keep both fear and greed in check and be more consistent.

MARKET INSIGHT

If inconsistent traders use the same strategies and approaches tomorrow that they used today, they will get the same results—inconsistent profits. To become more consistent, analyze every aspect of your trading, locate problems, and fix them.

CHAPTER 13

Preparing for the Trading Day

A neat row of silver surgical tools sits atop a small metal table on the right side of the bed. Nurses scurry around the operating room to complete final preparations for the medical procedure that is scheduled to begin momentarily. Suddenly the door swings open and Dr. Bishop steps into the room. He immediately takes his position beside the ailing patient and calls for the scalpel.

"Sir, with all due respect, the patient was involved in a horrible auto accident, and he is not yet prepped for surgery. Also, we have done some essential preliminary tests and do not yet have the information we need to begin. We must have more data before we start the surgical procedure."

"I don't need that information. I came to operate. Let's get this show on the road. All of that other stuff would just confuse me."

Not a doctor one wants to handle his critical care needs.

When a defendant faces the death penalty, he does not want his lawyer to casually step into the courtroom unprepared for the case. He wants an advocate who knows the facts and the law and is ready to argue them for the benefit of the client. If the attorney intends to have even a fighting chance, he or she must have spent many long hours getting ready for the courtroom appearance.

When preparing the tax filings for a blue-chip corporation, a CPA knows the tax codes and has identified the pertinent sections. The accountant has studied the financial records of the business and gathered the necessary corporate documentation to support the client's deductions. To take advantage of every legal opportunity to save money, the savvy CPA does the research and crunches the numbers.

Trading is no different from any other profession. Those who are successful are trained and prepared every day. "If I had eight hours to chop down a tree, I'd spend six hours sharpening my ax." That is reputed to be Abraham Lincoln's view of preparation for a task. As a trader, one must also understand and respect the degree of preparation that is required. Before I trade, I analyze market data and get ready to win. Those who do not do the hard job of analysis before placing their trades will pay for their laziness, because the market will gladly and easily take their money.

Every day I go through the same routine. In the following pages I explain the steps I take to get ready for the battles between the bulls and the bears.

STEP 1: CHECK FOR GLOBAL NEWS

Nothing can torpedo a winning trade faster than the release of a news report. I remember numerous times when I was in a winning trade, news would break, the market would react, and my trade would go down the tubes. Sometimes I was only seconds from getting paid, but I never saw those profits because some news story spooked traders. Financial markets respond to news. The difficult part of the scenario is predicting how they will respond. Sometimes news may seem good, but if the markets anticipated better numbers, prices will probably fall. Or, data may appear on the surface to be very negative, but if the markets are prepared for it to be even worse, the markets will rally. There is no way to determine what the response will be. However, one thing is certain, if the news is significant enough, there will be a reaction, and it will happen very quickly.

In addition to the DTI web site (www.dtitrader.com), I have two favorite sites that contain news calendars: *Barron's* at www.Barrons.com and *DailyFx.com* at www.dailyfx.com. The second is a site for currency trading, but it has an economic calendar that can be used for trading all markets.

Never trade without knowing the times when news reports are scheduled to be released. That should become habit for any trader, and it is an elementary step to get ready for the day. I check for news because I do not want to be sabotaged by it. I exit my positions prior to the scheduled news release.

There are two types of news: breaking news and scheduled news. If a bomb goes off in New York, or a diplomat is killed in Asia, there is no warning. You cannot prepare for such an unexpected and random event. The only way to safeguard your assets from such occurrences is by using protective stops. Always have a stop in place to remove you from the market if prices move sharply against you.

In addition to unexpected news events, there are many regularly scheduled reports that are released by educational facilities and governmental agencies. Therefore, the first thing I want to know before I begin trading is what news is scheduled to be released, and when the release will take place. I rely on *Barron's* for most of my domestic news and *DailyFx* for international news.

There are dozens of reports released each month. Remember that financial reports and news are common to all developed nations. There is a central bank in Germany and in Japan. Also, the same economic data that are gathered in the United States are also gathered in other nations around the globe. Therefore, if you are trading in foreign markets or are anticipating making a big play in the United States when foreign markets are trading, it is wise to check the international news and be prepared. If the story is big enough, repercussions may be felt on our shores.

Sometimes the market will react violently to a particular news release and a month or two later, there will be no response to similar news. It just depends on the economic situation and the importance that traders place on that particular report under those specific economic circumstances. I consider these five domestic reports to generally be market movers (remember to check world news when you are trading international markets):

1. Releases from the Federal Reserve
2. Consumer Price Index (CPI)
3. Gross Domestic Product (GDP)
4. Producer Price Index (PPI)
5. Consumer sentiment gauges: Michigan Consumer Sentiment Index (MCSI) and the Consumer Confidence Index (CCI)

Announcements or News Released by the Federal Reserve

If the chairman of the Federal Reserve or a member of the board of governors issues a statement or a report, be careful. The financial markets will probably respond irrationally. The Federal Open Market Committee (FOMC) sets interest rates. During each of its regularly scheduled meetings, traders around the globe sit in front of their computer screens with hands on their mouses ready to react to any rate changes. In fact, there will likely be some significant market response even if there is no change. That is how important interest rates are for the global economy.

Generally, when the FOMC issues its report, stock prices move franticly—jumping up and down wildly. There is no way to predict the direction the market will take when the news breaks. The site of the Federal Reserve is http://federalreserve.gov/.

The interest rate set by the Federal Reserve is one of the most important benchmarks for our economy. If the rate is too low, inflation may run rampant—but if it is too high, the increased interest may siphon out too much cash from the economy and halt growth or usher in recession. The FOMC holds eight formal meetings each year.

If you are a novice, I strongly suggest that you stay out of the market when the Fed is reporting. As noted, the market can move very quickly and be extremely volatile during these times. If you are on the wrong side of the move, you will pay a heavy price. If you do not exit your positions before the FOMC reports, be certain that you have a firm stop in place for your protection. If you decide to trade the news, wait for the initial shock to hit the markets and give prices a few minutes to settle down. I confess that I generally trade this news, but remember that I have a couple of decades of experience. My best advice for a novice is to stay clear of it; watch and learn.

The Consumer Price Index (CPI)

Generally viewed as the most significant gauge of core inflation, the CPI has the power to move markets. The Department of Labor releases the report each month. The numbers are based on prices for a specific basket of goods and services. As prices change from month to month, those prices are noted and reported. The goods and services are purchased in urban metropolitan areas and the basket always contains the same items. By constantly tracking these essential products and services, economists are able to make generalizations about the overall economic outlook.

The Department of Labor releases the CPI around the middle of each month. The release dates should be available on the Web site for the U.S. Department of Labor, Bureau of Labor Statistics at http://www.bls.gov/cpi/. However, the release dates are sometimes changed. Therefore, check with *Barron's* or some other source to determine the exact date of the CPI each month. This is an important economic release, and you need to be prepared.

Gross Domestic Product (GDP)

This is another big news release for the markets because traders and economists generally deem it to be the best gauge of the general health of our economy. If the economy is growing, one expects the GDP to reflect that growth. The reverse is also true. If the economy is stagnant, the GDP will tell the story. The GDP is compiled and reported by the Bureau of Economic Analysis of the U.S. Department of Commerce. It measures the total output of goods and services produced by labor and materials located in the United States and provides a broad and comprehensive picture of supply and demand. For additional information about this report see www.bea.gov.

The Producer Price Index (PPI)

Like the CPI, the Producer Price Index (PPI) tracks price changes over time for a specific set of goods and services. However, there are some significant differences between the two indexes. The CPI gauges consumer prices and the PPI gauges producer prices. There are thousands of PPIs. Every industry within the U.S. economy has a PPI. All of these individual indexes are weighed and reflected in one big PPI that is released by the Department of Labor monthly.

One of the major uses of the PPI is as an early warning economic indicator. The PPI captures changes before they appear in the retail sector. The PPI foreshadows price changes. This information is used for many things, but one of its major uses is by the Federal Reserve in determining fiscal and monetary policy.

Like the CPI, the PPI is released on various dates, but is usually released sometime in the middle of the month. Also like the CPI, depending on the particular circumstances, the PPI may have a significant impact on the market. Know when it is being released and be prepared.

Michigan Consumer Sentiment Index (MCSI) and the Consumer Confidence Index (CCI)

Each month the University of Michigan conducts a survey to determine how consumers feel about the economy. Specifically, it is designed to determine how consumers feel about spending. Are they buying cars, houses, clothes, and other goods and services, or are they holding tightly to their purse strings? Five thousand households are surveyed each month, and the final survey results for the prior month are released on the first business day of each month. A preliminary report is released on the tenth of each month, except for weekends.

The MCSI is a lagging indicator—that is, it is responding to how the economy has already changed. Nevertheless, it can be very important because it can confirm an economic pattern. Are consumers continuing to spend month after month? Or are there signs of a recession and a pull back in consumer spending? Manufacturers, retailers, banks, and governmental agencies and entities may make financial decisions based on this indicator. If consumers are slowing their spending, businesses may decide to freeze hiring or reduce personnel. They may reduce inventories or slow production. The reverse may also be true. If the numbers are strong, businesses may choose to expand. They may invest more in production and personnel in order to meet consumer expectations.

Another measure of consumer confidence is the Consumer Confidence Index (CCI). These data are collected and released by the Consumer Confidence Board. Like the Michigan report, it is just a survey. There are no data collected on actual spending. Consumers are surveyed about their plans to spend or not to spend.

These are only a few of the important economic news releases that are published each month. In addition, there are reports on construction, housing, employment, fuel, and other aspects of our economy. Knowing about these reports and being aware of when they are released is vital to good trading. My rule of thumb is that I am out of my positions prior to the new release. It usually takes the markets several minutes to digest the information and respond. Only after the data have been digested will I reenter the market. Otherwise, it is too easy to be misled and fall for a false play.

> *Always check for scheduled news releases before trading.*

STEP 2: GET ALL SYSTEMS UP AND GOING

Technology is a wonderful thing, but when it does not work correctly it can be more than a headache. I get to the office early enough to be sure that my trading systems are working correctly. Each day I check my analytical systems. In particular, I open and view my RoadMap software. I will rely on it for my trading data and charts, and it must be operating correctly. Am I receiving data from my data feed provider? Do all of these systems seem to be functioning correctly? I also use a stock program, *The Stock Box*, and

I check to be certain that it is ready to go. Then I open my trading platform. When I am ready to place a trade, the equipment must be going and running correctly.

I have learned from experience that if I am having a technical problem, I need to stay out of the market. It is hard enough to trade when things are working correctly. It is impossible when there are technical issues that cause distractions and anxiety.

STEP 3: GET A GENERAL SENSE OF THE MARKETS SENTIMENT

Scan the night action and get a sense of what the markets have been doing. How did Asia and Europe trade during their sessions? If Asia and Europe experienced a move of 1 percent or greater during their trading, it may be an early warning signal that a trending market is developing. The move may be up or down. The direction does not matter, but the agreement between both Asia and Europe and the degree of the move in major indexes across the world is the significant factor.

STEP 4: GATHER DATA FROM SEVEN MAJOR MARKETS

Because my trading method relies heavily on key numbers, I identify the numbers or price points that I believe will be important within the day's likely trading range of the products that I intend to trade. I always look at the S&P 500 futures, Nasdaq, Dow, Dax, crude oil, gold, and bonds.

I review the yearly open and the monthly opens. I keep ongoing trend lines that allow me to see the data at a glance. In relation to these yearly and monthly prices, is the particular market bearish or bullish? This gives me a big picture view of the action. Then I look at the weekly data. Where did the gold or crude trade this week? In relation to the big picture, where are we trading today? Now I focus on the short term. What were the high and the low of yesterday's trading? What were the high and low during the night session? Having this information helps me identify support and resistance. What are the pivot points that are important in each market? If I go long, I will do so once resistance has been broken. If I go short I will wait for support to be passed.

In light of this information, I plan my trading strategy. I identify the items that I plan to trade. Then I focus on the places that I will consider going long and the areas where I will go short. At the time the numbers are hit, I look at the indicators and the time of day and decide whether I will take that particular trade.

STEP 5: THINK POSITIVELY

Psychology plays a huge role in trading. I believe that most people do not understand how significant it is. Therefore, each day before I begin, I try to get my brain thinking positively. I read an uplifting quote or consider something that has positively impacted me. *Investors Business Daily* usually has some positive news or stories of success, and I read one of them, or I scan a passage from a favorite book or read an inspiring quote. For a special thought each day, you may want to visit dtitrader.com.

After reading some uplifting words, I think on them for a minute and get in a money-making frame of mind. Now I'm like Jonathan Livingstone Seagull—I'm flying.

STEP 6: CLEAR MY HEAD

Finally, after all systems are up and running and are checked, after the numbers are gathered and the markets analyzed, after I have tried to raise my thought process above the hum-drum of daily life, I get up and walk around. I clear my head and think about how beautiful the day is or how much I enjoyed last night's dinner.

Now I am ready to wage war with the bulls or the bears.

REVIEW

Successful trading is not a random process. Like every profession, trading requires training and planning. Traders have to be prepared for each day so that they can maximize the opportunities offered by the markets. Before I execute any trade, I do the following things:

1. Check for news
2. Get systems up and running

3. Survey the Global Markets

4. Gather Numerical Data and Plan My Trades

5. Think Inspiring Thoughts

6. Clear My Head so I Can Think Positively

Winners do not fly by the seat of their pants. They plan and prepare to win!

MARKET INSIGHT

When the battle begins, be ready!

CHAPTER 14

Mind over Matter

Breaking through the Psychological Barriers

66 I f you think you can, you can and if you think you can't, you're right."
Henry Ford understood the psychological power of believing in
yourself and your pursuits. I am convinced that a huge part of winning at the trading game is psychological. Over the years I have grown to respect the role of attitude and balance in trading. If your mind is not in the right place, you can be expertly trained and analytically sharp, but you will somehow manage to sabotage your efforts and you will ultimately lose. Winners are psychologically ready to accept success. Here are some of the most powerful psychological aspects of trading. I believe that if you unleash your potential, you can win.

FIND THE MIDDLE GROUND

Years ago in college, I remember reading Greek mythology. I recall wondrous stories of adventure, courage, exploration, and searching. In my memory, one principle stands out from these many great tales, and it has served to guide my life in business and most especially in trading. It is the Greek word *sophrosene*, or "balance." As the wise Greek writers knew, in all human endeavors, true success is attained when one learns to stay in balance.

Learning this lesson is, in my judgment, the first critical step to becoming a successful trader. It is key to overcoming a natural obstacle all traders face. I call it the "greed/fear syndrome" or the "going to the moon/going below ground" tendency. Greed is a natural human emotion. People want as much money as they can get, and they want to maximize each trade. But for traders, greed can be toxic. They get in a trade and things start going their way. The trade is working and paying. Once they are making money, however, they see no reason to get out of the market. Suddenly, they are shooting for the moon. Greed blinds them, and the next thing they know, the market reverses, and instead of making money, they are down. Winning trades can turn quickly into losing ones. Traders must learn when to exit.

Greed's opposite may also consume traders: fear. Once in the market, the realization grips traders that they really aren't certain about the direction that prices will take. They sense loss and ponder the effects of parting with their capital. Losing money is painful, and everyone wants to avoid it. They begin thinking that maybe the risk is too great and perhaps they should exit the trade now before the loss becomes a reality. They convince themselves that the trade probably isn't going to work. A quick click of the computer mouse and they are safe, but without the profits to which they are entitled. A few minutes of indecision for the market and the trade pays— or it would have paid, had the fearful trader not bailed. Remember the old adage about ships: A ship sitting in a harbor may be safe, but ships are made to sail, not to float uselessly in the safety of a port. Traders have to be in the market to make money trading.

In addition to causing traders to exit winning trades too early, fear also leads to indecision and paralysis. When fear takes control, trades never look good enough. The risk is always too great. The fear of losing money prevents them from taking advantage of winning opportunities. If traders overthink every trade and wait for the perfect opportunity where profits will be guaranteed, they will never trade.

Both greed and fear, in the extreme, destroy beginners. Yet, both are completely natural. The key to overcoming these two potentially destructive emotions is to keep them both under control. Balance fear and greed. Understand that trading is not all wins with no losses. Trading involves bad trades and losing days. Aspire for success but know that there will be failures. Remember that pigs get fat but hogs get slaughtered. And, remember, too, that he who hesitates is lost.

Learning how to balance these two natural and highly dangerous human emotions is among the most important lessons that I teach my students. Indeed, its importance to my own trading is one of the reasons that I started DTI. I find that by teaching others, I constantly force myself to remember what I know to be true, but what all traders find so hard to master—the art of balance, overcoming fear but avoiding greed. I learn from my mistakes and from my successes, and if you aspire to become a better trader, you must also do so.

One of the strategies that I use to help me balance fear and greed is to trade multiples so that I am able to concede part of my trade to fear and hold part for greed. For example, if I am trading a stock, I generally buy or sell 3,000 shares. I select my entry point very carefully and I also enter at a time when I know prices will likely be volatile and the market liquid. If I have chosen the right entry point at the right time, prices will move my way rapidly. Then, I exit at least one-third of my positions with profit. That is my concession to fear. I have lightened my load and put some profits on my side to offset any potential losses. Then, as prices continue to move my way, I soon exit another one-third of my positions. Now I have enough profits to safeguard my trade. I am trading with the market's money. I move my protective stop at or near my break-even point and ride the remaining positions for additional profits. This is my concession to greed.

Experience has taught me that if I take an all-or-nothing approach, too often I will get nothing. Therefore, I phase out of positions and do not allow either fear or greed to control me. In this way I am able to stay focused, concentrate on the numbers, and make more money.

STAY POSITIVE

The glass is half full; I focus on seeing it that way. I avoid pessimists and pessimistic thinking. I am certain that a negative attitude will destroy my trading, and I stay away from those who choose to see the world in gloomy terms. I experienced first hand the power of a negative thinking when I suffered a major financial reversal in 1987.

Because I did not consider the risk of the market, I was holding a very large long options position when the market crashed on October 19, 1987. Following the crash, I was totally broke. And, it wasn't only my bank account that had a negative balance; my faith in my abilities was destroyed. After the crash I continued to trade, but with little success. Each day when the market opened, I expected to lose money, and I lost it. I worked very hard. I analyzed market data extremely carefully, I read everything that I could find about the markets, but nothing helped. Now I realize that the problem was not the analysis or even the execution; the problem was imbedded in my brain. It was my attitude of failure. Like Henry Ford said, I thought I could not succeed and I was right. When I placed each trade, I did so with a negative attitude and an expectation of a financial loss. My poor attitude and my belief that I could not succeed were self-fulfilling prophecies. Day after day, I ended up empty handed.

It took years for me to emerge from that dark cloud, but finally I did it. Now I understand the power of attitude and the role that psychological factors play in trading. If you want to make money in the financial markets, you have to get your mind in the right space and you have to be willing and able to embrace success.

THE MARKET PAYS WHAT YOU THINK YOU ARE WORTH

Assume that a job applicant reports for an interview. He wants the position badly, and he is highly qualified for it. He could be a great employee and an asset to the firm. However, he does not have faith in his abilities and fears that he cannot do the job well. Therefore, he constantly downplays his skills and verbally exhibits his insecurity and lack of faith in himself.

The CEO explains the significance of the position, "This job is very important to the firm. We need someone who understands marketing and is able to identify and implement strategies to move our company forward."

The applicant has done well in all academic pursuits and has many ideas about how to overcome the challenges faced by the company. Yet, he expresses fear and doubt.

"I guess I could do it. I mean...I did well in school. This company is so big and it is different than anything I studied, though. But, I think I could do it." The tone in his voice captures his doubts.

"If you are hired for the position, what are your salary requirements?"

"I have so much to learn that I am not expecting top dollar. I just really want a chance to get some experience and join a good firm. My salary requirements are negotiable."

This guy is not going to get the job at any price because he lacks faith in himself. He thinks he is worth nothing, and with his attitude he is probably right.

Many traders are like the applicant. They have studied the markets and know how to trade. Yet they question their abilities and their value. They do not believe that they rate as traders. They expect to earn very little and they get paid what they expect.

Each day you approach the markets you should anticipate financial rewards. That does not mean that you have unrealistic expectations. Keep expectations in line with your skills. But, never expect to lose. Expect to win and prepare to do so. Remember that the market will pay what you think you are worth.

VISUALIZE SUCCESS

What does success look like? One needs to consider a winning trade. How do prices move? What do the indicators show? How are the charts forming? Think about every aspect of the trade and see it. Mentally take profits and relish them. Visualizing success is very important. It helps to believe in yourself and your abilities. It also helps to identify money-making opportunities when they are available. When the indicators point the way and the numbers support a trade, you will be ready. I suggest that beginning traders spend time on a regular basis picturing themselves as winners and visualizing winning traders. In fact, it probably is a good practice for experienced traders as well. Not only will it improve your trading, but it will also lift your spirits and attitude.

ACCEPT LOSSES GRACEFULLY

Every trader has losses. In fact, if you are always right, you are probably not taking enough risk. No one has a crystal ball, and no one can predict with certainty the direction of the markets. Traders must analyze each situation as best they can and then act on the basis of the analysis. Sometimes you will be right and sometimes you will be wrong. The trick is to maximize profits when you are right and minimize losses when you have made a mistake.

One of the most dangerous times for most traders to get into the market is after they have suffered a financial loss. Their mind is focusing on the loss and not on the current market action. Also, their goal is not to get a good trade but to get their money back. This leads them to take trades that are far too risky and dangerous. Remember that the markets never sleep. They will be open tonight, tomorrow, and next week. If there is not a good opportunity right now, there will be one later. It may be in a day or two, but a good trade will come. Be patient and wait for it. You can make more money, but maybe not in the next hour, or even the next day or week.

Accepting loss is hard; no one likes to do it. But, if you intend to trade for the long term, you must understand and accept the reality that losing is a part of trading.

BALANCE CONFIDENCE AND HUMILITY

Having faith in your abilities is good, but stubbornly refusing to accept your errors is deadly. You must manage your ego. If the indicators and the numbers say that you are wrong, accept the fact that you have made a mistake and exit your position. Prior to entering a trade, you should have carefully analyzed it. But things change, and sometimes they change quickly. The financial markets have the ability to shift in a heartbeat. One minute the scene is bullish and the next minute it is bearish. Every trader has seen dramatic changes in market sentiment over very short periods of time. Therefore, pay attention. Constantly read the indicators. If the picture changes and the trade is no longer a winning one, get out. Never sit and hold a loser. You might want prices to go higher, but the market does not care what you want. Being stubborn and refusing to accept the fact that you were wrong will not change the situation. All that will happen is that you will lose a lot of money. Therefore, be stubborn about something else, but not the markets. Temper confidence with humility and understand that even the world's best traders are sometimes wrong.

KEEP THINGS IN PERSPECTIVE

The last trade was a loser. So what? If you are a trader, each trade is just one of thousands of trades that will be made. One trade does not define a career or even a month or week of trading. Use each trade—the winners and the losers—as learning tools. I suggest that traders keep a diary or trading journal. At the end of each trading day, sit down and record the trades that you made. Write down the reasons for the trade and all of the details that you can remember. What did the indicators say? What time was the trade taken? Was the trade a good one or a loser? How much money was made or lost?

If the trade was successful, identify the elements that made it so. What were the triggers that contributed to the play? How could you have made even more money? Did you take profits too early or trade too few shares or contracts? How can you respond in the future to do even better?

If the trade was a loser, why was it? Did you misread indicators? Did news break and destroy the trade? Was the time wrong? Was the size of your positions too great? Analyze each trade carefully and work to identify the problem areas. Then use that information to improve. Do not waste time regretting your losses. That will not recoup one single dime. Learn from both losses and successes, and that will make you a better trader.

I believe that if you keep a journal you will force yourself to review your trading habits and work to improve them. Not only will you learn from each trade, but you will also hold yourself accountable—and that is a big part of trading.

TAKE RESPONSIBILITY

"I took the trade because a friend gave me a tip."

"I knew it was a bad trade, but the analyst on television was really bullish on that stock. He is an expert, and he should know what he is doing. I decided to go for it. He gave me a bum steer, and that loss was really his."

"I was going to sell my shares, but my broker said that everything was okay."

Over the years I have heard every excuse in the book for losing money in the financial markets. The bottom line is that each individual is responsible for the financial decisions that he or she makes. If you choose to take a tip from a friend or even an expert, the decision is your own and you have to live with the result.

The only way to become a better trader is to take personal responsibility. Own your trades. Then work to make them better. Listen to the advice that others give; if it seems good, you might want to take it. If not, politely let it go. Always remember who owns the money and the account, and constantly work to protect your investments.

REVIEW

Psychological factors play a huge role in trading. One of the most difficult challenges faced by traders is balancing fear and greed. Fear paralyzes you and keeps you from taking good trades. Fear may also lead you to exit winning trades prematurely just because you are down a tiny bit on the trade. On the other hand, greed leads you to stay with trades too long. A winning trade may turn into a loser if the market shifts. Keeping greed and fear in balance will produce far better results. One of the strategies that I use is to exit part of my position quickly as a concession to fear. Then, I hold a portion of the position to maximize profits and allow greed to run.

Traders must also stay positive. A negative attitude will lead to negative results. Visualize success and expect it. Believe me, having a positive attitude will make you a better trader. Every trader has losses, accept them gracefully. Take personal responsibility for your trades. Until you do that, you will not improve.

MARKET INSIGHT

Traders will be paid what they think they are worth.

CHAPTER 15

You Still Have Time to Sleep

ack in 1996, when I got my hands on a Globex terminal, I was so excited. I saw that terminal as my gateway to the world. With the Globex, I was finally able to trade around the clock from my office. I had the capability to place my own trades electronically—without having to call a trading desk hundreds of miles away. I felt like Aladdin riding across the sky on his magic carpet. The financial markets of the world were open to me like never before and I understood the power of it.

No kid was ever happier with a new toy than I was with that Globex terminal. I wanted to trade constantly. I stayed at the office at night with a fellow broker friend of mine, Bill, and we actually took turns trading. One of us slept on the old sofa in the receptionist's area while the other one manned the machine. We acted like long-distance truckers making a run from one coast to the other. Someone had to constantly be at the wheel.

When Bill and I finally exhausted ourselves, I hired two college boys to watch the Globex all night and learn everything that they could. One of those young men is Chuck Crow, who still works for DTI. Not only did the fellows who manned the night crew make observations about prices and markets, but they also placed trades at my direction. I did not want DTI, or myself, to miss a single market opportunity.

Technology is changing our world very quickly. Within a couple of years, my high-tech Globex terminal was no longer needed. Today, anyone has access to the night markets. All that is needed is a computer, a data feed provider, the right type of account, and a trading platform (I personally

219

like Ninja Trader for execution and DTN for data, and have had good success with them). With a couple of clicks of the mouse, the markets of the
world are open for trading—around the clock.

After I had the capability to trade overnight without a big bulky
Globex terminal, I tried again to be a marathon trader. I had my laptop and
my trading programs and I tried to trade virtually 24 hours a day. I felt
as though I had to make every trade in every trade zone and every time
segment. I was trading at 4:00 PM and again at 6:00 PM or 8:00 PM. When
German markets fired up, I was there—sitting at my computer watching the prices on the Dax futures run. I was also there at 4:00 AM when
European economic news was released; and I was still there at 8:30 AM
when the NYSE and the CME and CBOT opened. Then, I continued to trade
all day long. I had to observe every market that I could and make every
play possible.

Needless to say, that trading style did not work. Soon, I was totally
exhausted. I was not making more money; I was making less because I was
not thinking clearly. Successful trading requires a clear head. When traders
are weary, they buy instead of sell, execute limit orders instead of stop
orders, buy the wrong product, or make any number of other errors. I actually remember a day when I realized I was in the market, but was not certain what I was trading. I had enough clarity to immediately focus and
realize that I was long the yen. Did I mean to be long yen? No, I did not pur-
posefully go long or short the Japanese bills, and I was shocked to find
myself trading them. Somehow, I made a couple of wrong clicks and I was
in the market. At that point I did not even try to evaluate the situation. I
simply exited all positions.

Technology offers many new and exciting trading opportunities, but
no single individual has the ability to take advantage of all of them. That is
just common sense. Frankly, I should have never tried it. Thankfully, I
regained my senses and altered my schedule. Now I use the 24-hour clock,
but I certainly do not trade around the clock. I take time to rest, analyze,
and think. The majority of the trading day should be spent thinking. Only a
small portion of the day should be spent trading.

> *Technology offers many new and exciting trading opportuni-
> ties, but no single individual has the ability to take advan-
> tage of all of them.*

EVEN TRADERS NEED TO SLEEP

Sleep is an essential part of good health. Without it, one's mind and body deteriorate. Therefore, traders must give themselves adequate time for rest and recreation. Some traders need to execute their trades during the late-night hours. That's fine, but they still must find some time for sleep. The schedules of others mandate that trading be an early-morning pursuit. Still others have the entire day to make their plays. Each trader must evaluate his or her personal time restraints and select trading times accordingly. Be certain that there is time not only for trading but also for proper analysis and for adequate rest.

Earlier I mentioned Reid, one of my friends and students. Reid has a very demanding full-time job. But, he enjoys trading. Therefore, the best time for him is the early morning. He trades while the sun is rising. He likes trading the Dax futures or trading U.S. markets that are operating hours before his hectic workday begins. Reid may check on market action during the day session, but he is rarely able to trade. He is just too distracted at those times. Therefore, he found a time that fits his schedule.

Earl, another student and friend is retired. He lives in the United States and has the pleasure of trading any time he wishes. However, he enjoys trading the Dax during the early morning hours. Earl's goal is to make his money before the U.S. markets open. Therefore, he starts trading around 3:30 or 4:00 AM. By 8:30 AM, he is finished trading and ready to enjoy the rest of his day. Trading does not rule his life. Instead, he fits trading into his schedule and he still has time to go for a walk, take a leisurely bike ride, enjoy lunch with friends, and rest whenever he wants.

Traders must evaluate their personal time restraints and select trading times accordingly.

Trading requires attention. If there are phones ringing, clients waiting, and business to conduct, it is impossible to trade well. Reid knows the problems encountered when trying to trade while running another business. He knows because he tried it and learned the hard way that it does not work. Therefore, I suggest that one not try to trade unless he is able to devote his full attention to it. Reid solved his problem. Each trader must do the same.

Because I have the luxury of trading during the day, I like to trade the day market. That is, I start trading early—generally around 6:00 AM Central—and I continue trading until New York and Chicago close. I go to bed early and if I think there may be a good opportunity for trading around 4:00 AM, I get up and look at the tape.

It is not necessary to constantly look at market prices. In fact, that is a very bad thing to do. There is a much easier way to monitor the action. Software programs can do the job while traders sleep. My RoadMap software, driven by DTN, a data feed provider, tracks prices and stores the information. When I get up in the morning, I easily find the current price of the German Dax or anything else that I need. And, I can get the other numerical information required. I know the opening price at 1:00 AM, and the high and the low, and everything in between. While I am sleeping, the program and the technology gather and store the numbers for me (see Figure 15.1). It certainly is not essential that you have my software, but I recommend that you have a software program that accomplishes the essential tasks of gathering, storing, and displaying the data necessary to make your trading decisions. In that way, you can get a good night's sleep while knowing that you are also continuously tracking the market's progress.

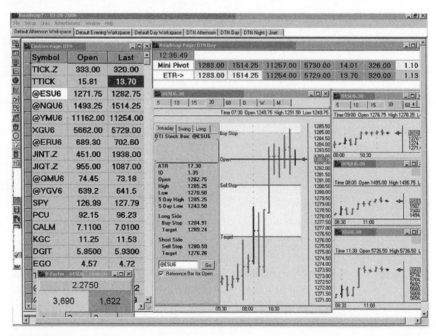

FIGURE 15.1 The software that I use organizes market data for me. I can step to my computer, pull up the software, and quickly read the tape.

SPEND 90 PERCENT OF THE TIME THINKING

The big question that a trader must answer is whether to be long, short, or out of the market. Most of the time, a trader should be out. With each gray hair, I learn the importance of analysis. Because I spend so much of my time looking for the right market approach and because I have so many gray hairs, some of my friends call me *The Silver Fox*. The vast majority of my time is spent in analysis. Likewise, most of your trading day should be spent gathering numbers and scrutinizing them in the context of the economic landscape.

Before you execute a trade, you should have a well-thought-out plan. Where should you buy or sell? Where will resistance and support likely step into the picture? If the bulls win the battle and that first point of resistance is broken, where will the bulls likely be challenged again? Also, consider the strength of the bears and locate the price points where they will gain strength. Know what the reasonable profit targets will be. Identify points of entry if things turn bullish and points of entry if the bears steal the show. With each possible entry point, know how to respond if the play is wrong. That let's you know where to place protective stops.

Trading is not about taking every play. It is about taking winning plays and making money. Therefore, the secret is to select trades carefully and take only a few trades each day. Good traders verify the numbers, check the indicators, and select the ideal time for entering and exiting the market. They do not try to execute marathon trading sessions. Overtrading is the single easiest way to lose money.

REVIEW

Technology allows traders to execute buy and sell orders virtually 24 hours a day. However, only a foolish player tries to do so. Traders need a great deal of time for analysis and a relatively small amount of time for trading. Therefore, you must plan your day with that in mind. Also, adequate rest is essential. Only when your mind is clear are you able to come head to head with the best minds of Wall Street.

 MARKET INSIGHT

Spend 90 percent of your time analyzing and 10 percent trading.

CHAPTER 16

So You Want to Be a Trader

Profile of a Winner

I have seen them come and go. Most begin with enthusiasm and high hopes of success. Yet many never reach their goals; they lack the ability to stick with the program and pay the price that must be paid for success. Why do some accomplish their goals while others fail? What separates the winners from the losers? I believe that in order to succeed as a trader (or just about anything else), you have to possess a core of traits or characteristics that will allow you to face the adversities present in trading, meet them head on, and persist. This chapter details a few of the qualities that good traders possess.

PERSISTENCE

"Continuous effort—not strength or intelligence—is the key to unlocking our potential." I think Winston Churchill had it right. I have seen many intelligent people who were not successful in their trading because they simply did not have the will to be persistent. Effort and perseverance define winners. A small loss or two, and many would-be traders give up. Perhaps their intelligence has made life too easy for them. Perhaps they cannot admit that trading involves skills that they need to develop and hone. For whatever reason, they lack the one skill that is absolutely critical to becoming a winning trader, and that is persistence. As the old adage goes, "When the going gets tough, the tough get going."

Trading the markets is not easy. In fact, it is not just hard, it is *very* hard. Every trader will make mistakes and suffer losses. That is all part of the learning process. How you react to those losses and errors will determine your fate. Losers quit, and winners make the most out of every losing situation by analyzing it. What was the mistake? Could it have been avoided? How? What can I do in the future to gain a better result? That is the response of a winner. One fact is certain—quitters won't win.

> *Quitters never win. Be persistent.*

INDUSTRY

As Abraham Lincoln said, "Things may come to those who wait...but only the things left by those who hustle." Winning traders are hustlers. When New York and Chicago come to life, they are ready. They know major levels of support and resistance; they have identified the key numbers in the current trading range. If the market shows strength, they know where they will buy, and if they see weakness, they know where they will sell. They have done their homework, and they are prepared to become winners. You will never be a winner at the trading game until you put forth the effort required to win.

You can't sit and wait for success. I doubt that success will come knocking at your door. Those who win are those who work and prepare to win. They study the markets, get a trading education, read, prepare, and are able to identify winning trades and take them when they see them. I operate an educational facility where I teach the art of trading. Educating yourself is rarely cheap, and learning about the financial markets is no exception. You spend money for the education that you receive. With that in mind, it would seem that those paying the tuition would approach their educational experience with zeal and effort. Most do. However, there are always a few who just refuse to put forth the effort. If class begins at 8:00 AM, they arrive at 8:15 AM and haven't completed the class preparation. They do not understand the importance of exerting the requisite effort to win.

A lot of folks see trading as an easy and somewhat lazy lifestyle. Believe me, that is not the case. Traders rise early and work late. Those who approach the financial markets in a dispassionate and casual manner will get out of it what they are putting in it. They will not last long in the trading game, because those who are industrious and serious about the craft will pick their pockets faster than a bolt of lightning shoots across a stormy Alabama sky.

A DESIRE TO WIN

David defeated Goliath. The small guy can win, but he has to be determined to do it. He can't just run from every challenge. There are a lot of Goliaths in the marketplace. They have deeper pockets than most of us, and maybe a lot more education and training, too. However, that does not mean that they will always win in the end. If you have a desire to learn to trade and the perseverance and determination to succeed, you can. Attitude and determination will decide how well you play the trading game.

DISCIPLINE

Why bother to develop a strategy or trading method if you are not going to follow it? Once you have a proven strategy, you must discipline yourself to adhere to your own rules and only take those trades that fit within your trading plan.

I believe that the inability to be disciplined is the single biggest reason that most traders fail. They know what they should do, but they cannot or will not do it. If a stock price bobbles up, they jump into the market. Never mind that the time of day is bad or that the indicators are not supporting the move. Without giving the trade much thought or analysis, they click the mouse and take the trade. Most of the time, trades taken hastily are not winners. True, sometimes traders can jump at the market and make a few bucks, but far more often than not, they are losers.

I have observed a lot of traders, and I think men have a tendency to be cowboys. They like the risk and embrace the danger of the market. Women, by contrast, tend to be more deliberate and wait for the right set-up. They follow their rules and often achieve their goals. One of my students, Michelle, exemplifies this. She understands that following the rules pays. Michelle and many others strive for discipline and get the rewards that accompany it. Taking unnecessary risk and approaching the markets in an undisciplined and reckless manner may be fun for a while, but the excitement will soon end when the trading account is empty. If you want to be a cowboy, you should go to the rodeo. If you want to be a trader, trade the markets calmly and deliberately, with a disciplined approach.

> *Good trading requires discipline.*

ABILITY TO ACCEPT MISTAKES

"It ain't what you don't know that gets you into trouble. It's what you know for sure that just ain't so." Perhaps Mark Twain could have been a trader. At least he knew that sometimes we all believe we are right when we are absolutely wrong. I used to suffer from that problem myself. Years ago when I was a young broker, I thought I knew everything. I would take a trade and when the market told me I was wrong, I just would not listen. As price moved against me, I added to my position. When the message was sent again and prices continued to move against my trade, I would add to my position again. I was certain that I was right and the market would eventually reverse and make me a hero. Far too often, there was no reversal and I dug a deep hole for myself by not recognizing my error and admitting my mistake.

Every trader makes mistakes. Sometimes the analysis is wrong. Sometimes the trade is not correctly executed. Sometimes the market just misbehaves. At any rate, there will always be situations in which traders will find themselves on the wrong side of the market. Identify the error as quickly as possible, admit the mistake, and exit the trade. That is the only way to preserve your capital and your objectivity.

ABILITY TO LEARN FROM MISTAKES

Traders must use their mistakes to get better. When you take a losing trade, use that opportunity to learn from it. I believe that traders should keep a trading diary and record each trade. If you are making so many trades that you cannot write them down, you are trading too much. I suggest that you jot down the time a trade is taken and also the entry point of the transaction. Why did you decide to buy or sell? What was the basis for putting your money at risk? Did the trade succeed? Why or why not? If there was a loss, try to determine the likely reason for it. If money was made, could profit totals have been even greater? As you analyze both the winners and losers, you can gain insight and understanding that will help you become a better trader.

EMOTIONAL STABILITY

Trading is emotionally charged. Money is on the line. Every trader wants to make money—lots of money. After all, that is the reason that you are trading. However, sometimes the greed factor gets too strong and leads you to take unnecessary risk or hold on to winners or losers too long. You might want to make $1,000 or $10,000 from a trade, but the market may be unwilling to pay the price. The market does not care what you want. That is irrelevant. Set reasonable profit targets and take pride in reaching them. Greed has destroyed many traders.

Another emotional enemy is fear. Beginning traders are often too fearful to take any trades, even the very good ones. They identify an entry point and the market comes to it, but they can't pull the trigger. The trade is missed because they lacked the courage to take it. Fear can be a good thing, but having too much fear is deadly. Trading is about taking risk. However, if you limit your exposure and take only those trades where the odds of success are on your side, you need not be afraid. If you have made a mistake, you can always bail the trade. If you always sit on the sidelines and wait, you can never make money. Respect fear, but hold it in check. If the trade is right, the time is right, the numbers are right, and the indicators support the move, take the trade.

> *Emotional stability is essential if you want to win.*

FLEXIBILITY

The financial markets constantly change. A trade that worked like a charm last month may not work today. A support level that the market could not cross last week is effortlessly passed now. The trading vehicle that paid so well last month may be too stingy to return a penny this month. That is the nature of the markets; they constantly change. In early 2006, the S&P futures had an average daily range of only 10 or 11 points. However, the scene greatly changed in late spring when a daily range of 18 or even 20 points became common.

Traders have to adapt to changing market conditions. If something is not working, do not continue to do it. Adapt to the changing conditions. There will be times when the market is highly volatile and you have to accept greater risk and place protective stops farther away from the entry price than you would like. There will be times when prices don't move very far during a trading session. You might have to accept smaller profits than usual. Or, huge moves might allow you to take far greater profits than you were able to eke out of a slow market. The point is, the market changes, and if you are to succeed as a trader, you have to change with it. Flexibility and adaptability are essential if you are going to last as a trader.

COMPOSURE

The markets can be scary places. Sometimes a trade moves against your position. In fact, all experienced traders have seen many times when a trade moved against their position. Stay calm. Just because the trade is down a few bucks does not mean that the world is ending. Stop and analyze the situation. If the indicators and the key numbers are expressing a view that is contrary to the trade—get out. But, do so calmly. Otherwise, you will make a mistake and buy when you mean to sell, or make some other foolish error.

Trading is not for the faint of heart. It requires a steady head. The best way to remain calm is to be prepared. Know at what point the trade will be bailed. Don't be like the deer caught in the headlights. The deer likely did not survive. Be a survivor.

RESPONSIBILITY

"I didn't think that entry point was good, but Tom felt so strongly about it that I went long anyway. He gave me bad advice." Or—"I took the recommendation from the expert on CNN and he was wrong. I could have done better myself." Over the years I have heard every excuse, and then some. Generally, people do not want to take responsibility for their actions. It is far easier to blame me, or the trader in the chat room, or their broker, than to blame themselves. Each person has a responsibility to make his or her own trading decisions and take responsibility for them. Sometimes those decisions will be good and sometimes they will be bad.

Ben Franklin once said, "He who is good at making excuses is seldom good for anything else." In trading, that is definitely true. You do not have time to blame your errors on others. The only way to get better is to take responsibility for your trades. Own your trades and work to make them better and better. Otherwise, you will never step up to the plate and consistently hit those home runs that make trading both fun and profitable. Sometimes it is hard to admit that you have misread the indicators or lost money because you took a losing trade, but the only way to get better is to accept responsibility. As Winston Churchill said, "The price of greatness is responsibility." Always take ownership of your trades. That is the price of becoming a good trader.

OPTIMISM

Optimistic people make better traders. They look for good trades, expecting to find them. They understand that sometimes their trades will not work, but they are not devastated by a few losses. They always look for the silver lining in every bad experience and generally they find it. If I see two traders and one is pessimistic and the other optimistic, I know which one is likely to succeed as a trader. Having a good attitude cannot be overrated.

REVIEW

Being a successful trader requires a variety of skills. You must be persistent. That is, you can't quit just because you have a few bad days, or even a few bad weeks. When you face adversity, you have to meet it head on and overcome the things that are holding you back. One fact is certain: If you quit, you will never win. Another essential trait of a winner is industry. It takes effort to play with the big boys on Wall Street. Many traders are highly skilled, very intelligent, and loaded with dough. So what? That does not mean that they cannot be beaten. However, it does mean that you have to work hard to beat them. Before you join the varsity team, you need to be willing to put forth the effort to win.

Another essential characteristic of a winner is the desire to win. You must want to seize the prize. If you do not have the spirit and drive to win, you will too easily become defeated. Discipline is another critical trait. You may have the best trading strategy in the world and be a truly great trader when you apply your strategy. But, if you do not have discipline and jump in and out of the market at every whim, you will not be able to become a winner. Trading requires that you have rules and you follow them. Sometimes that may mean that good trades are missed because the time was not right or the indicators were not accurate. So be it. Gaining a strong sense of discipline will pay in the long run.

Everyone makes mistakes, and that is okay. Use those mistakes and losing trades as learning experiences. Study, analyze, and benefit from them. Remember that every trade you make is just that—one trade among many trades. After a losing trade, focus, analyze, and work harder to make the next trade a winner.

Trading is an emotional roller coaster. Constantly fight to balance greed and fear, glee and desolation, winning and losing. You must analyze each trade carefully, and know how you will react if the trade moves against you. Determine in advance the point at which you will bail out of the market. Also, know before entering the trade what is expected as far as profits. What is the daily average range of this stock or this futures index? What will you do when the profit target is reached? Preparation is the best way to survive the emotional roller coaster of trading.

Many traders like to follow a trading system. They search and find a system that they believe will work for them day in and day out. However, the markets do not work like that. The financial markets continuously change. For that reason, you must have a well-developed trading strategy that is flexible and changes as market conditions change. The problem with most "systems" is that they work in only one type of market environment. When the landscape changes, the system fails. Being flexible and having the ability to identify changes in the marketplace and adapting to them is essential if you are going to be a long-term player.

Finally, to succeed, you must take responsibility for your trading. You cannot blame the analyst on television or the friend who offered the trading tip. If you decided to take the trade and it is a loser, the only person to blame is yourself. Only by taking responsibility can you take the necessary actions to improve and achieve your trading goals.

 MARKET INSIGHT

Traders who take responsibility for their trades improve because they address their problems, correct them, and make money.

CHAPTER 17

Wrapping It Up

Technology opens up the world to new and exciting trading opportunities. With a click of the mouse, modern traders have the ability to travel around the world and take advantage of market moves in Asia or Europe, or elsewhere. Not only does technology allow traders to expand their geographical reach, but it also allows them to extend their trading hours. Thanks to the Internet, a trader can sit at home and trade virtually 24 hours a day. In the 1950s, Bill Haley sang about rocking around the clock. Today traders have the opportunity to trade around the clock.

Trading follows the sun as it makes its path across the sky. Trading will be most active in areas of the world where the sun is shining brightest. When folks on the east coast of the United States are eating dinner, Asia is trading. When those same traders are snoring soundly in their beds, Europe takes over and trading continues. Finally, when that bright ball of red fire moves over our shores, New York and Chicago open their trading pits and the United States steals the show. If a trader has the knowledge and the technology, he or she can trade virtually 24 hours a day.

As with most technology, the 24-hour trading comes with advantages and disadvantages. The biggest disadvantage is that if you are not careful, you might be too easily drawn into the market when you should stay out of it. Knowing that electronic markets are active is a big temptation for some traders. They feel the need for greed and they overtrade.

The simple way to solve the problem is to select the optimum times for trading and maximize the opportunities within those times. Some traders like trading at night while others only trade day markets. Some like to trade exclusively U.S. products while others look for global opportunities. I especially enjoy trading the German Dax Index futures. Regardless of your preference, you should limit your trading to only good trades and remember that you need rest and a clear head if you want to make money.

For me, the most exciting aspect of electronic markets is that I can take advantage of a global timeframe. If I wish to do so, I can trade in the evening, at night, or during the early morning hours. Also, technology provides me with information. Asia starts trading when I am eating dinner. It may be Monday in the U.S., but in Tokyo, Tuesday's workday has started. The Nikkei in Japan is one of the first global markets to welcome each new day. The Hang Seng in Hong Kong starts trading a couple of hours later. The market sentiment of Asian traders is expressed on those indexes. That means that traders in the U.S. have an opportunity to see a dress rehearsal of market sentiment before our markets even start trading.

The German Dax, French CAC, London FTSE—the prices on these indexes reflect the sentiment of the bulls and bears across the Atlantic. That information is important to me because it gives me information that I am able to use to plan my trading day, limit my risk, expand my trading opportunities, and be a more consistent trader.

I do not sit in front of a computer screen 24 hours a day. However, I have software that gathers the important numbers and data for me. When I step to the computer and look at the RoadMap, I can read the tape quickly and know whether I need to pay attention to the market's rock or walk away.

Trading has changed so much during the two decades that I have been involved in it. When I started trading, I called orders to pit traders on the floor of the exchange and they executed them for me. There was no computerized trading. I stayed on the phone all day and nearly burned up the phone lines. Now with just a click of a computer mouse I can place my trades. And, I can do that at almost any hour of the day or night. Furthermore, I can trade products that are listed on exchanges or indexes on the other side of the globe.

I cannot imagine why anyone would not take advantage of such possibilities. Even if traders have no interest in trading a foreign index or product, they can still gain so much knowledge and information by taking a global approach.

Because I know the markets never sleep, I am able to be a better trader. I hope that the insights and information offered in this book make your trading experience more profitable and more consistent.

 MARKET INSIGHT

Tuesday's trading day began Monday afternoon.

Index